ARE YOU READY FOR YOUR
BUSINESS
TRANSFORMATION?

MICHAEL J. VITALE

ISBN: 978-1-7329311-0-7 (sc)
ISBN: 978-1-7329311-1-4 (e)

X4MU
2567 Willow Field Xing
Marietta, GA 30067
(404) 509-1867
X4MU, LLC

Library of Congress Control Number: 2019904032

Lulu Publishing Services rev. date: 06/20/2019

To my loving wife, Stacy. Thank you. Without your encouragement
and support, I would have never achieved my goal.

Contents

Preface

Business transformations bring about innovative new capabilities and improvements in the way you engage your customers and operate your business. However, they require a significant investment in time and resources, and they create business disruption. The disruption is caused by extensive change throughout the transformation. Most companies are not ready for this level of change.

This book provides a way to overcome the challenges of large-scale business change. The method introduced in this book is business transformation readiness. Business transformation readiness helps companies test their readiness for change through comprehensive assessments and, if necessary, helps them achieve change readiness through disciplined preparation steps. The objective is to help companies be ready for the change accompanying its transformation.

The stakes are high in a business transformation. There is huge potential for performance improvement, but the current rate of success is staggeringly low. Fortunately, the challenges most companies experience can be overcome. As leaders of change, you have already taken the first step toward addressing these challenges—you are preparing *yourself* for the change.

Introduction

FOUNDATION

Give me six hours to chop down a tree and I will spend the first four sharpening the axe.
—Abraham Lincoln

Fred West questioned his dream. He was a baker at heart and the owner of a small chain of bakeries called Let Us Eat Cakes. Fred had a lifelong dream of running a bakery enterprise with a local neighborhood feel. Within ten years, Fred owned five moderately successful bakeries throughout the metropolitan area. Each of them was nestled into its respective neighborhood and provided freshly baked pastries, pies, cookies, and custom-decorated cakes. Customers were happy with Let Us Eat Cakes and considered the local bakery a favorite spot to satisfy their collective sweet tooth and catch up with friends.

Let Us Eat Cakes was a pickup/dine-in bakery. In addition to the regular assortment of baked goods, customers could get made-to-order cakes. The custom cakes could be ordered at any of the five locations or via telephone and would be available for pickup when the customer arrived. Business was good, but it could always be better. Well, it needed to be better. Customers have many choices for baked goods, and some now value their time as much as their sweets.

Fred was sure he could double or even triple revenues by servicing on-the-go customers through an online ordering system. The online system would provide Let Us Eat Cakes with a mobile-enabled website to order the regular bakery items as well as the specialty cakes. Customers would pay in advance with a credit card, making it quick and convenient for commuters.

Fred secured funding and launched a modernization effort to add the online capability. It would be piloted in the original Let Us Eat Cakes bakery and then rolled out to the remaining bakeries. Eight weeks into the project, the website was coming along nicely. The software company contracted to develop the online site really understood the mobile customer experience. The images of the baked goods looked exceptional and made it easy to make a choice and quickly check out. If this was as successful as planned, Fred would seek private equity funding to expand outside the metropolitan area.

However, after about four months, some issues emerged. None of these were anticipated. They were the natural consequences of adding the online presence. During a recent staff meeting, Sarah—the bakery manager for the pilot store—asked how they were going to handle the on-the-go customers with their modest-sized store footprint. The additional volume would surely overflow both the sales and dining areas. Also, the customers who paid online expected to quickly pick up their orders and be on their way. That was the point of the modernization, after all. Someone suggested adding a dedicated paid-order pickup/checkout area. This added cost and still took up space in the store, and additional parking would be needed.

Fred asked Sarah to take some time to uncover all the issues so they could be addressed at once. After a few days, Sarah had a long list of items to discuss with Fred. In addition to the space required for online customer pickup, their restaurant supply vendor had to change its delivery schedule to avoid the customer rushes. Someone would need to monitor online orders placed in the evenings to ensure they were ready for fulfillment. That would mean adding a second shift. A shelving system was required to stage orders for pickup. It wasn't clear whether customers wanted assistance in designing specialty cakes—and if they needed assistance, how much. The customer credit card data had to be handled securely, and a system administrator had to be hired to take care of the new website. Indeed, the list was long.

How did this happen? Fred became frustrated and unsure whether they should continue with their effort to modernize the bakery. A lot of money had already been spent. Fred West questioned his dream.

Fred's case is not unique. Modernization is one of the many large-scale changes a business can undertake to improve sales and operations. It's not uncommon for companies to undergo several of these changes over their lifetimes. In today's vernacular, they are called *business transformations*. If the changes leverage technology to redefine the customer experience or operating model, they are called *digital transformations*. To understand the dilemma at Let Us Eat Cakes, Fred West needs to instead ask, "Why did this happen?"

Let Us Eat Cakes began its investment to modernize before its owner understood all the implications. Furthermore, it had no way to know whether it had uncovered all the implications. Let Us Eat Cakes needed a way to assess its readiness to take on its modernization effort—before it implemented it.

This book deals with business transformation readiness. It answers the questions "How do you know if you're ready?" and—if you are not ready—"What can you do about it?" The first question is addressed through the *readiness assessment*, and the second question is addressed through the *readiness preparation*. If Let Us Eat Cakes had conducted a readiness assessment prior to implementing its modernization effort, it would have known what readiness meant and would have clearly known it wasn't ready.

Now to address the second question: "What can you do about it?"

At the Crossroad

Fred knew Let Us Eat Cakes needed to support on-the-go customers with an online order/pay website. He also knew the additional sales volume was a necessity. Canceling the modernization effort was not a viable option. Furthermore, about one-third of its modernization budget had already been spent to develop the website.

On the other hand, there were a lot of issues that needed to be addressed, and Fred was not sure they knew them all yet. Moving forward *as is* caused Fred a lot of anxiety. At this point, the uncertainty had paralyzed his modernization effort. Let Us Eat Cakes was at a crossroad, and the decision fell to Fred.

Suppose Fred had conducted a readiness assessment. He would still be at a crossroad, but he would at least know the extent of the impacts from the modernization effort. Most importantly, he would know whether Let Us Eat Cakes was prepared to deal with these impacts. He would know whether his business was ready for the transformation.

Fred knew deep down that Let Us Eat Cakes was not ready for its transformation. There were several outstanding operational design items, clarification was still needed around custom cakes, and operational support had not been considered at all. They were all solvable, but Fred did not know how to solve them. That is addressed by readiness preparation.

Readiness preparation allows you to move forward on more than just the hope that issues will somehow be resolved. Readiness preparation frees you from the plague of paralysis. It helps ensure your business is ready for your transformation before moving forward. When you know you're not ready, readiness preparation answers the question "What can you do about it?"

What This Book Is About

Business transformations are complex, large-scale changes to your company's business capabilities and behaviors. Their purpose is to bring about significant and sustainable improvement in performance. As with any worthwhile and complex human endeavor, business transformations are filled with challenges.

The results from a McKinsey Global Survey on transformations (Jacquemont, Maor, & Reich, 2015) show that few executives (just 26 percent) considered their business transformation a success. This was up just slightly from a similar survey conducted in 2012. In these studies, success was defined as improving performance and equipping the organization for sustained, long-term performance.

While the inherent complexity of a transformation contributes to the low rate of success cited in the McKinsey survey, there are other challenges as well. This book characterizes the most significant challenges and shows how they can be overcome through disciplined business transformation readiness, that is, by conducting readiness assessments and carrying out readiness preparations. Methods, tools, and examples are provided throughout the book. They serve as how-tos for addressing the challenges. Much of the content is presented with the rigor required for a large-scale business transformation. However, the methodology can be applied to smaller business change efforts as well. The Let Us Eat Cakes example will be used throughout the book to illustrate the techniques.

Finally, while project management, software development, and business strategy are important disciplines, they will only be treated as adjacent topics in this book because there are many great sources of material on these subjects.

Who This Book Is For

This book is primarily intended for business leaders with the responsibility for planning, implementing, and optimizing business transformations within their companies. It is also intended for practitioners providing professional help to companies undergoing transformations. Finally, it is for anyone who seeks to broaden his or her general understanding of business transformations, including why they are necessary, the challenges experienced in carrying them out, and how to address these challenges.

Organization

Some chapters of this book are required to set up the context for the business transformation readiness methodology, some chapters describe the methodology, and others contain reference material on the various techniques and tools. The descriptions below help you determine the best way to approach the content.

Chapter 1: Business Transformation Change

This chapter characterizes change in a business transformation. It begins by examining the reasons businesses undertake transformations and describes the type of changes initiated during a transformation. It then looks at the resulting change impacts and introduces a way to measure the degree of impact in a transformation. This method of analysis allows a company to predict the change impact from its transformation.

Chapter 2: The State of Business Transformation Research

This chapter presents a summary of the research on business transformation failures, including an analysis of the reasons for high failure rate and what is being done to improve the chances for success. A simple three-phase business transformation life cycle (planning, implementing, and optimizing) is introduced to assist in analyzing the challenges arising during a business transformation.

Chapter 3: Business Transformation Readiness

This chapter shows how the challenges plaguing a business transformation can be framed as a "lack of readiness" to address the accompanying change. The concept of business transformation readiness is introduced to address these challenges. Business transformation readiness tests your readiness for change through readiness assessments, and if necessary, it helps you to become ready by carrying out related readiness preparations.

Chapter 4: Planning Phase Readiness

This chapter presents the details of business transformation readiness for the two objectives of the planning phase: purpose and scope. Readiness assessments and preparations are introduced to help achieve the readiness goals for the planning phase. Examples are presented, as is a methodology for producing the assessments and preparations.

Chapter 5: Implementing Phase Readiness

This chapter presents the details of business transformation readiness for the two objectives of the implementing phase: design and execution. Readiness assessments and preparations are introduced to help achieve the readiness goals for the implementing phase. Examples are presented, as is a methodology for producing the assessments and preparations.

Chapter 6: Optimizing Phase Readiness

This chapter presents the details of business transformation readiness for the two objectives of the optimizing phase: achievement and enhancement. Readiness assessments and preparations are introduced to help achieve the readiness goals for the optimizing phase. Examples are presented, as is a methodology for producing the assessments and preparations.

Chapter 7: Putting Readiness to Use

This chapter brings together the business transformation readiness concepts to address the challenges at Let Us Eat Cakes. It concludes with a perspective on how to get started using the readiness techniques within your own company.

Appendix

The appendix includes a summary of the research findings on business transformations.

Companion Guide

The readiness methodology explained in chapter 4, chapter 5, and chapter 6 is made actionable in acompanion guide available for download from the author's website at www.X4MU.com/.

Chapter 1

BUSINESS TRANSFORMATION CHANGE

The only way you survive is you continuously transform into something else. It's this
idea of continuous transformation that makes you an innovation company.
—Ginni Rometty

This chapter characterizes the change in a business transformation. It begins by examining the reasons businesses undertake transformations and describing the types of changes initiated during a transformation. It then looks at the resulting change impacts and introduces a way to measure the degree of change impact in a transformation. This method of characterization allows a company to predict the magnitude of change impact for its transformation.

The Business Transformation Change Cycle

Business transformations are complex, large-scale changes to your company's business capabilities and behaviors—to bring about significant improvement in performance. You can find many variations of this definition in books, articles, and websites, but they all share the notion of change. A significant part of the company must change during a transformation; otherwise, it's hardly worth undertaking. Some of the changes are obvious, and others are not so obvious. It is important to understand both types.

Business change can be characterized as a continuous cycle that never ends. One way to represent this cycle is shown in figure 1 (below).

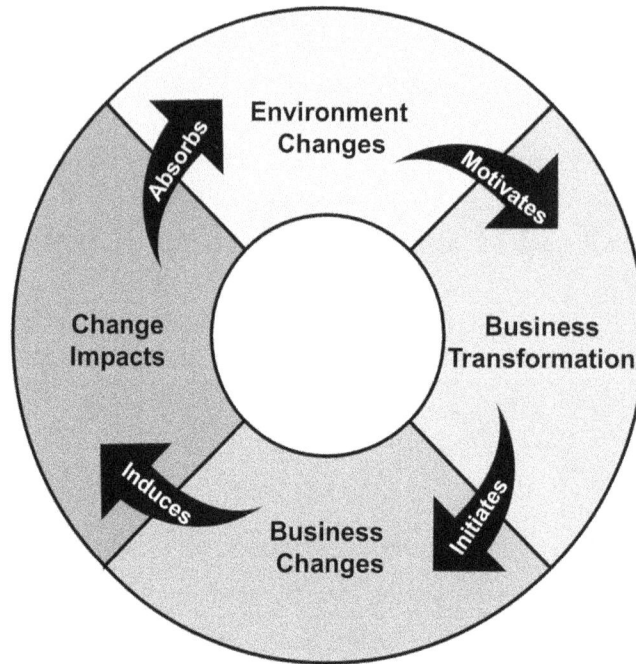

Figure 1. The Business Change Cycle

The business change cycle is interpreted from the perspective of your company. Beginning at the top, changes naturally occur in your business environment. These environment changes serve to motivate your business to undertake a transformation. A business transformation is under your company's control but is a response to something that has occurred in your business environment.

Your business transformation will then initiate one or more changes in your business. Business changes are the changes you elect to make as part of your transformation. They are the most visible and easily recognized changes. The business changes serve as the transformation's focal point.

The transformation becomes more complicated as business changes induce impacts on your business. The change impacts are not always visible or obvious. They require effort to identify and effort to determine their influence on your company. Quite often, they are ignored completely—at the detriment of the business transformation.

Finally, your business must absorb the impacts of these changes. Absorbing change impacts means your business has internalized them, making them part of your operation. This completes the cycle and positions your business to experience new changes in the environment.

The business change cycle is complex enough as a single sequence of change. However, multiple cycles can occur simultaneously. Before your business has fully absorbed the changes and impacts of your transformation, the environment can change again. This is indeed the case in our rapidly changing world.

There is value in characterizing change using the business change cycle. The relationships within the cycle allow a business to understand the scope of change and even predict the magnitude of change impact. This is a powerful tool for transformation readiness.

Why Most Business Transformations Fail

The rate of success (or failure) in business transformations has been studied for more than a decade. Highlights of these studies are covered in chapter 2. While many factors contribute to the poor success rate, a single theme is woven throughout the failures: the breadth and depth of change in a business transformation is unwieldy. The argument made in this book is that most businesses are simply not ready for this level of change. Fortunately, all is not lost as there are methods for assessing whether you are ready, and if not, what you can do to be ready. As stated in the opening, much of this book elaborates on these methods. For the time being consider the following basic readiness deficiencies.

- Willingness: Business transformations are not the purpose of a company. A company's purpose is to profitably service its customers. Senior business leaders would like to get this change completed as quickly as possible and get back to running their businesses.
- Ability: Business transformations are not something most companies do. Consequently, they do not have the right skills in sufficient quantity to address the change.

These deficiencies result in a gross underestimation of the change associated with a business transformation and dooms the transformation before it is started. If you're going to expend the resources to undertake a transformation, it's worth it to adequately prepare for the change. The best place to begin is with the reason for undertaking a transformation.

Why Business Transformations Are Necessary

If business transformations are so challenging, why do we do them? In short, because the business environment is constantly changing, and your business must adjust accordingly. In the past decade, the environment has changed at an accelerated pace, due to advances in technology and ever-increasing customer expectations. In many instances, the business model on which the company operates no longer reflects reality.

A business transformation is your response to the changes affecting your business—it allows you to regain some control over the changing environment. A company can either be proactive or reactive in undertaking a corresponding business transformation. Proactive is preferable, but it is not always possible.

Since business transformations result in considerable change to your company, it is critical to clearly understand and express the reason(s) for undergoing the disruption (Kotter, 1995). Seventeen reasons, or motivators, will be considered here. They are arranged into three categories based on where in the business environment the change occurs: competitive environment, external environment, or internal environment. The seventeen motivators are shown in figure 2 (below)[1] and discussed in the next three sections.

Competitive Environment Motivators

The competitive environment motivators originate with respect to your competitors and their objectives to win business within your segment. The five most significant competitive environment motivators for a business transformation include underserved customer expectations, losing customers or market share, arrival of better positioned competitors, emergence of substitute products, and changes in industry structure.

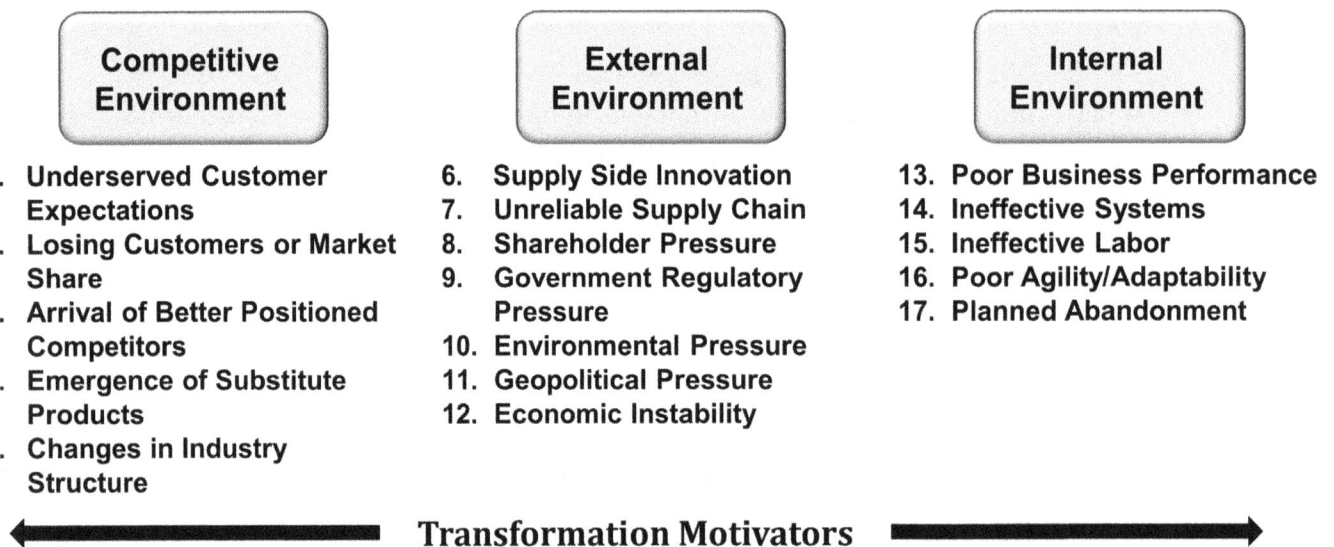

Competitive Environment	External Environment	Internal Environment
1. Underserved Customer Expectations 2. Losing Customers or Market Share 3. Arrival of Better Positioned Competitors 4. Emergence of Substitute Products 5. Changes in Industry Structure	6. Supply Side Innovation 7. Unreliable Supply Chain 8. Shareholder Pressure 9. Government Regulatory Pressure 10. Environmental Pressure 11. Geopolitical Pressure 12. Economic Instability	13. Poor Business Performance 14. Ineffective Systems 15. Ineffective Labor 16. Poor Agility/Adaptability 17. Planned Abandonment

← **Transformation Motivators** →

Figure 2: Business Transformation Motivators

Underserved Customer Expectations

An underserved customer expectation is a product, service, or experience the customer desires but has not received. This can happen to a single company that has not kept up with the pace of customer

---

[1] This list of motivators is compiled from various studies on business transformations. It does not exist elsewhere in one place or organized in this manner.

demand, or it can happen to all companies serving the entire customer segment when customer demand shifts.

Sometimes customers can articulate their underserved expectations, and sometimes they cannot. For example, a customer may ask for a product or service your competitors already have on the market. There are also examples of products and services (e.g., smartphones and social media) that were developed ahead of customer expectations. In either case, an underserved customer expectation is an opportunity for you to out-service your competitors—or to be out-serviced by your competitors.

Entire industries have been created and have disappeared due to underserved customer expectations. For example, the DVD movie rental industry was disrupted when Netflix transformed itself into a streaming movie rental service.

Losing Customers or Market Share

Companies can lose customers or market share for several reasons—price, quality, product or service mix, and availability. Customer and competitor analytics can be used to determine the reasons this occurs, but then they must be addressed quickly. The nature of a transformation to address lost customers or market share is determined by the scope/speed of customer and market share loss.

Arrival of Better Positioned Competitors

Better positioned competitors are those that have created an advantage in their commercial offering or their operating cost relative to the other companies in the market segment. This occurs primarily through commercial or operational innovation from the emerging competitor. It can also occur when a company effectively lobbies regulatory agencies to provide an advantage over its competitors. Either case will result in the loss of profitability, market share, or both. Typically, the better positioned competitor has already undergone a transformation. The other competitors within the segment may respond with a transformation of their own.

Emergence of Substitute Products

Substitute products are products (or services) from another industry that offer similar form and function as those by the companies within the industry. For example, listening to live music is a substitute for going to a movie theater. The substitute product may or may not be intended to compete with the original product. Sometimes changing economic conditions can induce consumers to seek out substitutes. One example is an import tariff on foreign goods.

The substitute product generally impacts all competitors within the industry, causing a loss of sales or profitability. As in the case of the arrival of better positioned competitors, the emergence of the substitute product could have been the result of a transformation. The impacted companies in the industry may then respond with a similar transformation.

Changes in Industry Structure

Changes in industry structure include mergers, acquisitions, divestitures, and in extreme cases, breakups of an entire industry segment. Mergers and acquisitions generally provide a competitive advantage to the merging or acquiring company, including access to new products, services, and markets. Divestitures improve the divesting company's profitability or focus its strategic scope. Industry breakups are taken to mean the separation of a company into two or more pieces as is the case when mandated by a government regulatory agency.

The impact to the industry depends on the nature and magnitude of the structural change. For example, when a product distributor acquires a professional services company, that distributor can then become a better positioned competitor within that industry. Another company may divest an unprofitable business unit, thereby improving its own competitive position. However, it may also result in an opportunity for the divested business unit to be acquired by a company with a better strategic fit. In all cases, the competitive landscape within the industry is changed. The transformation may either be the change in industry structure or the response by the companies competing within that industry structure.

External Environment Motivators

The external environment motivators originate with respect to factors occurring outside of your and your competitor's organizations—and often outside of the industry segment in which you compete. There are seven significant external environment motivators for a business transformation: supply-side innovation, unreliable supply chain, shareholder pressure, government regulatory pressure, environmental pressure, geopolitical instability, and economic instability.

Supply-Side Innovation

Supply-side innovations consist of new products, services, technologies, and other supplier developments that have the potential to change a company's or an entire industry's business model. Supply-side innovation occurs (thankfully) because companies are continually developing new products and services.

Consider the creation of a plug-in credit card reader for smartphones. This allowed mobile/ temporary storefronts to process credit card transactions—clearly an opportunity for those businesses. It also allowed new competitors to quickly emerge with a mobile customer experience. Supply-side innovation driven transformation brings opportunities to some businesses and introduces better positioned competitors to others.

Unreliable Supply Chain

A company's supply chain is considered unreliable when the company experiences disruptions in the expected flow of goods and services. This can occur when suppliers discontinue products, services, or operations, when supplier quality falls below service level expectations, or when there are changes in regulations governing supply chain products and activities. An unreliable supply chain impacts sales, profitability, and customer service. The decision to pursue a business transformation depends on the nature, frequency, and severity of the supply chain reliability issues.

Shareholder Pressure

Shareholder pressure in publicly traded companies is a proxy motivator for a business transformation. It indicates dissatisfaction with the performance or direction of the company. Recommendations by commercial investment analysts can impact a company's stock price, and in extreme cases, create a transformation of ownership structure, such as changes in the board of directors or company executives.

Government Regulatory Pressure

Government regulations include the policies and statutes governing every aspect of a business—from labor, to materials, to commercial licensing, to operational and financial practices. Furthermore, government regulations can vary by the scope of jurisdiction—city, county, state, and country. Regulations are intended to establish fair business practices, protect consumers and other groups, and provide revenues for the governing organizations. Their effectiveness at accomplishing these objectives will not be considered here, but their impact will.

Government regulations are constantly changing. It's expensive to comply with these changes as well as the existing regulations. Companies must create data tracking and gathering systems, reporting capabilities, and in some cases, adjust their organizational structures. Regulations can also limit revenue growth and profitability. As a transformation motivator, government regulatory pressure is considered a necessity of doing business.

MICHAEL J. VITALE

Environmental Pressure

Environmental pressure is a special case of government regulation. It includes regulations that impact the environment in which the company operates—air quality, energy, waste products, and plant/animal habitats. Environmental regulations have legal statutes, and as with government regulations, they constantly change, create a compliance expense, and are considered a necessity of doing business.

Geopolitical Instability

Geopolitics includes the influence of political and economic geography on the national power, foreign policy, and economy of a state. Geopolitical instability increases operational risk through increased government regulations, political/social instability, restrictive trade policies, violation of intellectual property rights, commodity price fluctuation, increased public debt, and discontinuity in the supply chain.

Global businesses must pay close attention to geopolitics as the impact can be devastating—consider the case where the host country nationalizes a foreign company's operations. A transformation motivated by geopolitical instability seeks to offset the instability with some form of risk mitigation.

Economic Instability

Economic stability is the absence of excessive fluctuations in the macroeconomy—that is, an economy with fairly constant output growth and low/stable inflation. The converse is economic instability—an economy with rapid inflation/deflation, credit volatility, asset bubbles/bursts, and large cycles of economic growth and recession.

Economic instability occurs when there is a significant and increasing imbalance between the demand of goods/services (including money) and their supply. Governments will try to create stabilization by varying its budgetary and monetary policies. A transformation motivated by economic instability seeks to offset the instability, with some form of risk mitigation.

Internal Environment Motivators

The internal environment motivators originate with respect to controllable conditions inside the organization itself. Left unaddressed, these conditions create an operational disadvantage that needs to be corrected. The five most significant internal environment motivators for a business transformation include poor business performance, ineffective systems and infrastructure, unreliable internal labor, poor agility/adaptability, and planned abandonment.

8

Poor Business Performance

Poor business performance is exemplified in the metrics used to indicate how well a company is doing relative to its peers within the same industry segment. They include sales growth, gross margin, operating expense, working capital, cash flow, and capital structure. Poor performance is due to decisions/actions taken by the current or prior management team. The implications range from suboptimal value creation to operating losses to bankruptcy. A corresponding transformation will depend on the metrics affected, their severity, and the amount of change the company can absorb.

Ineffective Systems and Infrastructure

Systems include the collection of tools, technologies, and methodologies a company uses to carry out its operations. Infrastructure includes properties, buildings, and other equipment. Ineffective systems and infrastructure fail to provide a business advantage and can even create a significant disadvantage.

Systems and infrastructure become ineffective over time. The business can also outgrow their capabilities. In some cases, the systems/infrastructure were poorly conceived to begin with. Furthermore, the pace of technology is accelerating and driving the need to continuously refresh systems.

Regardless of the reason, ineffective systems or infrastructure create an operational cost that outweighs the related benefits and negatively impacts a company's competitiveness. Many companies are motivated in whole or in part to transform their business because of ineffective systems and infrastructure.

Ineffective Labor

Labor includes the full-time and contracted personnel utilized to carry out the operations of the company. Ineffective labor fails to provide the skills, experience, reliability, availability, attitudes, and relationships required by the business. Labor can become ineffective over time, or as with systems/infrastructure, the labor model is poorly conceived to begin with.

Regardless of the reason, ineffective labor is caused by ineffective management and is the sole responsibility of management to remediate. Left unaddressed, ineffective labor erodes operational productivity, creates public relations and legal liabilities, and damages morale and culture. The decision to pursue a business transformation depends on the nature and severity of the labor issues.

Poor Adaptability/Agility

Adaptability is the ability to adjust to new business conditions. Agility is the ability to easily and quickly adapt to these new business conditions. Conversely, a business with poor adaptability or agility will find it difficult if not impossible to adjust to new business conditions.

Poor adaptability/agility occurs in organizations that lack the proper motivation to adjust, lack the capabilities to adjust, or both. Businesses with poor adaptability/agility have the greatest difficulty undergoing transformations. They do not have the resiliency required to effectively carry out the myriad changes in the transformation. If a company plans to take on a business transformation and it knows that adapting to change has been difficult in the past, the company can first undergo an effort to improve its adaptability/agility.

Planned Abandonment

The final internal environment motivator is planned abandonment—the intentional termination of a less effective product, service, market, and capability—to make room for a more effective one. Planned abandonment allows a company to conserve its resources for more productive uses and is one of the ways to improve agility. In a sense, planned abandonment is the part of a transformation that turns off something that was turned on in a prior transformation.

Poorly Defined Motivators

Just as it was valuable to understand the valid motivators for a business transformation, it's equally valuable to look at some of the invalid motivators. A motivator is poorly defined if it fails to capture an objective business reason to undertake the transformation. Poorly defined motivators lead to poorly defined business transformations. The three most significant poorly defined motivators include "Be more innovative," "Management differentiation," and "Everyone is doing it."

Be More Innovative

The challenge in using "Be more innovative" as a motivator for a transformation is the meaning is vague and not associated with a specific business reason to transform.

Innovation

1. The introduction of something new
2. A new idea, method, or device: novelty

When a company says it wishes to be more innovative, it is not clear why the company needs to be innovating, what exactly needs to be innovated—and to what degree—or what the outcome will be. A new product, service, or method may in fact be detrimental if it fails to create any perceivable value. Value is not in the novelty innovation can bring, but in the improvement it can bring.

There of course are many innovation success stories. In particular, (Vullings & Heleven, 2015) many companies created cross-industry mashups to create a better customer experience. BMW borrowed from the video gaming industry to create a simple and easy-to-use media navigation system.

There are many more examples, however, of companies setting out on a "Be more innovative" transformation without clearly defined improvement objectives. A well-known example is the Coca-Cola Company's launch of "New Coke." This was the first innovative change to the Coca-Cola formula in ninety-nine years. The product was introduced in April 1985. Three months later—because of consumer backlash—the company returned to the original formula rebranded as "Coca-Cola Classic."

Management Differentiation

Management differentiation as a motivator means a newly appointed C-level leadership team is initiating a business transformation to be perceived as transformational. When this occurs, it is unlikely the new leadership team will explicitly express their desire to differentiate themselves from the prior team. Rather, the purpose of the transformation will be vague and will not be associated with specific business reasons to transform. As in the case of the "Be more innovative" motivator, management differentiation without clearly defined improvement objectives will fail to create any perceivable value.

Everyone Is Doing It

The last example of a poorly defined motivator is pressure from industry peers carrying out their own business transformations. There may be legitimate reasons for all peers in the industry segment to take on a transformation. For example, better positioned competitors could be entering the segment— or there could be an emerging substitute product. However, without clearly defined improvement objectives that are specific to the company, the "me too" motivator will fail to create perceivable value. The transformations will suffer incohesive changes.

Example: Let Us Eat Cakes

Let Us Eat Cakes took on a transformation to improve its business. Their business environment changed, and Fred West is now equipped to articulate those changes and ultimately the motivation for taking on a transformation. Several sentences from the opening few paragraphs of the case provide clues as to the motivation. Consider the following. The numbers refer to the motivators in figure 3 (below).

1. "Business was good, but it could always be better. Well actually, it needed to be better."
   a. [13] Poor Business Performance

2. "Customers have many choices for baked goods, and some now value their time as much as their sweets."
   a. [4] Emergence of Substitute Products
   b. [1] Underserved Customer Expectations

3. Fred was sure he could double or even triple revenues by servicing the on-the-go customers through an online ordering system. The online system would provide Let Us Eat Cakes a mobile-enabled website to order the regular bakery items as well as the specialty cakes.
   a. [6] Supply-Side Innovation

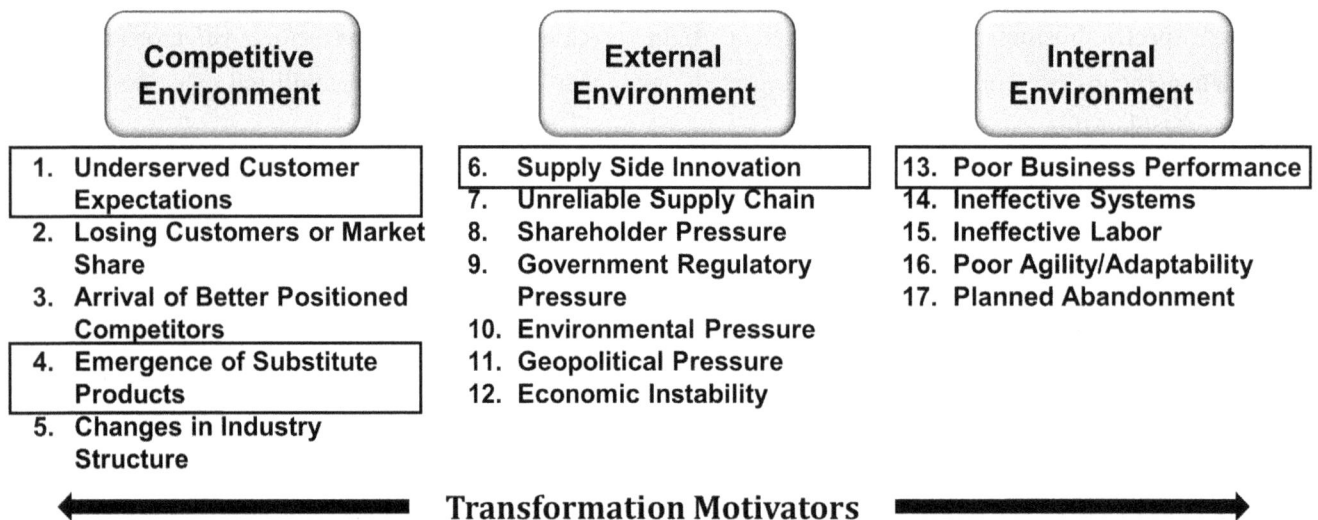

Competitive Environment

1. Underserved Customer Expectations
2. Losing Customers or Market Share
3. Arrival of Better Positioned Competitors
4. Emergence of Substitute Products
5. Changes in Industry Structure

External Environment

6. Supply Side Innovation
7. Unreliable Supply Chain
8. Shareholder Pressure
9. Government Regulatory Pressure
10. Environmental Pressure
11. Geopolitical Pressure
12. Economic Instability

Internal Environment

13. Poor Business Performance
14. Ineffective Systems
15. Ineffective Labor
16. Poor Agility/Adaptability
17. Planned Abandonment

← **Transformation Motivators** →

Figure 3: Let Us Eat Cakes Business Transformation Motivators

Business Changes Initiated during a Transformation

Once a company has established the motivation for a business transformation, it must determine—at a macro level—the set of changes it will make. These changes represent the levers the business can manipulate during the transformation. They are initiated in response to the changes in their business environment and are frequently used to communicate the scope of the transformation to stakeholders. Fifteen common business changes will be considered here. They are shown in figure 4 (below)[2] and described in the next section. Later in this chapter, a relationship will be created between the motivators and the initiated business changes.

Common Business Changes

1. Product Scope
2. Service Scope
3. Industry/Market Served
4. Customer Experience
5. Technology Platform
6. Cost Structure
7. Ownership Structure
8. Internal Organization
9. Sales/Distribution Channel
10. Core Capabilities Definition
11. Outsourcing & Insourcing
12. Risk Profile
13. Regulatory Profile
14. Geographic Structure
15. Corporate Culture/Values

Figure 4: Common Business Changes Initiated during a Business Transformation

The Common Business Changes

Each of these business changes represents a core dimension of the business that can be directly controlled. Several of these changes can be combined to produce even more complex business change. For example, by controlling insourcing and outsourcing, you can indirectly control your supply chain.

---

[2] This list of common business changes is compiled from various studies on business transformations. It does not exist elsewhere in one place or organized in this manner.

Product Scope

Product scope pertains to the set of all salable items a business offers to its customers. When a business initiates a change in product scope, it intends to expand, contract, or modify its commercial product offering.

Service Scope

Similarly, service scope pertains to the set of all salable tasks/activities a business offers to its customers. When a business initiates a change in service scope, it intends to expand, contract, or modify its commercial service offering.

Industry/Market Served

The industry segment is the set of all companies providing similar products or services. The market segment is the set of all customers who require the products and services within an industry segment. When a business initiates a change in the industry it participates in, it changes the set of companies with which it competes. This is typically done by changing the set of products/services offered. When a business initiates a change in the market segment it serves, it changes the set of customers with which it commercially engages. Again, this is typically done by changing the set of products/services offered.

Customer Experience

The customer experience pertains to how your customers perceive their interactions with your company. Businesses initiating changes in their customer experience seek to improve the quality of interactions by using knowledge about customers to personalize the experience and anticipate their needs. Consumerization of online digital capabilities has precipitated a movement to totally rethink the customer experience.

Technology Platform

Technology platforms include the infrastructure, applications, tools, and methodologies used to operate the business and transact commercially. Technology has been evolving at a breakneck pace, enabling new capabilities and implementation challenges at that same pace. Changes in a company's technology platform are primarily initiated when they enable a business advantage.

However, sometimes, the changes are required by the platforms themselves, as in refreshes, upgrades, and ongoing maintenance.

Cost Structure

Cost structure pertains to the types of cost in a company as well as the composition of those costs. When a company changes its cost structure, it will alter either the types themselves or their proportion in the total mix. Companies will initiate changes in cost structure as a result of mergers, acquisitions, and divestitures, other competitive/industry restructuring, or financial performance challenges.

Ownership Structure

The ownership structure pertains to the entities holding claims to the company's equity and the distribution of the equity among those entities. Ownership structure changes are initiated during mergers, acquisitions, divestitures, sales, purchases, becoming a public company, taking a public company private, or bankruptcy.

Internal Organization

Internal organization means the composition of functional roles, the arrangement of those roles with respect to their interrelationships and responsibilities, and the allocation of human resources to the roles. Companies initiate changes to their internal organization for a variety of reasons—some of which are more rational than others. When they are initiated, they result in changes to the size, scope, and structural relationships of the functional groups.

Sales/Distribution Channel

A sales channel is the method of bringing products or services to a market segment so they can be purchased by customers within that segment. A distribution channel refers to the way products and services are disseminated from the creator to the end consumer. The scope of the distribution channel for a company depends on how that company chooses to operate its business. When a company initiates a change to either its sales or distribution channels, it will add a new channel, modify a current channel, or discontinue the use of a channel.

Core Capabilities Definition

Core capabilities are the activities a company performs together with the assets it uses to perform them for the purposing of driving value or sustaining their competitive position. When a company initiates a change to its core capabilities, it will add a new capability, modify an existing capability, or—in some cases—discontinue a capability.

Outsourcing and Insourcing

All companies have some form of supply chain on which they depend to carry out the sales and delivery of products and services. The supply chain is configured as a combination of their own internal operations and the operations of external companies. When a company initiates outsourcing, it means they are moving some internal portion of the supply chain to external companies. Conversely, when a company initiates insourcing, it means they are moving some external portion of the supply chain into their own internal operations.

Risk Profile

A risk profile is an assessment of a company's willingness to take risks as well as the threats to which they are exposed. Companies do not intentionally increase risk to their operations—just the opposite. However, risk increases over time due to actions outside the company as well as actions the company has taken. When a company initiates a change to its risk profile, it intends to eliminate the source of the threats or reduce the company's exposure.

Regulatory Profile

A regulatory profile is the aggregate of all regulations a company is exposed to—through its geopolitical presence, operational practices, or business relationships. As with risk profiles, companies do not seek to increase regulations on their operations. Regulations increase over time due to actions outside the company as well as decisions/actions the company has taken. When a company initiates a change to its regulatory profile, it intends to reduce the amount of regulation to which it is exposed.

Geographic Structure

Geographic structure pertains to the structure and arrangement of business offices and operations in different geographic locations. When a company initiates a geographic structure change, it can either expand or contract its geographical footprint.

Corporate Culture/Values

Corporate culture/values refers to the shared attitudes, standards, and beliefs that characterize what is important to the company and ultimately guides its behavior. When a company initiates a change in corporate culture/values, it will do so through changes in business goals, strategies, structure, relationships with employees, customers, suppliers, and investors, and the community in which it operates.

The next step in analyzing business transformation change is to form a relationship between the motivators for a business transformation and the common business changes initiated during a transformation. This relationship serves as a reference for the potential changes a company could make when responding to changes in its business environment.

Relating Competitive Environment Motivators to Business Changes Initiated

The relationship between the five competitive environment motivators and the fifteen potential business changes initiated will be captured in the matrix shown in figure 5 (below).

Transformation Motivators (Reasons for your Transformation)	1. Product Scope	2. Service Scope	3. Industry/Market Served	4. Customer Experience	5. Technology Platform	6. Cost Structure	7. Ownership Structure	8. Internal Organization	9. Sales/Distribution Channel	10. Core Capabilities Definition	11. Outsourcing & Insourcing	12. Risk Profile	13. Regulatory Profile	14. Geographic Structure	15. Corporate Culture/Values
Competitive Environment — 1. Underserved Customer Expectations															
2. Losing Customers or Market Share															
3. Arrival of Better Positioned Competitors															
4. Emergence of Substitute Products															
5. Changes in Industry Structure															

Figure 5: Relating Competitive Environment Motivators to Common Business Changes

Underserved Customer Expectations

In responding to underserved customer expectations, a company may initiate some combination of the following business changes in its transformation:

- product scope
- service scope
- industry/market served
- customer experience
- technology platform
- sales/distribution channel
- core capabilities definition

Consider companies choosing to address underserved customer expectations by launching ecommerce. Their transformations will initiate a new sales/distribution channel and changes to their technology platform. They could also initiate changes to their product and service scope in the process, but they don't necessarily have to. Most certainly, their customer experience will change as will their core capabilities to support the e-commerce platform. Finally, they may change the industry/market served, but they may choose to initiate those changes later.

Every company must select the specific changes it will initiate. The matrix depicted in figure 6 (below), shows the changes most likely to be initiated in addressing underserved customer expectations.

Transformation Motivators (Reasons for your Transformation)	1. Product Scope	2. Service Scope	3. Industry/Market Served	4. Customer Experience	5. Technology Platform	6. Cost Structure	7. Ownership Structure	8. Internal Organization	9. Sales/Distribution Channel	10. Core Capabilities Definition	11. Outsourcing & Insourcing	12. Risk Profile	13. Regulatory Profile	14. Geographic Structure	15. Corporate Culture/Values
Competitive Environment 1. Underserved Customer Expectations	●	●	●	●	●				●	●					
2. Losing Customers or Market Share															
3. Arrival of Better Positioned Competitors															
4. Emergence of Substitute Products															
5. Changes in Industry Structure															

Figure 6: Business Changes Associated with Underserved Customer Expectations

Losing Customers or Market Share

In response to the loss of customers or market share, a company may initiate some combination of the following business changes in its transformation:

- product scope
- service scope
- industry/market served
- customer experience
- cost restructure
- sales/distribution channel

As with underserved customer expectations, the exact combination of changes initiated depends on the nature of the loss and the environment in which the company competes. Every company must choose which specific changes it will initiate. Figure 7 (below) illustrates the changes most likely to be initiated in addressing losing customers of market share.

Arrival of Better Positioned Competitors

In response to the arrival of better positioned competitors, a company may initiate some combination of the following business changes in its transformation:

- product scope
- service scope
- industry/market served
- customer experience
- technology replatform
- cost restructure
- core capabilities redefinition

This is the nature of a competitive business environment, and to some extent, every company eventually faces a better positioned competitor. Their response can be reactive or proactive and will determine which specific changes they will initiate. Figure 7 (below) illustrates the changes most likely to be initiated in addressing the arrival of better positioned competitors.

Emergence of Substitute Products

In response to the emergence of substitute products, a company may initiate some combination of the following business changes in its transformation:

- product scope
- service scope
- industry/market served
- customer experience
- core capabilities redefinition

As in the case of better positioned competitors, the response can be reactive or proactive, and it will determine which changes get initiated. When a company is too slow or incapable of responding, the impact can be devastating. Consider this example from McKinsey: "In the electric-power industry, battery improvements are bringing down storage costs faster than expected, allowing customers to 'defect' from grids—with disruptive consequences." (Frankel & Wagner, 2018) Figure 7 (below) illustrates the changes most likely to be initiated in addressing the emergence of substitute products.

Changes in Industry Structure

In responding to changes in industry structure, a company may initiate some combination of the following business changes in its transformation:

- industry/market served
- technology replatform
- cost restructure
- ownership restructure
- internal reorganization
- outsourcing and insourcing
- geographic structure

Responses are generally reactive due to the privacy of the structural transaction. They can range from "do nothing"—when a merger/acquisition creates no competitive advantage—to a flurry of "fast follower" mergers/acquisitions when a competitive threat materializes. The US auto industry experienced the "fast follower" style with Japanese car manufacturing partnerships in the eighties and nineties. Figure 7 (below) illustrates the changes most likely to be initiated in addressing changes in industry structure.

Transformation Motivators (Reasons for your Transformation)	1. Product Scope	2. Service Scope	3. Industry/Market Served	4. Customer Experience	5. Technology Platform	6. Cost Structure	7. Ownership Structure	8. Internal Organization	9. Sales/Distribution Channel	10. Core Capabilities Definition	11. Outsourcing & Insourcing	12. Risk Profile	13. Regulatory Profile	14. Geographic Structure	15. Corporate Culture/Values
Competitive Environment — 1. Underserved Customer Expectations	●	●	●	●	●					●	●				
2. Losing Customers or Market Share	●	●	●	●		●				●					
3. Arrival of Better Positioned Competitors	●	●	●	●	●	●					●				
4. Emergence of Substitute Products	●	●	●	●							●				
5. Changes in Industry Structure			●		●	●	●	●			●			●	

Figure 7: Business Changes Initiated for Competitive Environment Motivators

Relating External Environment Motivators to Business Changes Initiated

The relationship between the seven external environment motivators and the fifteen potential business changes initiated are captured in the matrix shown in figure 8 (below).

Transformation Motivators (Reasons for your Transformation)	1. Product Scope	2. Service Scope	3. Industry/Market Served	4. Customer Experience	5. Technology Platform	6. Cost Structure	7. Ownership Structure	8. Internal Organization	9. Sales/Distribution Channel	10. Core Capabilities Definition	11. Outsourcing & Insourcing	12. Risk Profile	13. Regulatory Profile	14. Geographic Structure	15. Corporate Culture/Values
External Environment — 6. Supply Side Innovation															
7. Unreliable Supply Chain															
8. Shareholder Pressure															
9. Government Regulatory Pressure															
10. Environmental Pressure															
11. Geopolitical Pressure															
12. Economic Instability															

Figure 8: Relating External Environment Motivators to Common Business Changes

Supply-Side Innovation

In responding to supply-side innovations, a company may initiate some combination of the following business changes in its transformation:

- product scope
- service scope
- customer experience
- technology platform
- cost structure
- core capabilities definition

Many factors will determine the combination of changes a business initiates in its transformation including the nature of the business, the supply-side innovation, and the pace at which the competitive environment can adopt the innovation. Figure 9 (below) illustrates the changes most likely to be initiated in addressing supply-side innovation.

Unreliable Supply Chain

Supply chain issues do not always require a transformation. However, when reliability is severely impacted, such as in the case when a key product is banned, or when an energy producer is subject to regulatory rationing, a company may initiate some combination of the following business changes in its transformation:

- product scope
- service scope
- technology platform
- cost structure
- core capabilities definition
- outsourcing and insourcing
- risk profile
- geographic structure

Consider a company using a hazardous material in its manufacturing process. Their supply chain includes a hazardous waste disposal service for retrieving and managing the manufacturing waste byproducts. If a subsequent environmental regulation prohibits the usage/disposal of this material, the waste disposal company can disrupt the manufacturers supply chain. The manufacturing company may then initiate a change to its manufacturing processes to eliminate the need for the hazardous material; it may even relocate its manufacturing process to a geography without this regulatory limitation. Figure 9 (below) illustrates the changes most likely to be initiated in addressing an unreliable supply chain.

Shareholder Pressure

In responding to increased shareholder pressure, a company may initiate some combination of the following business changes in its transformation:

- cost restructure
- ownership restructure
- core capabilities redefinition
- risk profile
- geographic structure
- corporate culture/values

Consider the case of Home Depot. Home Depot spent several years building its wholesale segment to diversify their offering and spark growth. However, in late 2006, some investors voiced strong dissatisfaction with the wholesale distribution business unit, calling it a diversion from the retailer's core business. In February 2007, Home Depot announced it would consider a spin-off of their wholesale distribution business. The transaction was completed later in the year. Figure 9 (below) illustrates the changes most likely to be initiated in addressing shareholder pressure.

Government Regulatory Pressure

In responding to changes in government regulations, a company may initiate some combination of the following business changes in its transformation:

- product scope
- industry/market served
- sales/distribution channel
- core capabilities definition
- outsourcing and insourcing
- regulatory profile
- geographic structure

Consider the impact of Sarbanes-Oxley (SOX) on companies in the United States. SOX compliance required companies to develop new controls, procedures, tracking, and reporting systems to manage financial data and practices—and then annually certify that these systems met the standards laid out in the SOX regulations. As in the case of all other motivators, the changes initiated will depend on the nature of the regulations and the company's ability to navigate them. Figure 9 (below) illustrates the changes most likely to be initiated in addressing government regulatory pressure.

Environmental Pressure

In responding to increased environmental pressure, a company may initiate some combination of the following business changes in its transformation:

- outsourcing and insourcing
- risk profile
- regulatory profile
- geographic structure
- corporate culture/values

In the United States, the Environmental Protection Agency has instituted laws and regulations governing the agriculture, automotive, construction, electric utilities, oil and gas, and transportation industries. These industries have responded by initiating transformational changes including the use of green business materials, sustainable energy sources, waste, and water recycling. Figure 9 (below) illustrates the changes most likely to be initiated in addressing environmental pressure.

Geopolitical Instability

In responding to increased geopolitical pressure, a company may initiate some combination of the following business changes in its transformation:

- outsourcing and insourcing
- risk profile
- regulatory profile
- geographic structure
- corporate culture/values

A most recent example is in the United Kingdom. Their vote to leave the European Union created uncertainty surrounding future trade negotiations between the UK and the EU—and operational risk for all multinational businesses. These businesses could respond to the geopolitical instability by initiating changes to their outsourcing and insourcing mix as well as their geographic structure. Figure 9 (below) illustrates the changes most likely to be initiated in addressing geopolitical instability.

Economic Instability

When there is economic instability, the impact on a given business depends on the magnitude of the instability and the structure/operating model of that business. Even though the effects of economic instability are usually on a macro scale, a business can mitigate some of the risk by initiating some combination of the following business changes:

- cost structure
- ownership structure
- outsourcing and insourcing
- risk profile
- geographic structure

Consider the effects of the housing boom in the United States in the early 2000s. A change in mortgage lending rates artificially induced demand for new homes. Home prices rose in response to the demand until the supply of new homes met the demand. The boom was not sustained, however. When the home construction asset bubble burst, it contributed significantly to the recession in 2009.

During this period, the home construction industry experienced a rapid rise encouraging massive business investment, inventory buildup, and many new competitors. This was followed by an even faster decline creating huge industry adjustments including bankruptcies, divestitures, and structural contraction. Figure 9 illustrates the changes most likely to be initiated in addressing economic instability.

Transformation Motivators (Reasons for your Transformation)		1. Product Scope	2. Service Scope	3. Industry/Market Served	4. Customer Experience	5. Technology Platform	6. Cost Structure	7. Ownership Structure	8. Internal Organization	9. Sales/Distribution Channel	10. Core Capabilities Definition	11. Outsourcing & Insourcing	12. Risk Profile	13. Regulatory Profile	14. Geographic Structure	15. Corporate Culture/Values
External Environment	6. Supply Side Innovation	●	●		●	●	●				●					
	7. Unreliable Supply Chain	●	●			●	●				●	●	●		●	
	8. Shareholder Pressure						●	●			●		●		●	●
	9. Government Regulatory Pressure	●		●						●		●		●	●	
	10. Environmental Pressure											●	●	●	●	●
	11. Geopolitical Pressure											●	●	●	●	●
	12. Economic Instability	●	●	●			●	●				●	●		●	

Figure 9: Business Changes Initiated for External Environment Motivators

Relating Internal Environment Motivators to Business Changes Initiated

The relationship between the five internal environment motivators and the fifteen potential business changes initiated are captured in figure 10 (below).

Transformation Motivators (Reasons for your Transformation)		1. Product Scope	2. Service Scope	3. Industry/Market Served	4. Customer Experience	5. Technology Platform	6. Cost Structure	7. Ownership Structure	8. Internal Organization	9. Sales/Distribution Channel	10. Core Capabilities Definition	11. Outsourcing & Insourcing	12. Risk Profile	13. Regulatory Profile	14. Geographic Structure	15. Corporate Culture/Values
Internal Environment	13. Poor Business Performance															
	14. Ineffective Systems															
	15. Ineffective Labor															
	16. Poor Agility/Adaptability															
	17. Planned Abandonment															

Figure 10: Relating Internal Environment Motivators to Common Business Changes

Poor Business Performance

In responding to poor business performance, a company may initiate some combination of the following business changes in its transformation:

- product scope
- service scope
- industry/market served
- customer experience
- technology platform
- cost structure
- ownership structure
- internal organization
- sales/distribution channel
- core capabilities definition
- outsourcing and insourcing

As implied above, a business can initiate many changes to address poor performance. The set chosen will depend on the business performance characteristics affected, their severity, and the amount of change the company can absorb.

For example, consider a company wishing to improve gross product profitability with respect to its peers. A transformation could consist of changing the mix of products in its offering to include more high-margin products and fewer low-margin products. The company could also discontinue lower-margin products, bundle low-margin products with higher-margin services, or introduce higher-margin privately branded products. Figure 11 (below) illustrates the changes most likely to be initiated in addressing poor business performance.

Ineffective Systems and Infrastructure

In responding to ineffective systems and infrastructure, a company may initiate some combination of the following business changes in its transformation:

- technology platform
- cost structure
- core capabilities definition
- outsourcing and insourcing
- risk profile
- geographic structure

For example, consider a company that is growing beyond a small startup. It will eventually exhaust the capabilities of an off-the-shelf packaged accounting system. At some point, the company will need to consider introducing an enterprise resource planning system (ERP) to manage sales, purchasing, logistics, and financial information. This is not a small endeavor since the ERP also embodies the processes and methods for transacting business. All users must master the new processes and methods after introducing the ERP. The company must initiate changes in its technology platform, cost structure, core capabilities definition, and possibly outsourcing and insourcing as well as its risk profile. Figure 11 (below) illustrates the changes most likely to be initiated in addressing ineffective systems and infrastructure.

Ineffective Labor

In responding to ineffective labor, a company may initiate some combination of the following business changes in its transformation:

- technology platform
- cost structure
- internal organization
- outsourcing and insourcing
- regulatory profile
- geographic structure
- corporate culture/values

Consider the case where a business fails to train its employees on emerging technology. It will find over time that its workforce is less productive and less satisfied than that of its competitors. The solution is not to simply hire new employees with better skills. That would create a workforce consisting of both skilled and unskilled employees and would introduce multiple operational procedures/methods as well as deteriorate morale. Over time, the productivity of the higher-skilled employees would atrophy relative to that of the competition since there is no training-refresh program. A better option would be to initiate changes in corporate culture/values to make training employees a priority, and then include the changes in cost structure and other areas as part of a transformation. Figure 11 (below) illustrates the changes most likely to be initiated in addressing ineffective labor.

Poor Adaptability/Agility

If a company plans to take on a business transformation, and it knows that adapting to change has been difficult in the past, the company can first undergo an effort to improve its adaptability/agility. This can take the form of several smaller business changes (from the set below) with enough time in between the changes to allow the organization to recover:

- technology platform
- cost structure
- internal organization
- sales/distribution channel
- core capabilities definition
- outsourcing and insourcing
- corporate culture/values

As an example, consider a company that is interested in transforming from "products only" to "products and services." Even with well-defined services that are tailored to a market segment, if this company lacks the technology, core capabilities, and sales/distribution channels to support a services business, the transformation will be very challenging. The company may decide first to support the services by initiating an outsourcing agreement until it is able to build out the technology platform, core capabilities, and sales/distribution channels. It, in effect, spreads the change to a services business over time, allowing itself to adapt. Figure 11 (below) illustrates the changes most likely to be initiated in addressing poor adaptability/agility.

Planned Abandonment

In a sense, planned abandonment is the part of a transformation that shuts down what was built in a prior transformation. To carry out planned abandonment, a company may initiate some combination of the following business changes in its transformation:

- product scope
- service scope
- industry/market served
- cost restructure
- sales/distribution channel
- core capabilities redefinition

- outsourcing and insourcing
- risk profile
- regulatory profile
- geographic structure

General Motors exercised planned abandonment when it eliminated its Saturn, Pontiac, and Hummer automobile lines in 2010, and around the same time, it entered the China market with Baojun and Jiefan automobile lines. More than just a product change, GM initiated an exit of the markets for the Saturn, Pontiac, and Hummer, and it initiated an entrance into the new markets and countries with Baojun and Jiefan. Figure 11 (below) illustrates the changes most likely to be initiated in addressing planned abandonment.

	Transformation Motivators (Reasons for your Transformation)	1. Product Scope	2. Service Scope	3. Industry/Market Served	4. Customer Experience	5. Technology Platform	6. Cost Structure	7. Ownership Structure	8. Internal Organization	9. Sales/Distribution Channel	10. Core Capabilities Definition	11. Outsourcing & Insourcing	12. Risk Profile	13. Regulatory Profile	14. Geographic Structure	15. Corporate Culture/Values
Internal Environment	13. Poor Business Performance	●	●	●	●	●	●	●	●	●	●	●				
	14. Ineffective Systems					●	●					●	●	●	●	
	15. Ineffective Labor					●	●		●			●		●	●	●
	16. Poor Agility/Adaptability					●	●		●			●	●			●
	17. Planned Abandonment	●	●	●			●			●	●	●	●	●	●	

Figure 11: Business Changes Initiated for Internal Environment Motivators

Figure 12 (below) aggregates all the business changes most likely to be initiated during a transformation addressing motivators from any of the three environment categories.

Transformation Motivators (Reasons for your Transformation)	1. Product Scope	2. Service Scope	3. Industry/Market Served	4. Customer Experience	5. Technology Platform	6. Cost Structure	7. Ownership Structure	8. Internal Organization	9. Sales/Distribution Channel	10. Core Capabilities Definition	11. Outsourcing & Insourcing	12. Risk Profile	13. Regulatory Profile	14. Geographic Structure	15. Corporate Culture/Values
Competitive Environment															
1. Underserved Customer Expectations	●	●	●	●	●					●	●				
2. Losing Customers or Market Share	●	●	●	●		●				●					
3. Arrival of Better Positioned Competitors	●	●	●	●	●	●					●				
4. Emergence of Substitute Products	●	●	●	●							●				
5. Changes in Industry Structure			●		●	●	●	●			●			●	
External Environment															
6. Supply Side Innovation	●	●		●	●	●					●				
7. Unreliable Supply Chain	●	●			●	●					●	●	●	●	
8. Shareholder Pressure						●	●				●		●	●	●
9. Government Regulatory Pressure	●		●						●		●		●	●	
10. Environmental Pressure											●	●	●	●	●
11. Geopolitical Pressure											●	●	●	●	●
12. Economic Instability	●	●	●			●	●				●	●		●	
Internal Environment															
13. Poor Business Performance	●	●	●	●	●	●	●	●	●	●	●				
14. Ineffective Systems					●	●					●	●	●	●	
15. Ineffective Labor					●	●			●		●		●	●	●
16. Poor Agility/Adaptability					●	●			●		●	●			●
17. Planned Abandonment	●	●	●			●				●	●	●	●	●	

Figure 12: Business Changes Initiated for All Motivators

Example: Let Us Eat Cakes

Recall from figure 3 that the business transformation motivators for Let Us Eat Cakes included:

- underserved customer expectations
- emergence of substitute products
- supply-side innovation
- poor business performance

The business changes that could be initiated during its transformation can be found by relating the motivators to the business changes using the matrix in figure 12. If you do this, you will get the business changes shown in figure 13 (below). Let Us Eat Cakes may elect to initiate some or all of these changes in their business transformation. Several sentences in the opening paragraphs of the case provide clues as to the changes they initiated. The numbers [#] refer to the common business changes in figure 13 (below).

1. Fred was sure he could double or even triple revenues by servicing the on-the-go customers through an online ordering system.
   a. [3] industry/market served
   b. [9] sales/distribution channel

2. The online system would provide Let Us Eat Cakes a mobile-enabled website to order the regular bakery items as well as the specialty cakes. Customers would pay in advance using a credit card, making it quick and convenient for commuters.
   a. [2] service scope
   b. [5] technology platform
   c. [4] customer experience

Let Us Eat Cakes has not yet decided to initiate a change to its product scope. However, at some time in the future, they could expand their offerings through the new sales channel.

Transformation Motivators (Reasons for your Transformation)	1. Product Scope	2. Service Scope	3. Industry/Market Served	4. Customer Experience	5. Technology Platform	6. Cost Structure	7. Ownership Structure	8. Internal Organization	9. Sales/Distribution Channel	10. Core Capabilities Definition	11. Outsourcing & Insourcing	12. Risk Profile	13. Regulatory Profile	14. Geographic Structure	15. Corporate Culture/Values
Competitive Environment															
1. Underserved Customer Expectations	●	●	●	●	●				●	●					
2. Losing Customers or Market Share															
3. Arrival of Better Positioned Competitors															
4. Emergence of Substitute Products	●	●	●	●						●					
5. Changes in Industry Structure															
External Environment															
6. Supply Side Innovation	●	●		●	●	●				●					
7. Unreliable Supply Chain															
8. Shareholder Pressure															
9. Government Regulatory Pressure															
10. Environmental Pressure															
11. Geopolitical Pressure															
12. Economic Instability															
Internal Environment															
13. Poor Business Performance	●	●	●	●	●	●	●	●	●	●	●				
14. Ineffective Systems															
15. Ineffective Labor															
16. Poor Agility/Adaptability															
17. Planned Abandonment															

Figure 13: Let Us Eat Cakes Potential Business Changes Initiated

The business change cycle has been updated in figure 14 (below) to reflect the notion that a transformation initiates "business changes." The next step in the analysis of the business change cycle is to examine the change impacts induced within a company when business changes are initiated.

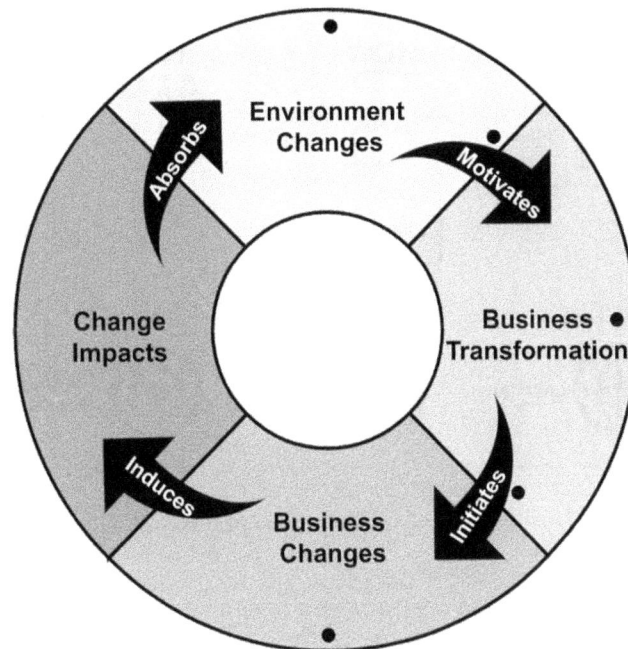

Figure 14: The Business Change Cycle Updated

Business Impacts Induced during a Transformation

While it is necessary to understand the range of business changes a company could initiate during a transformation, it is not the complete story. Business changes are the sources of the change experienced during a transformation, and the resulting change impacts are the effects of the transformation. Business change impacts are what you must deal with when you undertake the transformation—they are what happens to your business. A company undergoing a business transformation must be aware of the change impacts and must effectively address them during the transformation.

Business Change Impacts

A business change impact is something that affects your business as a result of a change. Change impact analysis is facilitated via a framework to capture all dimensions of a business that could be impacted. One framework that is simple to understand, and which will be used here, is shown in figure 15 (below): what, how, who, where, when, and why.

Each of the dimensions represents an aspect of business behavior that could experience a change impact. The actual impact is an addition to, modification of, or discontinuation of some portion of the business dimension.

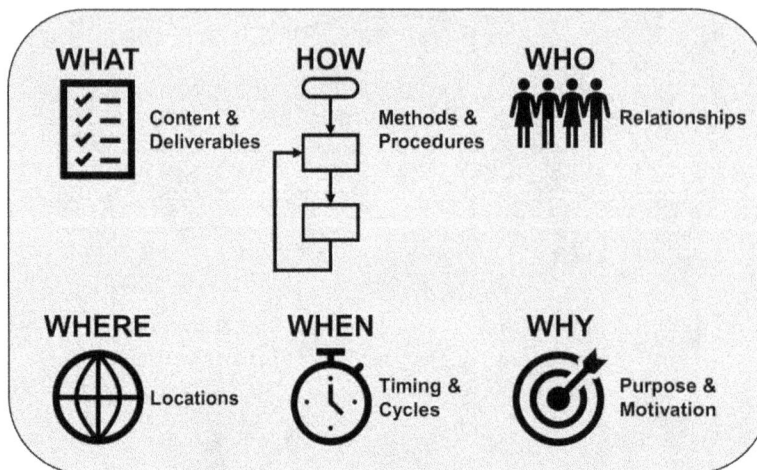

Figure 15: Change Impact Framework

What

The what dimension represents the content or the deliverables of a business. It includes the products and services a business offers its customers as well as the intermediate products and services used in producing the commercial offering. Impacts to the what dimension include adding new products/services, modifying existing products/services, and discontinuing existing products/services.

How

The how dimension represents methods, policies, or procedures used to perform work by a business. It includes the methods/policies/procedures used in producing work content and deliverables as well as those used in the administration of the business. Impacts to the how dimension include adding, modifying, or discontinuing methods, policies, or procedures.

Who

The who dimension represents the relationships through which work is performed by a business. It includes internal, reporting, customer, supplier, regulatory, and other external entity relationships. Impacts to the who dimension include adding, modifying, or discontinuing relationships with any of the entities engaged during the performance of work.

Where

The where dimension represents the locations at which work is performed by a business. It includes offices, workspaces, customer and supplier sites, and other external entity sites. Impacts to the where dimension include adding, modifying, or discontinuing locations where work is conducted.

When

The when dimension represents the time at which work is performed by a business. It includes the start/stop time of business activities as well as patterns or cycles of activity. Impacts to the when dimension include adding, modifying, or discontinuing timing, cycles, or patterns for work activities conducted by the business or external entities interacting with the business.

Why

The why dimension represents the reason work is performed by a business. It includes the purpose or motivation for performing a business activity. Impacts to the why dimension include adding, modifying, or discontinuing a reason work activity is performed by the business.

Business Change Impact Profile

Business change impacts do not occur without cause. Change impacts are induced by the changes a business chooses to initiate during a transformation. The relationship between the changes initiated and the change impacts induced can be expressed in a change impact profile. The change impact profile indicates the impacts you could experience in each of the business dimensions—whenever you initiate a business change.

The change impact profile is summarized for the fifteen common business changes in figure 16 (below). This is a qualitative representation that provides a directionally correct expression for the impact on a business. Harvey Balls are used to indicate significant change impact, moderate change impact, or minimal change impact to each business dimension. A rationale is provided in the next few sections for each of the common business changes.

Product Scope

Companies frequently change the mix of products they offer. When a business expands, modifies, or contracts its product offering, it will then experience subsequent expansions, modification, or contractions in the work content and procedures for supporting the product changes. Quite often, the business can experience corresponding changes to active customers and suppliers—and possibly operating locations. For these reasons, what, how, who, and where impacts can be induced whenever a company initiates a change to its product scope.

#	Business Changes	Change Impact Profile					
		What	How	Who	Where	When	Why
1	Product Scope	◀	◀	◀	◀	○	○
2	Service Scope	●	●	◀	◀	○	◀
3	Industry/Market Served	◀	◀	●	◀	◀	●
4	Customer Experience	●	●	●	○	○	●
5	Technology Platform	●	●	◀	○	○	◀
6	Cost Structure	●	●	●	◀	○	●
7	Ownership Structure	◀	◀	●	●	◀	●
8	Internal Organization	○	◀	●	◀	◀	●
9	Sales/Distribution Channel	●	●	●	●	◀	●
10	Core Capabilities Definition	●	●	◀	◀	◀	●
11	Outsourcing & Insourcing	◀	●	●	●	◀	●
12	Risk Profile	◀	●	◀	◀	◀	◀
13	Regulatory Profile	●	●	◀	◀	◀	◀
14	Geographic Structure	◀	◀	●	●	◀	◀
15	Corporate Culture/Values	◀	●	●	○	○	●

● Significant Change Impact   ◀ Moderate Change Impact   ○ Minimal Change Impact

Figure 16: Change Impact Profile for Common Business Changes

Service Scope

When a business expands its service offering or adds services for the first time, it can experience significant expansions in the work content and procedures for supporting the new services. The business may also experience changes to its active customers and suppliers—and possibly operating locations. Additionally, product businesses consciously undergo changes in business purpose when they choose to provide a service offering.

Similarly, as a business contracts its service offering, it will undergo contraction in the work content and procedures for supporting the existing portfolio of services. For these reasons, what, how, who, where, and why impacts can be induced whenever a company initiates a change to its service scope.

Industry/Market Served

Companies grow by offering new products and services, selling a larger basket of products and services to existing customers, or expanding into new industries and market segments. When a business chooses to service a new industry or market segment, it will experience a significant change in purpose as well as a significant change in active customers and suppliers. There may be accompanying expansions in both work content and procedures for supporting the new industry/market segment, as well as potential changes to operating locations and even active business hours. The business will see corresponding contractions in purpose, customers, and suppliers whenever it chooses to exit an industry or market segment. For these reasons, what, how, who, where, when, and why impacts can be induced whenever a company initiates a change to industry/market served.

Customer Experience

Consumerization of online digital capabilities has precipitated a movement to rethink the customer experience, including improving the quality of interactions, using knowledge about the customer to personalize their experience, and anticipating their needs. Many new businesses are centered entirely around creating an improved customer experience. When a business revises the way it engages its customers, it will experience significant changes in both work content and the procedures to support the new customer experience. The segments of customers served and the reasons for serving them can dramatically change as well. For these reasons, what, how, who, and why impacts can be induced whenever a company initiates a change to its customer experience.

Technology Platform

Companies must continuously be aware of emerging technology, choose the technologies that provide the greatest strategic advantage, and contend with the accompanying change. No sooner is a technology fully deployed, it is almost time to upgrade or enhance it. When a business modernizes/replaces current technology or introduces a new technology, there are significant changes to internal work content and the procedures for carrying out that work. These changes are often accompanied by changes in work relationships to support the technology, and depending on the technology platform, changes in business purpose as well. For these reasons, what, how, who and why impacts can be induced whenever a company initiates a change to its technology platform.

Cost Structure

Companies will make dramatic shifts in cost structure because of mergers, acquisitions, and divestitures, other competitive/industry restructuring, or financial performance challenges. When a business initiates changes to its cost structure, it can experience significant changes to internal work content, the procedures for carrying out that work, and quite often, the workforce and operating locations. In many cases, companies will also redefine their purpose within the industry segments they serve. For these reasons, what, how, who, where and why impacts can be induced whenever a company initiates a change to its cost structure.

Ownership Structure

Ownership restructuring includes mergers, acquisitions, divestiture, sales, purchases, becoming a public company, taking a public company private, and bankruptcy. In addition to the changes to its cost structure, a company can experience significant changes to work content, the procedures for carrying out that work, internal reporting relationships, the company's customers, suppliers, operating locations, and possibly even work timing. Frequently the company's purpose will change with the new ownership structure as well. For these reasons, what, how, who, where, when, and why impacts can be induced whenever a company initiates a change to its ownership structure.

Internal Organization

Internal reorganizations in general induce fewer change impacts than cost or ownership structure changes. However, they still induce impacts to work procedures and internal reporting relationships, and to a lesser degree operating locations and work timing. Sometimes the company will experience changes in purpose as that is often the reason for initiating the change to the internal organization. For these reasons, how, who, where, when, and why impacts can be induced whenever a company initiates a change to its internal organization.

Sales/Distribution Channel

Companies will consider adding a new sales channel or distribution channel to better service an existing market segment or reach new market segments. For example, in the past decade, many companies have added an online commercial presence. Other companies alter their distribution model and sell directly to the end customers of their products. This induces impacts to all dimensions of the change impact profile, including work content and procedures, customer relationships, and often internal and supplier relationships. Significant impacts can also occur in operating locations as well as the timing for conducting business. Furthermore, if the business model changes significantly with the new sales or distribution channel, the business will experience corresponding impacts in purpose as well. For these reasons, what, how, who, where, when, and why impacts can be induced whenever a company initiates a change to its sales/distribution channel.

Core Capabilities Definition

As described earlier, core capabilities are the activities a company performs to drive value and sustain their competitive position in the markets they serve. When a company adds a new core capability, it is generally in response to a change in purpose. New core capabilities and redefinition of existing core capabilities will also result in significant impacts to internal work content and method and can be accompanied by impacts to internal and external relationships—as well as changes to operating locations and work timing. For these reasons, what, how, who, where, when, and why impacts can be induced whenever a company initiates a change to its core capabilities definition.

Outsourcing and Insourcing

As companies rethink their core purpose, they consider initiating changes in outsourcing and insourcing elements of their supply chain. If they choose to implement one of these supply chain structure changes, they will experience corresponding impacts in each of the change impact profile dimensions—most notably in work procedures, internal and external working relationships, and operational locations. For these reasons, what, how, who, where, when, and why impacts can be induced whenever a company initiates a change to its outsourcing and insourcing.

Risk Profile

When mitigating or eliminating the source of business risk, a company can experience impacts to its internal work content as well as significant impacts to work procedures. There may be accompanying changes in both internal and external relationships, operating location, and timing, as well as changes to the purpose for undertaking some business activities. For these reasons, what, how, who, where, when, and why impacts can be induced whenever a company initiates a change to its risk profile.

Regulatory Profile

Regulations increase over time due to actions outside the company as well as decisions/actions the company takes. For example, a company is subjected to foreign regulations when it expands operations outside of the country in which it currently operates. When addressing new regulations, the company will experience significant impacts in internal work content and work procedures.

There may also be accompanying impacts in both internal and external relationships, operating locations, and timing. If a company significantly changes its core business to reduce regulatory burden, it will experience impacts to purpose as well. For these reasons, what, how, who, where, when, and why impacts can be induced whenever a company initiates a change to its regulatory profile.

Geographic Structure

Geographic structure changes include relocations, expansions, and contractions. The most significant impacts occur with the operating locations themselves as well as the internal/external working relationships. There can also be impacts to the internal work content and procedures, timing, and even strategic purpose. For these reasons, what, how, who, where, when, and why impacts can be induced whenever a company initiates a change to its geographic structure.

Corporate Culture/Values

Corporate culture and values are reestablished and sometimes adjusted whenever there is a significant change in structure, ownership, or vision. Companies undergoing changes to their culture, values, norms, and expectations typically will experience significant accompanying impacts in internal work content, procedures, and internal work relationships. Some culture/value changes will even impact the company's purpose. For these reasons, what, how, who, and why impacts can be induced whenever a company initiates a change to its corporate culture/values.

Quantifying the Change Impact Profile

The qualitative behavioral change impact profile can be quantified in an elementary, but relevant manner by assigning ten points to every full Harvey Ball, five points to every half ball, and zero points to every hollow one as shown in figure 17 (below).

#	Business Changes	Quantified Change Impact Profile						Total
		What	How	Who	Where	When	Why	
1	Product Scope	5	5	5	5	0	0	20
2	Service Scope	10	10	5	5	0	5	35
3	Industry/Market Served	5	5	10	5	5	10	40
4	Customer Experience	10	10	10	0	0	10	40
5	Technology Platform	10	10	5	0	0	5	30
6	Cost Structure	10	10	10	5	0	10	45
7	Ownership Structure	5	5	10	10	5	10	45
8	Internal Organization	0	5	10	5	5	10	35
9	Sales/Distribution Channel	10	10	10	10	5	10	55
10	Core Capabilities Definition	10	10	5	5	5	10	45
11	Outsourcing & Insourcing	5	10	10	10	5	10	50
12	Risk Profile	5	10	5	5	5	5	35
13	Regulatory Profile	10	10	5	5	5	5	40
14	Geographic Structure	5	5	10	10	5	5	40
15	Corporate Culture/Values	5	10	10	0	0	10	35
	Total Change Impact	105	125	120	80	45	115	590

● "10" Significant Change Impact   ◖ "5" Moderate Change Impact   ○ "0"Minimal Change Impact

Figure 17: Quantified Change Impact Profile for Common Business Changes

Quantifying in this way provides a metric for comparing the relative change impacts across a variety of business changes. The range of the metric begins at twenty for a change to only the product scope to 590 for all fifteen business changes. The change impact metric is depicted in figure 18 (below).

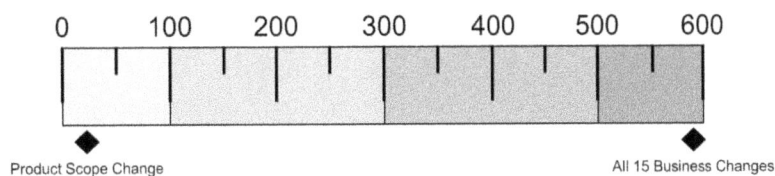

Figure 18: Change Impact Metric

Predicting Change Impacts

At this point, you have the tools you need to predict an upper boundary for the change impacts induced by your business transformation.

Step 1: Motivators

Changes in the business environment motivate your business to undertake a transformation. The business transformation motivators are shown in figure 2. You begin by identifying the motivators for your transformation.

Step 2: Business Changes

Your business transformation will in turn initiate one or more business changes. Business transformation motivators are related to the common business changes through the matrix shown in figure 12. You can use the matrix to identify the potential business changes you will initiate in your transformation. You won't necessarily initiate all the business changes in your transformation, but you can start from those identified in the matrix.

Step 3: Change Impacts

The business changes you choose to initiate will in turn induce one or more change impacts. Business changes are related to the change impacts through the change impact profile shown in figure 17. You can use the change impact profile to identify the potential change impacts in your transformation. You won't necessarily experience all the potential change impacts in your transformation, but you can start from those identified in the change impact profile. You can then calculate the magnitude of change impact for your transformation using the change impact metric shown in figure 18.

The three steps used to estimate the magnitude of change impact for a business transformation are shown as a flow diagram in figure 19 (below).

Step 1

Business Transformation Motivators

Step 2

Common Business Changes

Step 3

Change Impact Profile

Competitive Environment
1. Underserved Customer Expectations
2. Losing Customers or Market Share
3. Arrival of Better Positioned Competitors
4. Emergence of Substitute Products
5. Changes in Industry Structure

External Environment
6. Supply Side Innovation
7. Unreliable Supply Chain
8. Shareholder Pressure
9. Government Regulatory Pressure
10. Environmental Pressure
11. Geopolitical Pressure
12. Economic Instability

Internal Environment
13. Poor Business Performance
14. Ineffective Systems
15. Ineffective Labor
16. Poor Agility/Adaptability
17. Planned Abandonment

← Transformation Motivators →

	Quantified Change Impact Profile						
#	Business Changes	What	How	Who	Where	When	Why	Total
1	Product Scope	5	5	5	5	0	0	20
2	Service Scope	10	10	5	5	0	5	35
3	Industry/Market Served	5	5	10	5	5	10	40
4	Customer Experience	10	10	10	0	0	10	40
5	Technology Platform	10	10	5	0	0	5	30
6	Cost Structure	10	10	10	5	0	10	45
7	Ownership Structure	5	5	10	10	5	10	45
8	Internal Organization	0	5	10	5	5	10	35
9	Sales/Distribution Channel	10	10	10	10	5	10	55
10	Core Capabilities Definition	10	10	5	5	5	10	45
11	Outsourcing & Insourcing	5	10	10	10	5	10	50
12	Risk Profile	5	10	5	5	5	5	35
13	Regulatory Profile	10	10	5	5	5	5	40
14	Geographic Structure	5	5	10	10	5	5	40
15	Corporate Culture/Values	5	10	10	0	0	10	35
	Total Change Impact	105	125	120	80	45	115	590

0   100   200   300   400   500   600

Product Scope Change — All 15 Business Changes

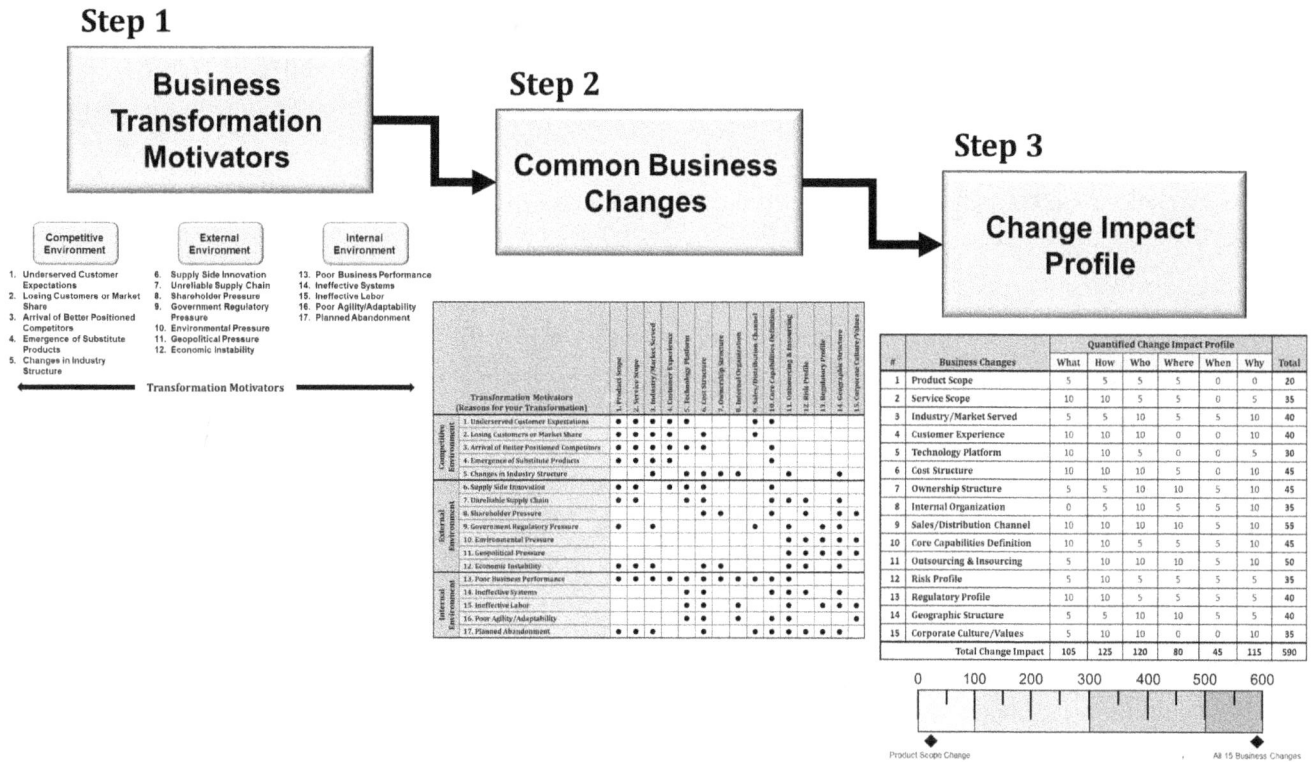

Figure 19: Predicting the Change Impact from a Business Transformation

Example: Let Us Eat Cakes

Continuing the example for Let Us Eat Cakes, recall their business transformation was motivated by the following environment changes (see figure 3).

a. [1] underserved customer expectations

b. [4] emergence of substitute products

c. [6] supply-side innovation

d. [13] poor business performance

Also, recall their business transformation motivators led them to initiate the following business changes (see figure 13):

a. [2] service scope

b. [3] industry/market served

c. [4] customer experience

d. [5] technology platform

e. [9] sales/distribution channel

Let Us Eat Cakes can use the change impact profile from figure 17 to relate the business changes initiated to the potential change impacts they would induce. This is shown in figure 20 (below). The magnitude of these change impacts total to two hundred as shown on the change impact metric in figure 21 (below).

To help understand how to interpret these results, consider the service scope business change, and the following excerpt from the case:

> The online system would provide Let Us Eat Cakes a mobile-enabled website to order the regular bakery items as well as the specialty cakes. Customers would pay in advance using a credit card, making it quick and convenient for commuters.

#	Business Changes	Quantified Change Impact Profile						Total
		What	How	Who	Where	When	Why	
1	Product Scope							
2	Service Scope	10	10	5	5	0	5	35
3	Industry/Market Served	5	5	10	5	5	10	40
4	Customer Experience	10	10	10	0	0	10	40
5	Technology Platform	10	10	5	0	0	5	30
6	Cost Structure							
7	Ownership Structure							
8	Internal Organization							
9	Sales/Distribution Channel	10	10	10	10	5	10	55
10	Core Capabilities Definition							
11	Outsourcing & Insourcing							
12	Risk Profile							
13	Regulatory Profile							
14	Geographic Structure							
15	Corporate Culture/Values							
	Total Change Impact	45	45	40	20	10	40	200

Figure 20: Let Us Eat Cakes Potential Change Impacts Induced

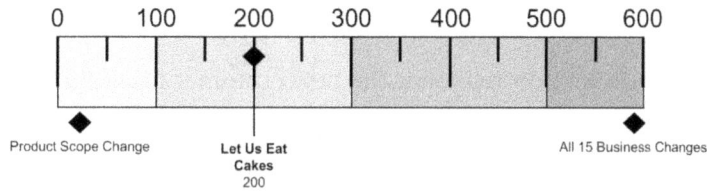

Figure 21: Let Us Eat Cakes Change Impact Profile

The Let Us Eat Cakes online system provides customers with self-service ordering and payment services. Consider how this single business change induces impacts to each of the dimensions in the change impact profile.

What

The impacts to the what dimension represent the new commercial service content for their business. Let Us Eat Cakes must now develop and support self-service ordering and payment services—including the detailed scope and prices for these services. This is a major addition to the work content and deliverables for their bakery. Furthermore, they will not eliminate any existing services. For example, they will continue to provide custom cake designs and order placement by phone or in person.

How

The impacts to the how dimension represent the new policies and procedures required to support the self-service ordering and payment services. Someone must monitor the self-service order queue to ensure orders placed online are added to the orders placed by phone and in-person. The online orders must then be incorporated into their daily order fulfillment process. Policies must be developed around cutoff times for custom orders as well as the handling of customer credit card payments.

Who

The impacts to the who dimension represent the new online customers as well as the new contact information that must be collected and maintained for any customer ordering and paying online. Once the online channel grows beyond the operating threshold for their staff, Let Us Eat Cakes may need to consider adding staff and creating new reporting relationships to manage the online services.

Where

The impacts to the where dimension represent the new customer locations at which the self-service activities are performed. Since ordering and payment processing now take place outside of Let Us Eat Cakes' physical locations, there could be sales tax implications.

When

The impacts to the when dimension represent the extended business hours required for self-service order placement and payment. Order placement for next-day fulfillment can now occur outside of the normal store business hours. Let Us Eat Cakes must consider staffing operations during this extended time frame.

Why

The impacts to the why dimension represent the reasons Let Us Eat Cakes is incorporating self-service into their commercial offering. The bakery is signaling a shift in its product/service mix to include more services. It's a subtle shift at this point, but it positions them to become a high-service customer experience business if they choose.

You can complete the example by carrying out a similar analysis of the change impact dimensions for the other business changes. The change impacts will be unique to each business change as they depend on the nature of the business change as well as the current state of the business. Even if the dimension occurs multiple times, it could introduce different impacts.

For example, the what dimension appears in all five business changes. However, the change impacts are different for the technology platform change as compared to the service scope change. The change impacts from the new online ordering system include setting up the data and applications to facilitate the online ordering system—and then supporting the data and applications once they are in service. Let Us Eat Cakes' internal work content will change significantly with the introduction of the new technology.

The business change cycle has been updated in figure 22 (below) to reflect the notion that business changes initiated through the transformation will induce change impacts to the business.

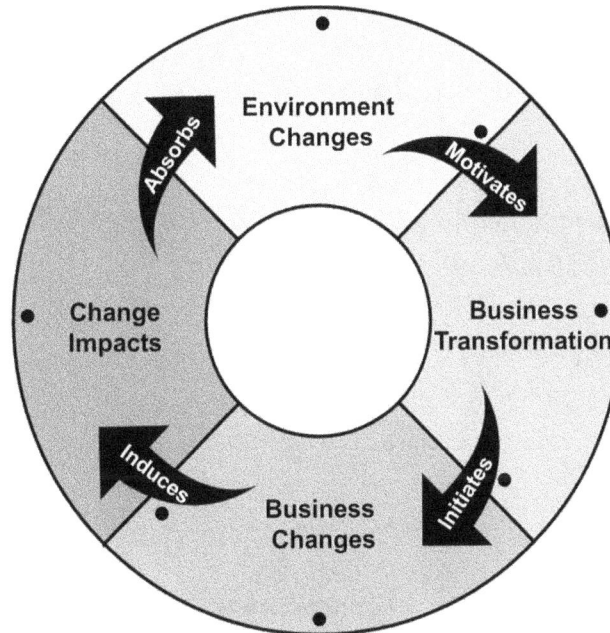

Figure 22: The Business Change Cycle Revisited

Change Impact Profiles for Actual Business Transformations

The change impact profile will now be used to determine the magnitude of change impact for a few well-known business transformations. This will help illustrate the value in quantifying the change impacts associated and allow relative comparisons among the example transformations. For each example, a description of the transformation will be given, along with the analysis of motivators, business changes, and change impacts. The examples were drawn from widely available sources.

IBM

In 1984, IBM's strategy of assembling low-cost hardware and software components essentially created the PC industry. By 1993, the market was flooded with cheaper clone computers from all over the world. IBM posted a loss of $8 billion that year.

IBM was now at a crossroads and chose to abandon the assembly/sales of low-cost PCs—the core of its business model—and instead to focus on providing IT expertise and computing services to other businesses.

By 2010, IBM acquired more than two hundred IT service companies, and by 2013, IBM became the number one provider of enterprise server solutions. (Roos, 2014)

The IBM transformation was motivated by at least three changes in their competitive and external environments (see figure 23):

> *By 1993, the market was flooded with cheaper clone computers from all over the world. IBM posted a loss of $8 billion that year.*

a. [3] arrival of better positioned competitors

b. [6] supply-side innovation

c. [2] losing customers or market share

Competitive Environment	External Environment	Internal Environment
1. Underserved Customer Expectations	6. Supply Side Innovation	13. Poor Business Performance
2. Losing Customers or Market Share	7. Unreliable Supply Chain	14. Ineffective Systems
3. Arrival of Better Positioned Competitors	8. Shareholder Pressure	15. Ineffective Labor
4. Emergence of Substitute Products	9. Government Regulatory Pressure	16. Poor Agility/Adaptability
5. Changes in Industry Structure	10. Environmental Pressure	17. Planned Abandonment
	11. Geopolitical Pressure	
	12. Economic Instability	

◀━━━━━━━━ **Transformation Motivators** ━━━━━━━━▶

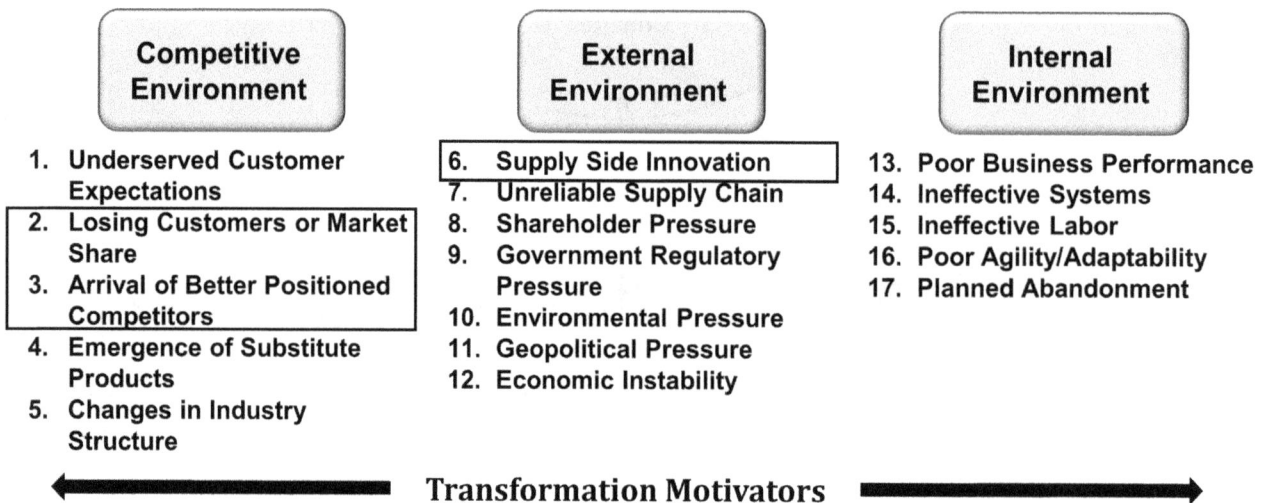

Figure 23: IBM's Potential Transformation Motivators

Using the matrix relating transformation motivators to potential business changes, IBM could have initiated some combination of the eight business changes in response to the changes in their business environment—shown in figure 24 (below).

Transformation Motivators (Reasons for your Transformation)	1. Product Scope	2. Service Scope	3. Industry/Market Served	4. Customer Experience	5. Technology Platform	6. Cost Structure	7. Ownership Structure	8. Internal Organization	9. Sales/Distribution Channel	10. Core Capabilities Definition	11. Outsourcing & Insourcing	12. Risk Profile	13. Regulatory Profile	14. Geographic Structure	15. Corporate Culture/Values
Competitive Environment															
1. Underserved Customer Expectations															
2. Losing Customers or Market Share	●	●	●	●		●			●						
3. Arrival of Better Positioned Competitors	●	●	●	●	●	●				●					
4. Emergence of Substitute Products															
5. Changes in Industry Structure															
External Environment															
6. Supply Side Innovation	●	●		●	●	●				●					
7. Unreliable Supply Chain															
8. Shareholder Pressure															
9. Government Regulatory Pressure															
10. Environmental Pressure															
11. Geopolitical Pressure															
12. Economic Instability															
Internal Environment															
13. Poor Business Performance															
14. Ineffective Systems															
15. Ineffective Labor															
16. Poor Agility/Adaptability															
17. Planned Abandonment															

Figure 24: IBM's Potential Business Changes

IBM's actual response to the changes in their business environment included the initiation of at least five business changes.

IBM was now at a crossroads and chose to abandon the assembly/sales of low-cost PCs—the core of its business model—and instead to focus on providing IT expertise and computing services to other businesses.

a. [1] product scope
b. [10] core capabilities definition
c. [2] service scope
d. [3] industry/market served

By 2010, IBM acquired more than 200 IT service companies, and by 2013, IBM became the number one provider of enterprise server solutions.

e. [7] ownership structure

The change impact profile for this transformation is an aggregation across all five business changes as shown in figure 25 (below) and represents the potential change impacts IBM could have experienced in carrying out its transformation. The resulting change impact profile metric of 185 is shown in figure 26 (below).

#	Business Changes	Quantified Change Impact Profile						Total
		What	How	Who	Where	When	Why	
1	Product Scope	5	5	5	5	0	0	20
2	Service Scope	10	10	5	5	0	5	35
3	Industry/Market Served	5	5	10	5	5	10	40
4	Customer Experience							
5	Technology Platform							
6	Cost Structure							
7	Ownership Structure	5	5	10	10	5	10	45
8	Internal Organization							
9	Sales/Distribution Channel							
10	Core Capabilities Definition	10	10	5	5	5	10	45
11	Outsourcing & Insourcing							
12	Risk Profile							
13	Regulatory Profile							
14	Geographic Structure							
15	Corporate Culture/Values							
	Total Change Impact	35	35	35	30	15	35	185

Figure 25: IBM's Potential Change Impact Profile

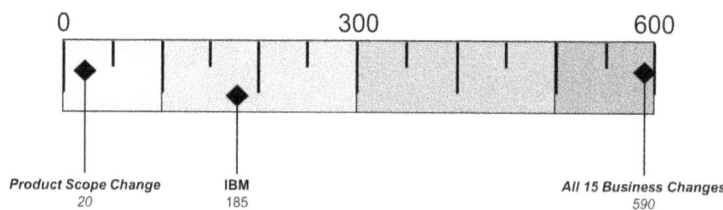

Figure 26: IBM's Potential Change Impact Metric

Armstrong World Industries

In 2015, the IT organization was viewed as "order takers," and lack of visibility into spend brought their value into question.

Later that year, the CIO initiated a transformation within the IT organization. They adopted lean and agile principles, providing visibility and instilling greater trust, and implemented several technology upgrades, including moving their ERP to the latest version of SAP, extending their Salesforce.com CRM suite to Asia and Europe, migrating their travel management system to Concur, and refreshing their customer-facing e-commerce platform.

In addition to improving spend transparency, these moves generated cost savings that were reallocated to improving cybersecurity.

The Armstrong transformation was motivated by at least four changes in their competitive and internal environments:

> *In 2015, the IT organization was viewed as "order takers," and lack of visibility into spend brought their value into question.*

a. [1] underserved customer expectations (internal customers of the IT function)
b. [13] poor business performance (of the IT function)

> *Later that year, the CIO initiated a transformation within the IT organization. They adopted lean and agile principles, providing visibility and instilling greater trust, and implemented several technology upgrades, including moving their ERP to the latest version of SAP, extending their Salesforce.com CRM suite to Asia and Europe, migrating their travel management system to Concur, and refreshing their customer-facing e-commerce platform.*

c. [16] Poor Agility/Adaptability
d. [14] Ineffective Systems

These are shown in figure 27 (below).

Competitive Environment

1. Underserved Customer Expectations
2. Losing Customers or Market Share
3. Arrival of Better Positioned Competitors
4. Emergence of Substitute Products
5. Changes in Industry Structure

External Environment

6. Supply Side Innovation
7. Unreliable Supply Chain
8. Shareholder Pressure
9. Government Regulatory Pressure
10. Environmental Pressure
11. Geopolitical Pressure
12. Economic Instability

Internal Environment

13. Poor Business Performance
14. Ineffective Systems
15. Ineffective Labor
16. Poor Agility/Adaptability
17. Planned Abandonment

◄———— **Transformation Motivators** ————►

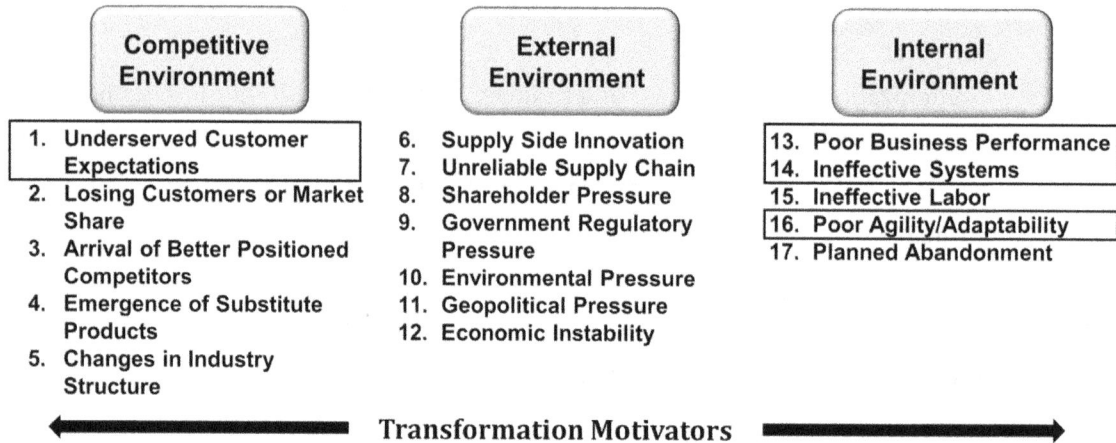

Figure 27: Armstrong's Potential Transformation Motivators

Using the matrix relating transformation motivators to potential business changes, Armstrong could have initiated some combination of the eight business changes in response to the changes in their business environment—shown in figure 28 (below).

Transformation Motivators (Reasons for your Transformation)	1. Product Scope	2. Service Scope	3. Industry/Market Served	4. Customer Experience	5. Technology Platform	6. Cost Structure	7. Ownership Structure	8. Internal Organization	9. Sales/Distribution Channel	10. Core Capabilities Definition	11. Outsourcing & Insourcing	12. Risk Profile	13. Regulatory Profile	14. Geographic Structure	15. Corporate Culture/Values
Competitive Environment 1. Underserved Customer Expectations	●	●	●	●	●				●	●					
2. Losing Customers or Market Share															
3. Arrival of Better Positioned Competitors															
4. Emergence of Substitute Products															
5. Changes in Industry Structure															
External Environment 6. Supply Side Innovation															
7. Unreliable Supply Chain															
8. Shareholder Pressure															
9. Government Regulatory Pressure															
10. Environmental Pressure															
11. Geopolitical Pressure															
12. Economic Instability															
Internal Environment 13. Poor Business Performance	●	●	●	●	●	●	●	●	●	●	●				
14. Ineffective Systems					●	●				●	●	●		●	
15. Ineffective Labor															
16. Poor Agility/Adaptability					●	●		●		●	●				●
17. Planned Abandonment															

Figure 28: Armstrong's Potential Business Changes

Armstrong's actual response to the changes in their business environment included the initiation of at least five business changes:

They adopted lean and agile principles providing visibility and instilling greater trust, and implemented several technology upgrades included moving their ERP to the latest version of SAP, extending their Salesforce.com CRM suite to Asia and Europe, migrating their travel management system to Concur, and refreshing their customer-facing e-commerce platform.

a. [10] core capabilities definition
b. [5] technology platform
c. [4] customer experience

In addition to improving spend transparency, these moves generated cost savings that were reallocated to improving cybersecurity.

d. [6] cost structure
e. [12] risk profile

The change impact profile for this transformation is an aggregation across all five business changes as shown in figure 29 (below) and represents the potential change impacts Armstrong could have experienced in carrying out its transformation. The resulting change impact profile metric of 195 is shown in figure 30 (below).

#	Business Changes	Quantified Change Impact Profile						Total
		What	How	Who	Where	When	Why	
1	Product Scope							
2	Service Scope							
3	Industry/Market Served							
4	Customer Experience	10	10	10	0	0	10	40
5	Technology Platform	10	10	5	0	0	5	30
6	Cost Structure	10	10	10	5	0	10	45
7	Ownership Structure							
8	Internal Organization							
9	Sales/Distribution Channel							
10	Core Capabilities Definition	10	10	5	5	5	10	45
11	Outsourcing & Insourcing							
12	Risk Profile	5	10	5	5	5	5	35
13	Regulatory Profile							
14	Geographic Structure							
15	Corporate Culture/Values							
	Total Change Impact	45	50	35	15	10	40	195

Figure 29: Armstrong's Potential Change Impact Profile

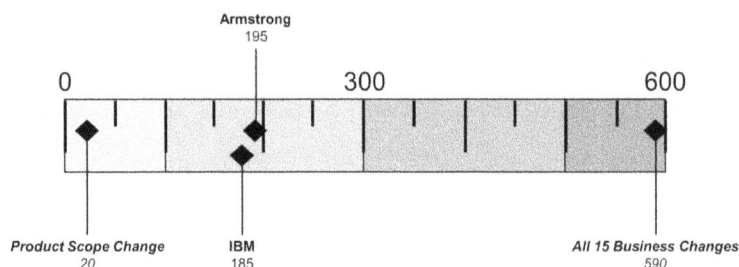

Figure 30: Armstrong's Potential Change Impact Metric

StubHub

In 2013, the ticket retailer's infrastructure could not keep up with their event ticket transaction volume (in the thousands per day). The CIO launched an effort to build a virtual private cloud that could scale to handle future growth. StubHub then moved this infrastructure into the public cloud to locate the processing closer to its now forty-four-country worldwide business.

New customer-facing applications were introduced to support the growing base of mobile device access (> 50 percent). Sellers can now use their smartphones to take a picture of their tickets and post them for online sale. StubHub is also reimagining their e-commerce presence as a destination website for music and other content, and to eventually serve as a social media ticket marketplace.

The StubHub transformation was motivated by at least three changes in their business environment:

In 2013, the ticket retailer's infrastructure could not keep up with their event ticket transaction volume (in the thousands per day).

a. [14] ineffective systems

New customer-facing applications were introduced to support the growing base of mobile device access (> 50 percent). Sellers can now use their smartphones to take a picture of their tickets and post them for online sale.

a. [1] underserved customer expectations
b. [6] supply-side innovation

These are shown in figure 31 (below).

Competitive Environment

1. Underserved Customer Expectations
2. Losing Customers or Market Share
3. Arrival of Better Positioned Competitors
4. Emergence of Substitute Products
5. Changes in Industry Structure

External Environment

6. Supply Side Innovation
7. Unreliable Supply Chain
8. Shareholder Pressure
9. Government Regulatory Pressure
10. Environmental Pressure
11. Geopolitical Pressure
12. Economic Instability

Internal Environment

13. Poor Business Performance
14. Ineffective Systems
15. Ineffective Labor
16. Poor Agility/Adaptability
17. Planned Abandonment

← **Transformation Motivators** →

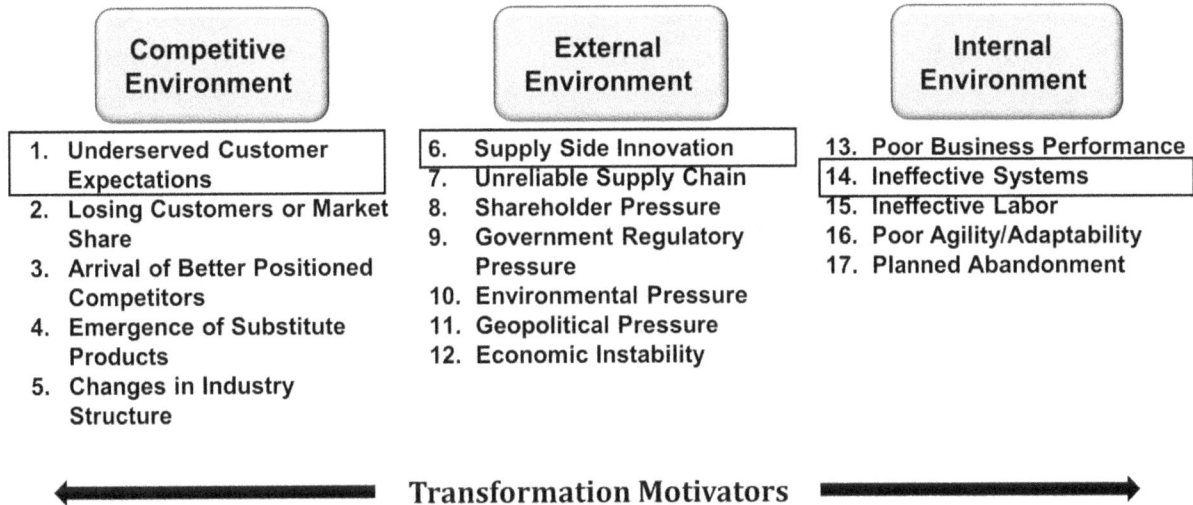

Figure 31: StubHub's Potential Transformation Motivators

Using the matrix relating transformation motivators to potential business changes, StubHub could have initiated some combination of the eleven business changes in response to the changes in their business environment—shown in figure 32 (below).

Transformation Motivators (Reasons for your Transformation)	1. Product Scope	2. Service Scope	3. Industry/Market Served	4. Customer Experience	5. Technology Platform	6. Cost Structure	7. Ownership Structure	8. Internal Organization	9. Sales/Distribution Channel	10. Core Capabilities Definition	11. Outsourcing & Insourcing	12. Risk Profile	13. Regulatory Profile	14. Geographic Structure	15. Corporate Culture/Values
Competitive Environment 1. Underserved Customer Expectations	●	●	●	●	●				●	●					
2. Losing Customers or Market Share															
3. Arrival of Better Positioned Competitors															
4. Emergence of Substitute Products															
5. Changes in Industry Structure															
External Environment 6. Supply Side Innovation	●	●		●	●	●			●						
7. Unreliable Supply Chain															
8. Shareholder Pressure															
9. Government Regulatory Pressure															
10. Environmental Pressure															
11. Geopolitical Pressure															
12. Economic Instability															
Internal Environment 13. Poor Business Performance															
14. Ineffective Systems				●	●				●	●	●		●		
15. Ineffective Labor															
16. Poor Agility/Adaptability															
17. Planned Abandonment															

Figure 32: StubHub's Potential Business Changes

StubHub's actual response to the changes in their business environment included the initiation of at least seven business changes:

The CIO launched an effort to build a virtual private cloud that could scale to handle future growth. StubHub then moved this infrastructure into the public cloud to locate the processing closer to its now forty-four-country worldwide business.

a. [5] technology platform
b. [14] geographic structure

New customer-facing applications were introduced to support the growing base of mobile device access (> 50 percent). Sellers can now use their smartphones to take a picture of their tickets and post them for online sale.

c. [1] product scope
d. [9] sales/distribution channel

StubHub is also reimagining their e-commerce presence as a destination website for music and other content, and to eventually serve as a social media ticket marketplace.

e. [2] service scope
f. [4] customer experience
g. [10] core capabilities definition

The change impact profile for this transformation is an aggregation across all seven business changes as shown in figure 33 (below) and represents the potential change impacts StubHub could have experienced in carrying out its transformation. The resulting change impact profile metric of 265 is shown in figure 34 (below).

#	Business Changes	Quantified Change Impact Profile						Total
		What	How	Who	Where	When	Why	
1	Product Scope	5	5	5	5	0	0	20
2	Service Scope	10	10	5	5	0	5	35
3	Industry/Market Served							
4	Customer Experience	10	10	10	0	0	10	40
5	Technology Platform	10	10	5	0	0	5	30
6	Cost Structure							
7	Ownership Structure							
8	Internal Organization							
9	Sales/Distribution Channel	10	10	10	10	5	10	55
10	Core Capabilities Definition	10	10	5	5	5	10	45
11	Outsourcing & Insourcing							
12	Risk Profile							
13	Regulatory Profile							
14	Geographic Structure	5	5	10	10	5	5	40
15	Corporate Culture/Values							
	Total Change Impact	60	60	50	35	15	45	265

Figure 33: StubHub's Potential Change Impact Profile

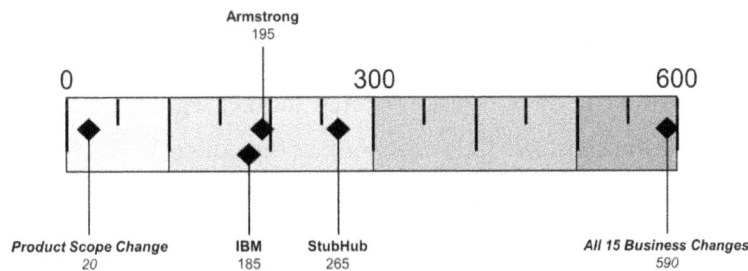

Figure 34: StubHub's Potential Change Impact Metric

It's interesting to note that in all three business transformation examples, the change impact metric was below three hundred. Do any companies take on business transformations where the change impact metric is above three hundred? Of course, it's possible to do so. However, given that the successful completion rate for business transformations is around 25 percent, it's unlikely that many transformations go much beyond three hundred. Three hundred represents a significant amount of change impact that must be absorbed by your business. If you are planning a business transformation with a change impact metric above three hundred, you could tackle the transformation in phases—moving to a subsequent phase only after successfully completing the prior phase.

What about transformations below two hundred or one hundred? When is a transformation not really a transformation?

Business Initiatives That Are Not Transformations

The change impact profile and accompanying metric provide a way to differentiate business transformations from less complex business initiatives. It's reasonable to consider one hundred on the change impact metric as the separator between business initiatives and business transformations. This is not a hard and fast rule, but a total change impact of one hundred covers at least two business changes (see figure 17). Also, note that at least five business changes can be initiated for every transformation motivator (see figure 12). Consider the following examples of business initiatives.

New Product Introductions

If a business routinely introduces new products to its current base of customers, then the introduction of a new product in a current product line will result in the product scope business change. Consequently, the change impact is low (twenty points on the change impact profile and metric), making this a business initiative and not a transformation.

Now suppose this same company is introducing a new product to address a different market segment. In addition to the product scope business change, this company will also experience a change in industry/market served. The change impact profile/metric now increases to sixty points, with twenty points for product scope and forty points for industry/market served. If this company also had to change distribution channels to reach the new market segment, fifty-five points would be added for new sales/distribution channel. This new product introduction would move from a business initiative to a business transformation as shown in figure 35 (below).

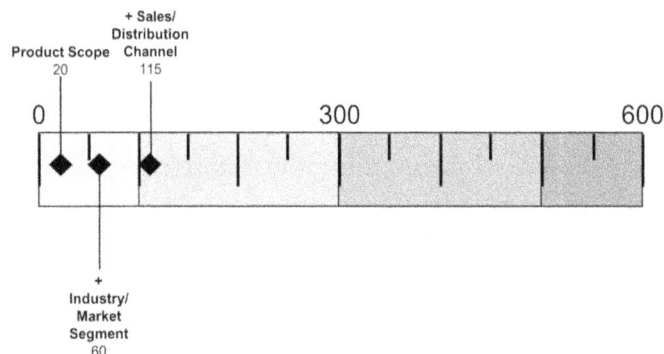

Figure 35: New Product Introductions Change Impact Metric

Technology Upgrades

Companies frequently upgrade elements of their technology platform—introducing new features, improving performance, addressing security concerns, and replacing obsolete components. Sometimes these upgrades can be implemented with little to no change impact. For example, adding network, server, or storage capacity can be frequently accomplished with little impact on business users outside of the information technology organization. Functional upgrades often require testing by the users of the technology, but user testing is already taken into consideration within the technology platform business change. The resulting change impact is still low (thirty-five points on the change impact profile/metric), making this a business initiative and not a transformation.

The change impacts are much greater when the technology upgrade enables new business processes or capabilities, which is frequently the case. For example, when the newest version of an accounting application introduces support for treasury and cash management, the company will also experience a change to their core capabilities definition—adding forty-five points on the change impact profile/metric. If the upgrade initiates a change to the customer experience as well (as in the case of online self-service invoice retrieval), an additional forty points are added. The technology upgrade now moves from a business initiative to a business transformation as shown in figure 36 (below).

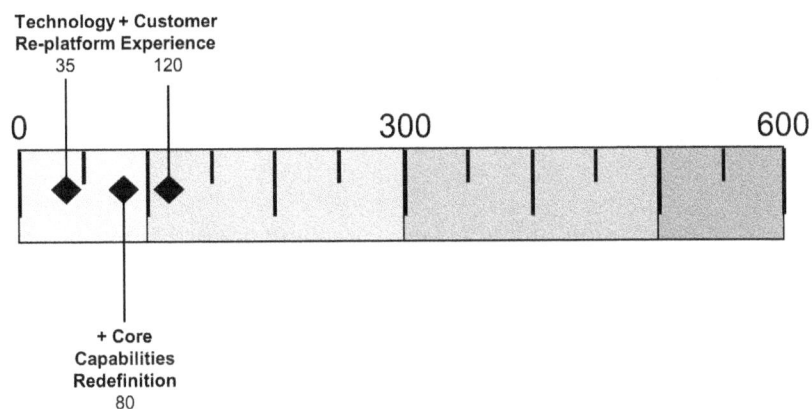

Figure 36: Technology Upgrades Change Impact Metric

Functional Cost Reductions

During a company's life cycle, operations will stabilize and mature. Companies frequently look for opportunities to reduce cost and improve operating leverage. For example, many companies standardize accounts payable processing, enabling a reduction in workforce for the same workload. Functional cost reduction is captured in the cost structure business change resulting in forty-five points on the change impact profile/metric—a business initiative.

However, a global company may decide to centralize the accounts payable function in a new office located in a lower-cost geography. This further reduces operating costs and provides dual time zone processing. The centralized office is considered a geographic structure business change and adds forty points to the change impact profile/metric. If the company decides to outsource accounts payable processing altogether, the outsourcing and insourcing business change is initiated, adding another fifty points to the change impact profile/metric. The functional cost reduction now moves from a business initiative to a business transformation as shown in figure 37 (below).

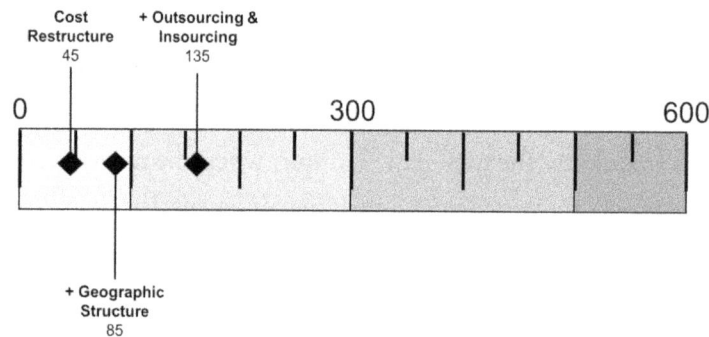

Figure 37: Functional Cost Reductions Behavioral Change Impact Metric

Chapter Takeaway Points

- The business transformation change cycle characterizes the change occurring in a business transformation.
- Most business transformations fail because the accompanying change is unwieldy, and most businesses lack the ability or willingness to manage the change.
- Business transformations are motivated by seventeen changes to the competitive, external, or internal business environment in which they operate.
- Some subset of the fifteen common business changes are initiated during a business transformation.
- A matrix is used to express the relationship between transformation motivators and the corresponding business changes.
- Business changes initiated during a business transformation will induce some subset of the six business change impacts.
- A change impact profile is used to express the relationship between business changes initiated and change impacts induced during a transformation.
- The quantified change impact profile and metric allows you to express the magnitude of change in your business transformation.

Chapter 2

THE STATE OF BUSINESS TRANSFORMATION RESEARCH

If you steal from one author, it's plagiarism; if you steal from many, it's research.
—Wilson Mizner

This chapter presents the results of other authors' studies on business transformation failures and identifies the reasons for such poor success. It then looks at the recommendations to address the failure rates and improve the odds of carrying out a successful transformation. A business transformation life cycle is formally defined and used to analyze the results of the studies.

Business Transformation Success and Failure Rates

The failure rate of business transformations is significant and has been known since the mid-1990s when John Kotter published the results of his ten-year study in the *Harvard Business Review*. Kotter analyzed more than one hundred companies undergoing transformations and discovered that very few had been successful, a few had been utter failures, and the rest fell somewhere in between—but primarily toward the failure end of the spectrum.

Kotter went further, stating that "motivation for the change" was the essential first step in any transformation. Without motivation, people won't help, and the effort is wasted. Kotter found that more than 50 percent of the companies he observed failed to establish proper motivation.

In 2014, McKinsey & Company discovered similar results. In a survey of nearly two thousand executives representing a full spectrum of regions, industries, and company sizes, only 26 percent of those responding said its transformations had been very or completely successful at improving and sustaining performance. A similar survey was conducted in 2012 in which executives reported slightly worse success rates—only 20 percent.

Other surveys analyze a slightly different scope. In a *Forbes* article, survey results showed that only 16 percent of digital transformations were successful, and 50 percent were utter failures. The conclusion is that somewhere between 50 percent and 80 percent of transformational efforts fail to deliver the expected value.

Reasons for the High Failure Rate

The failure rate of business transformations is catastrophic, especially given the significant investment and accompanying business disruption. It's therefore not surprising this topic has drawn so many to investigate why it occurs.

Organization of Results

The failure results are easier to comprehend with a tiny bit of organization. The method used here associates the failures with one of the three phases of a business transformation. The three phases are:

- Phase 1: Planning the Transformation—preparatory activities leading up to the transformation implementation.
- Phase 2: Implementing the Transformation—activities required to carry out the transformation.
- Phase 3: Optimizing the Transformation—activities to ensure the transformation yields value.

This three-phase life cycle will be formally defined later in this chapter, after considering some of the more widely known research studies into the cause of business transformation failures.

Kotter

Part of John Kotter's original report (Anderson & Anderson, 2010) includes an explanation for the high failure rate as well as a prescription for ensuring success. In his research, John Kotter found that transformations failed for eight reasons:

- not establishing a great enough sense of urgency
- not creating a powerful enough guiding coalition (transformation leadership)
- lacking a vision
- undercommunicating the vision
- not removing obstacles to the new vision (employee change obstacles)
- not systematically planning for and creating short-term wins (intermediate results)

- declaring victory too soon (before adoption is complete)
- not anchoring changes in the corporation's culture (institutionalizing the new way)

The first four reasons are associated with the planning phase of the transformation, the next two are associated with the implementing phase, and the last two are associated with the optimizing phase.

Change Leaders Network

The authors propose that the most common reason for transformation failures is that change leaders do not use the proper approach for leading transformational change. Three types of organizational change are presented:

1. Developmental—improving on what you currently do (simplest type of change).
2. Transitional—replacing the current with something new, which requires defining and implementing the "new."
3. Transformational—replacing the current with something that is not well known at the start, but will emerge during the transformation

Transformational change is considered the most challenging as it is very difficult to manage an emerging target using predetermined plans. Also, since the future is so radically different from the present, the people and culture must change during the transformation to implement it successfully.

The reasons given by these authors are associated with the planning phase of a transformation.

Forbes

In 2014, Forbes Media surveyed 106 executives across the business and industrial landscape on transformation leadership. The survey respondents indicated leadership limitations as the largest barrier to success. The top five barriers were:

- conflicting visions among executive leadership or decision-makers
- lack of internal talent to spearhead or execute business change
- resource/budget constraints
- inefficient execution or lack of formal process
- lack of adequate technology

The first two barriers are associated with the planning phase of a transformation, and the last three barriers are associated with the implementing phase.

McKinsey & Company—RTS

The authors at McKinsey first define transformation as an intense, organization-wide program to enhance performance and boost organizational health. Transformations are distinguished from other initiatives as they radically improve top-line growth, capital productivity, cost efficiency, operational effectiveness, customer satisfaction, and sales excellence. As such, they require enormous energy to realize transformational change. This is the significant barrier, and the average company does not have the necessary combination of skills, mind-sets, and ongoing commitment. These skills impact both the planning and optimizing phases of a transformation.

Harvard Business Review

The authors acknowledge that significant effort is required to plan the perfect change management initiative. However, they go a step further and state that change leaders need to first transform themselves—a planning phase activity. The authors argue that without significant "self-help," they may be provoked into exhibiting bad behavior. For example, the leaders would be less aware of how they will react during the change and how their own behaviors will impact others.

KPMG

KPMG conducted a study in 2016 of more than 1,600 senior executives across sixteen countries. From their analysis, they concluded the high rate of failure to achieve value from a transformation was due to the following five reasons:

- a failure to understand the complexity of the operating model and the changes necessary to affect its transformations
- the inability to innovate or create the processes and budgets required for innovation
- missing the cultural connection, or more precisely, their existing organizational culture was a barrier
- a failure to take a "business value first" approach to technology and building its transformations around specific technologies
- an inability to execute the transformation and operationalize a new target operating model

The first and fifth reasons for failure are associated with the planning phase of a transformation. Reasons 2, 3, and 4 are associated with the implementing phase.

Wipro Digital conducted a survey of four hundred US-based senior executives. The results released in 2017 indicated 50 percent of the senior executives polled believe their companies were not successfully executing against even half of their digital strategies. CIO.com conducted a follow-on analysis (based on this survey) to identify the following twelve impediments to completing a digital transformation:

1. Lack of consensus on what digital transformation means
2. Lack of CEO sponsorship
3. Lack of focus
4. Resistance to change
5. Trouble in articulating the what and how of the transformation
6. Lack of speed
7. Talent deficit—in technology and product management
8. Too strong of focus on back-office and infrastructure
9. Integration challenges
10. Isolating the digital transformation from the rest of the business
11. Insufficient funding
12. Lack of leadership continuity

Impediments 1, 2, 3, 5, 7, 8, and 11 are associated with the planning phase of a transformation. Impediments 4, 6, 9, and 10 are associated with the implementing phase.

In total, there are thirty-six reasons for transformation failure across these studies. The distribution across the three life cycle phases are summarized in figure 38 (below). As can be seen, most of the failures occur during the planning phase.

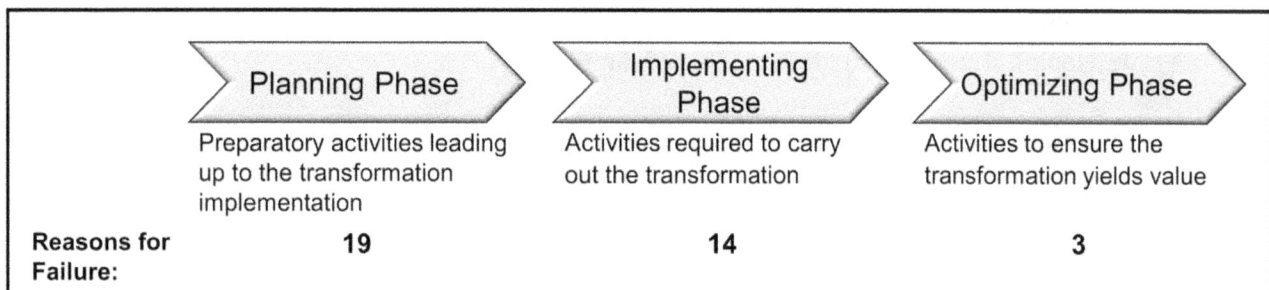

Planning Phase	Implementing Phase	Optimizing Phase
Preparatory activities leading up to the transformation implementation	Activities required to carry out the transformation	Activities to ensure the transformation yields value

Reasons for Failure:	19	14	3

Figure 38: Summary of Business Transformation Failure Reasons from Studies

What Is Being Done to Improve Success

The authors of the above studies attribute the low transformation success rates to a variety of causes, most of which fall into the broad categories of preparation and implementation. Some of these authors go on to recommend steps you can take to overcome transformation challenges and improve your chances for success. Here is a sample of some of the more widely known analyses into the actions a company can take to ensure success. The three phases of a business transformation will again be used to organize where the actions occur.

Kotter

John Kotter's original work on transformation failure rates rephrases the eight reasons for failure as eight steps to transforming your organization:

1. Establishing a Sense of Urgency

- examining market and competitive realities
- identifying and discussing crises, potential crises, or major opportunities

2. Forming a Powerful Guiding Coalition

- assembling a group with enough power to lead the change effort
- encouraging the group to work together as a team

3. Creating a Vision

- creating a vision to help direct the change effort
- developing strategies for achieving that vision

4. Communicating the Vision

- using every vehicle possible to communicate the new vision and strategies
- teaching new behaviors by the example of the guiding coalition

5. Empowering Others to Act on the Vision

- getting rid of obstacles to change
- changing systems or structures that seriously undermine the vision
- encouraging risk taking and nontraditional ideas, activities, and actions

6. Planning for and Creating Short-Term Wins

- planning for visible performance improvements
- creating those improvements
- recognizing and rewarding employees involved in the improvements

7. Consolidating Improvements and Producing Still More Change

- using increased credibility to change systems, structures, and policies that don't fit the vision
- hiring, promoting, and developing employees who can implement the vision
- reinvigorating the process with new projects, themes, and change agents

8. Institutionalizing New Approaches

- articulating the connections between the new behaviors and corporate success
- developing the means to ensure leadership development and succession

The eight steps for success are the converse of the eight reasons for failure. As such, the first four steps are associated with the planning phase of the transformation, the next two are associated with implementing phase, and the final two are associated with the optimizing phase. John Kotter has written several books that extended this research and institutionalized his approach.

KPMG

KPMG's study of business transformation failures included recommendations for improving the success of a business transformation. They identified the following three critical factors for success:

1. Focus on the customer: Understand your customers' evolving expectations and align them to what drives value in your organization.
2. Embed Continual Innovation: Create a culture of continuous innovation to create an enduring competitive advantage.
3. Learn to thrive on change: Build agility into your organization to allow adaptation to the innovations.

These success factors are not the converse of the reasons KPMG found for transformation failure. Rather, they reflect the competitive environment in which a business operates—continually adapting to the changing needs of customers through innovative solutions. The first critical factor for success is associated with the planning phase of a transformation, the second is associated with the optimizing phase, and the last factor is associated with the implementing phase.

Forbes

Part of Forbes Media's transformation leadership analysis identified several factors for ensuring a successful transformation. The top five factors for success were as follows:

1. Assigning the right employees to implement the project
2. The need to appropriate adequate resources from the start
3. Gathering data for metrics during the process
4. Accurate timely feedback from employees executing the program
5. Forming the right executive team to oversee the project

Factors 1, 2, and 5 are associated with the planning phase of a transformation, while factors 3 and 4 are associated with the implementing phase.

McKinsey & Company—RTS

When McKinsey defined transformation, they found the best predictor of success was a CEO who recognized the need for a new approach to dramatically improve the company's performance. To overcome resistance to this new approach, the company must also instill the following practices:

- stretch for the company's full potential
- change the pace/cadence with a formal transformation office, empowered to make decisions
- appoint a chief transformation officer (CTO) as a single leader to focus the effort
- remove barriers/create incentives to change past behaviors holding the organization back
- sustain the transformation by embedding a new culture of execution throughout the business

The first three practices impact the planning phase of a transformation, practice four impacts the implementing phase, and the last practice impacts the optimizing phase of a transformation.

McKinsey

McKinsey, in an article "How do I transform my organization's performance," recommended a five-frame process to address both organizational performance and long-term health during a transformation. The five frames cover key questions an organization should ask itself as it proceeds through the transformation.

1. Aspire: Where do we want to go?
2. Assess: How ready are we to embark on the journey?

3. Architect: What are the practical steps that will take us to our destination?

4. Act: How should we manage the journey itself?

5. Advance: Once we've completed the transformation, how do we keep it moving forward?

This is a variation from the other success recommendations as it is based on what needs to happen during a transformation as opposed to addressing specific failures. The first two frames impact the planning phase of a transformation, the next two impact the implementing phase, and the last one impacts the optimizing phase of the transformation.

PMI

The Program Management Institute (PMI) provided a program management perspective on transformations. Their program approach articulated four key success factors:

1. Business engagement—to socialize transformation objectives, clarify scope and objectives, and manage expectations and acceptance

2. Simplification—leadership uses the fit/gap approach to simplify solutions

3. Strong governance—including management of scope/plan/budget

4. Adopting proven solutions—improving integration

All four success factors impact the implementation phase of a transformation.

McKinsey & Company—Organization

Respondents to McKinsey's 2014 survey were asked whether their organizations followed twenty-four specific transformation practices. The results of this analysis showed that four of the twenty-four practices correlated highest with transformation success.

1. Leaders communicated effectively, especially about transformation progress.

2. Leaders were active and involved.

3. Employees were engaged, empowered, and held accountable.

4. The organization had plans for continuous improvement after the transformation.

The second practice impacts the planning phase of a transformation, the first and third practices impact the implementation phase, and the last practice impacts the optimizing phase of the transformation.

There are thirty-four actions to ensure transformation success across these studies; the distribution across the three life cycle phases are summarized in figure 39 (below). As can be seen, most of the actions for success occur during the planning and implementing phases.

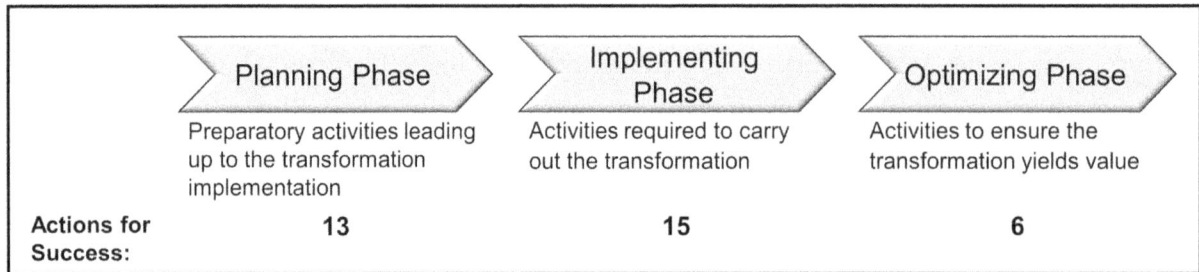

Planning Phase	Implementing Phase	Optimizing Phase
Preparatory activities leading up to the transformation implementation	Activities required to carry out the transformation	Activities to ensure the transformation yields value

Actions for Success:	13	15	6

Figure 39: Summary of Business Transformation Success Actions from Studies

The Three Phases of a Business Transformation

The life cycle of a business transformation was used (above) to facilitate the analysis of transformation failure reasons and actions to improve success. Throughout the rest of this book, the business transformation life cycle is used as a framework for organizing readiness assessments and preparations. This transformation life cycle will now be formally defined.

Other authors have introduced frameworks for analysis and organization. For example, in the McKinsey team defined five frames to organize business performance and health:

- Aspire: Where do we want to go?
- Assess: How ready are we to embark on the journey?
- Architect: What are the practical steps that will take us to our destination?
- Act: How should we manage the journey itself?
- Advance: Once we've completed the transformation, how do we keep it moving forward?

In (Maven Training, 2011), the authors introduced a four-phase transformation life cycle supports a change management offering:

1. Assessing the Change: Change impacts, vision, compelling results.
2. Planning the Change: Identify implementation and communication activities.
3. Implementing the Change: Change action activities, resourcing, managing the change.
4. Embedding the Change: Celebrate achievements, user adoption support.

The business transformation life cycle proposed here is a simple three-phase structure—planning, implementing, and optimizing—as shown in figure 40 (below).

Phase 1 Planning	Phase 2 Implementing	Phase 3 Optimizing
Activities setting the stage for the transformation	Activities required to carry out the transformation	Activities to ensure the transformation yields value

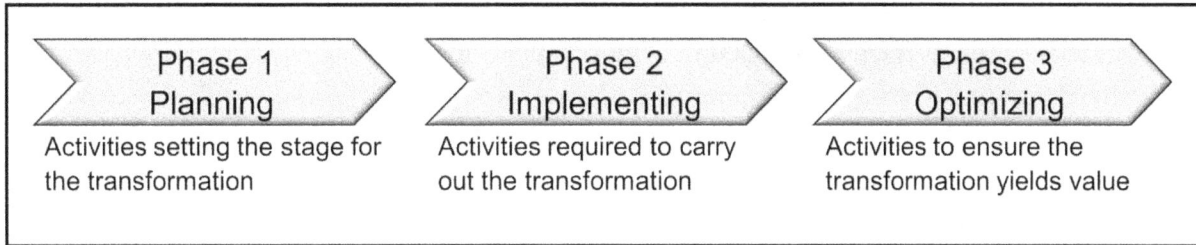

Figure 40: Three-Phase Business Transformation Life Cycle

The advantage in using a simplified life cycle is that it can be applied to the widest range of transformations without distorting the meaning of the phases. Most importantly, it will be shown in chapter 3 that readiness assessments and preparations are not isolated activities. They are specific to what happens within each phase.

Planning Phase

The planning phase is arguably the most important phase of the business transformation as it establishes the foundation for the transformation, defining the purpose, what it entails, why it is needed, and the value it will bring; this must be expressed in language understandable to all transformation stakeholders. Two primary objectives must be accomplished during the planning phase. You must establish the reason for your transformation and the extent of the transformation (purpose and scope).

Transformation Purpose

It may seem trivial to emphasize the need to clearly state the purpose of a business transformation. However, as the research findings show, six of the thirty-six reasons for failure can be related to purpose. They range from no vision, to poor definition, to lack of communication. If the purpose isn't clearly defined and communicated, it is extremely difficult to achieve anything of value and nearly impossible to tell.

Purpose-Related Transformation Failure Reasons

- not establishing a great enough sense of urgency
- lacking a vision
- lack of focus
- lack of CEO sponsorship

- conflicting visions among executive leadership or decision-makers
- lack of consensus on what digital transformation means

Transformation purpose is discovering and articulating the reasons for doing the transformation. In chapter 1, seventeen primary reasons (motivators) were described in detail and arranged in three categories based on their source—competitive, external environment, and internal environment. Companies undertaking a business transformation can begin here to understand the purpose for its transformation.

Transformation Scope

The scope is the extent to which the business will be transformed. The research showed that thirteen of the thirty-six reasons for failure were related to scope. They range from incomplete understanding of the change to aligning the proper resources to lead and implement the change. If the scope isn't clearly defined and communicated, it will be difficult to know whether the change supports the purpose—or if the change can even be implemented.

Scope-Related Transformation Failure Reasons

- unknown future state when you begin
- trouble articulating the what and how of the transformation
- too strong a focus on back-office and infrastructure
- not creating a powerful enough guiding coalition
- failure to understand the complexity of the operating model and the changes necessary to affect its transformations
- undercommunicating the vision
- the future state is radically different than the current state—the people and culture must change to implement it successfully
- lack of internal talent to spearhead or execute business change
- change leaders need to transform themselves first
- missing the necessary skills and mind-sets to execute the transformation
- talent deficit
- inability to innovate or create the processes and budgets required for innovation
- insufficient funding

Transformation scope is specifying all that needs to be included in the transformation. At this point in the transformation life cycle, you will not know every detail of your scope, but you should at least understand which of the fifteen common business changes (shown in figure 4) are required to achieve the purpose.

The two primary objectives of the planning phase of a business transformation are summarized in figure 41 (below).

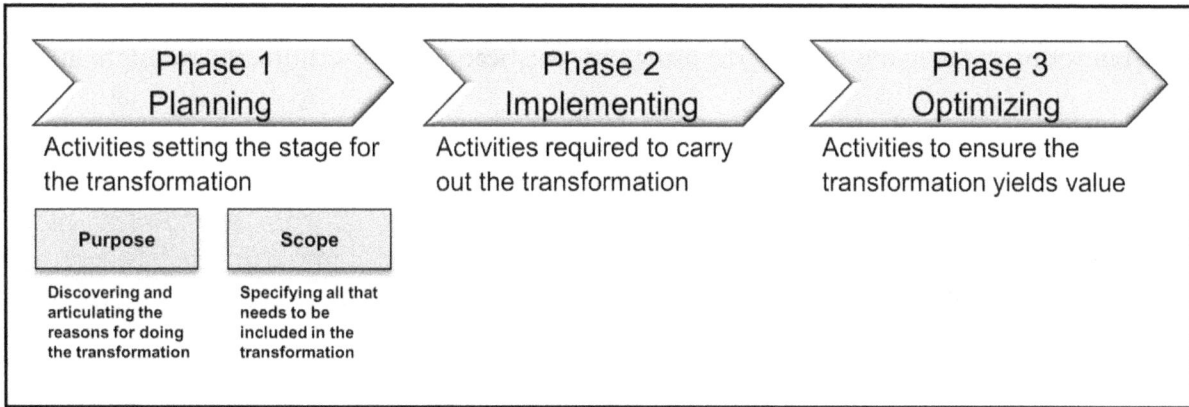

Figure 41: Objectives of the Planning Phase

Implementing Phase

The implementing phase is where the transformational change activities are carried out to achieve the purpose and scope defined in the planning phase. The transformational change must be specified in detail and completed in entirety; otherwise, the value expected is at risk. In extreme cases, an incomplete change impairs existing operations or creates discontinuity. Two primary objectives must be accomplished during the implementing phase. You must fully specify and carry out the transformational change—that is, design and execute the transformation.

Transformation Design

Design in this context means design of the transformation. This is an elaboration of the plans and specifications pertaining to the scope of change identified during the planning phase. The research only indicated three of the thirty-six reasons for failure were related to design. It's not surprising as there is a large body of existing knowledge around system requirements and design. However, it's important to remember that transformations include more than just system changes. Transformation design pertains to all that is changed during the transformation.

Design-Related Transformation Failure Reasons

- failure to take a "business value first" approach to technology
- not systematically planning for and creating short-term wins
- resource/budget constraints

Transformation design is creating the plans and specifications for executing the transformation.

Transformation Execution

Execution is the fulfillment of all the transformation changes included in the design. The research showed that eleven of the thirty-six reasons for failure were related to execution. They range from failure to implement sound project management practices to insufficient attention to change management. Execution is generally the longest, most resource-intensive, and hence most expensive part of the transformation. It is when the transformation comes into existence and creates both excitement and anxiety.

Execution-Related Transformation Failure Reasons

- isolating the digital transformation from the rest of the business
- inflexibility—managing transformation with predetermined, time-bound, and linear project plans
- inefficient execution or lack of formal process
- lack of adequate technology
- inability to execute the transformation and operationalize a new target operating model
- integration challenges
- not removing obstacles to the new vision
- existing organizational culture was a barrier
- resistance to change
- lack of speed
- lack of leadership continuity

Transformation execution is carrying out the plans and specifications for the transformation. The two primary objectives of the implementing phase of a business transformation are summarized in figure 42 (below).

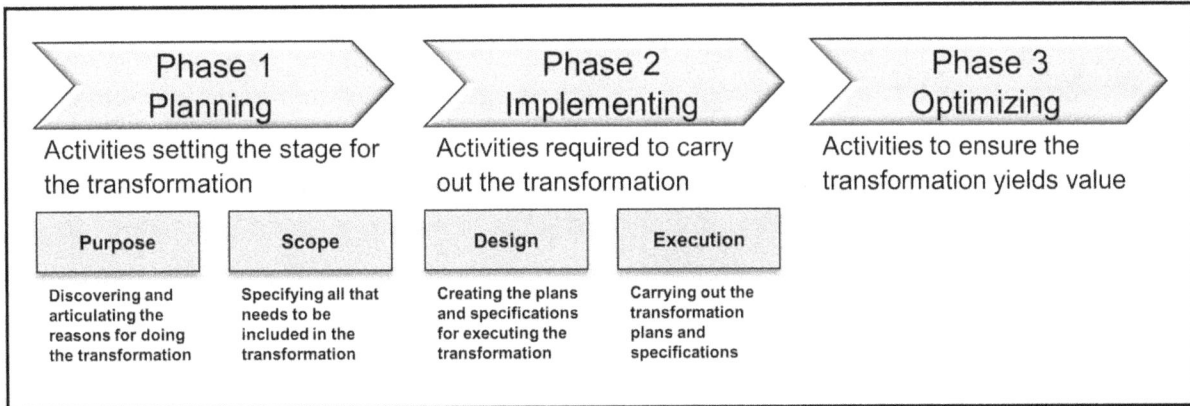

Figure 42: Objectives of the Implementing Phase

Optimizing Phase

The optimizing phase is where the value of the transformation is realized. The transformational change must be fully adopted within the business, the transformation's purpose must be fully achieved, and the business must attain an operational state of continuous improvement. Anything less yields only partial realization of value. Two primary objectives must be accomplished during the optimizing phase. You must complete the transformation and create lasting value—that is, achievement and enhancement of the transformation.

Transformation Achievement

Achievement means the purpose is achieved. The business has fully adopted all the changes required to realize the purpose, and the value of the transformation can be objectively measured. The research only indicated two of the thirty-six reasons for failure were related to achievement:

- declaring victory before adoption has been completed
- missing ongoing commitment to the transformation

Only a small set of companies reach this phase of its transformation. There are more than thirty reasons a transformation fails before it gets to the optimizing phase and not much advice on what can be done to improve the success rate. Chapter 6 is dedicated to the optimizing phase and will show how to define a pathway to achieving the purpose and value of the transformation.

Achievement is ensuring the purpose of the transformation is accomplished.

Transformation Enhancement

Enhancement means the business attains a new operating state—one in which the value of the transformation continues to increase over time. This is important as the disruption created by a transformation is not sustainable. However, incrementally improving an operating state is less disruptive and is sustainable.

Enhancement-Related Transformation Failure Reasons

- Changes Not Institutionalized in Company Culture

While there are negligible research findings surrounding enhancement after a transformation has been achieved, there are many continuous improvement methodologies such as Total Quality Management and Six Sigma.

Enhancement is creating lasting value and continuous improvement. The two primary objectives of the optimizing phase of a business transformation are summarized in figure 43 (below).

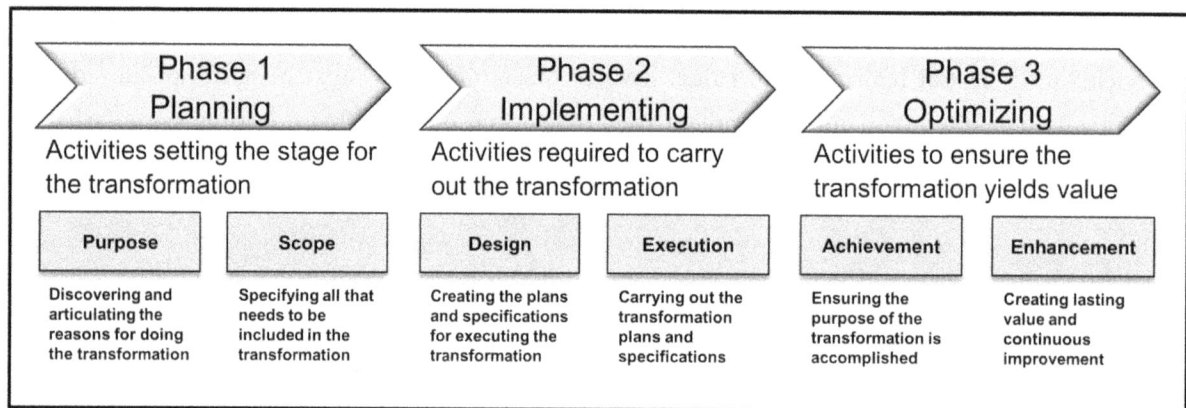

Figure 43: Objectives of All Three Phases

Implications from the Research

The formal business transformation life cycle can be used to classify the findings from the research studies. The thirty-six reasons for failure and thirty-four actions to ensure success are aligned to the objectives in the business transformation life cycle and summarized in figure 44 (below). The actual text for the failure reasons and success actions are summarized in the Appendix sections "Reasons for Business Transformation Failure" and "Actions to Ensure Success on a Business Transformation."

	Phase 1 Planning		Phase 2 Implementing		Phase 3 Optimizing	
	Activities setting the stage for the transformation		Activities required to carry out the transformation		Activities to ensure the transformation yields value	
	Purpose	**Scope**	**Design**	**Execution**	**Achievement**	**Enhancement**
	Discovering and articulating the reasons for doing the transformation	Specifying all that needs to be included in the transformation	Creating the plans and specifications for executing the transformation	Carrying out the transformation plans and specifications	Ensuring the purpose of the transformation is accomplished	Creating lasting value and continuous improvement
Reasons for Failure:	6	13	3	11	2	1
Actions for Success:	5	8	3	12	2	4

Figure 44: Findings from Research Organized by Life Cycle Phase and Objective

This book is not intended to be an exhaustive survey of the reasons transformations fail or even to identify all the actions you can take to ensure success. The objective of this book is to define a special type of activity called "readiness" and to demonstrate how readiness can address the reasons transformations fail and ultimately help ensure a transformation succeeds.

The research findings provide insights into where and when challenges occur in a business transformation. The next chapter generalizes the challenges specific to each phase and defines the concept of readiness to address those challenges. Chapter 4, chapter 5, and chapter 6 introduce readiness assessments and preparations for the challenges in the planning, implementing, and optimizing phases, respectively, and show how they are used to improve success in a business transformation.

Chapter Takeaway Points

- Thirty-six reasons for transformation failure were presented from the studies of other researchers. Most of the failures occur during the planning phase of a business transformation.
- Thirty-four actions to ensure transformation success were presented from the studies of other researchers. Most of the actions pertain to the planning and implementing phases of a business transformation.
- The three-phase life cycle of a business transformation was formally defined, including planning, implementing, and optimizing phases.
- The six objectives of a business transformation were formally defined, including purpose, scope, design, execution, achievement, and enhancement. The reasons for failure and actions for success from the research were aligned with the life cycle phases and the objectives.

Chapter 3

BUSINESS TRANSFORMATION READINESS

By failing to prepare, you are preparing to fail.
—Benjamin Franklin

This chapter characterizes the business transformation challenges that ultimately become the source of transformation failures. The concept of readiness is formally introduced as a tool to address the challenges and help ensure transformation success.

Life Cycle Phase Specific Challenges

The results of the research studies from chapter 2, together with the author's own experience with business transformations, can be generalized as a set of business transformation challenges. The challenges are specific to the phases and objectives of the transformation and encapsulate the reasons transformations fail. But, more importantly, they provide insight into why they fail and are therefore essential in formulating an approach to address them. The challenges are denoted as a "gap or deficiency," but can be rephrased as a "goal" to be achieved during the life cycle of the transformation.

Planning Phase Challenges and Goals

Planning phase challenges derail or impede the completion of the transformation's purpose and scope.

Transformation Purpose

The reasons a company will fail to establish the purpose of its transformation are condensed into four primary challenges:

- incomplete understanding of your business
- insufficiently defined reason for the transformation
- business leaders not aligned around the reason for the transformation
- the reason for the transformation is not communicated throughout your business

Understand Your Business

Understanding your business is the starting point of any strategic endeavor. Without a sufficient understanding of your own business, you cannot assess your performance with respect to the competitive environment in which you operate—or tell how well you are serving the expectations of your customers. Most importantly, a thorough understanding of your company's strengths and weaknesses is essential for defining the reason for taking on a transformation.

Define the Reasons for the Transformation

The biggest challenge in establishing the purpose of your transformation is to identify and clearly articulate the reason(s) you must undertake the transformation. The reasons must logically follow from the current state of your business and express a compelling next state that creates lasting value. The motivation should not reflect an invalid reason for undergoing the disruption—such as becoming more innovative. Finally, the reason cannot be vaguely stated or subject to interpretation.

Align the Business around the Reason

Once the reason is clearly established, it is essential for all stakeholders to agree it is the single most important thing the business needs to do. If your business leaders are not aligned on the reason for the transformation or do not believe it is critical to your company's future, the transformation will compete for time and resources and experience overt or covert resistance. You must know who the stakeholders are and ensure they understand the reason for the transformation and are committed to the goals and objectives.

Communicate the Reason throughout Your Business

Transformations impact everyone in the organization in one way or another. You will depend on some people to lead the changes and others to adopt the changes. Transformations are not intended to be secret, and you couldn't keep them that way for very long even if that was your intention. The success of the transformation depends on how well you mobilize your entire organization in the new direction. There may be aspects of the transformation that must be kept confidential for some period. However, a clear, concise statement of purpose reflecting the reasons for the transformation is essential for motivating the organization to change. This is the first step in ensuring the transformation is adopted.

Transformation Scope

The reasons a company will fail to establish the scope of its transformation are summarized as four primary challenges.

- have not completely identified what needs to change
- incomplete understanding of the impact of the change
- insufficient understanding of the investment required to change
- have not committed the required investment

Identify What Needs to Change

The most critical step in producing the scope of a transformation is to have a clear and complete understanding of everything that must change to achieve the transformation's purpose. This must include new products, new services, new industries, and new markets served, and any of the other common business changes shown in figure 4. Since this is a complete description of the changes, you must also know which of these products and services need to stop. Without a complete understanding of the required changes, it is impossible to have a full understanding of the impacts on the organization and impossible to determine the resources required to carry out the changes.

Understand the Impact of the Change

The impact of a transformational change is a quantification of the change impacts induced and which must be managed throughout the transformation. As shown in figure 15, change impacts include content and deliverables, methods and procedures, and relationships. This is a measure of how much change your organization will experience in carrying out your transformation. A complete understanding of the change impacts is critical for estimating the investment required to implement the transformation and in knowing whether your company can afford to make that investment.

Identify the Investment Required to Change

Transformations require a significant amount of resources in the form of internal/external labor, purchased/leased software, equipment, services, licenses, and facilities. The quantity of these resources will not be precisely known until after the design objective has occurred during the implementation phase. However, the resources can be estimated once a thorough understanding of the change impacts has been completed. The resource estimate is required to secure funding for the transformation and helps in understanding the return on investment.

Commit the Required Investment

Full commitment to the resources required for the transformational change is dependent on two factors: whether you are "able" to expend the resources and whether you are "willing" to expend them. Being able means you can secure the funding, devote the people, and absorb the impacts of the change. Being willing means it is a high-priority use of resources and your organization is ready to expend them. It makes no sense to go any further with your business transformation until you have full resource commitment.

Implementing Phase Challenges and Goals

Implementing phase challenges derail or impede the completion of the transformation's design and execution.

Transformation Design

The reasons a company will fail to establish the design of its transformation are summarized as five primary challenges:

- incomplete identification of required business capabilities
- incomplete specification of required business solution
- incomplete description of value realization
- incomplete description of capabilities/solution/value delivery
- insufficient resources for leading/executing

Identify Required Business Capabilities

A business capability is a competency or ability a company possesses and uses to carry out business activity. Capabilities are skills, physical assets, or relationships that provide the business a commercial advantage. Examples of business capabilities include product engineering and manufacturing, a mobile transactional website, a comprehensive distribution network, or the right to sell products and services in a foreign country.

When companies undergo a transformation, their business capabilities often change. New capabilities may be acquired, and existing capabilities may be enhanced—or retired. Business capabilities provide a formal way to represent what the company "needs to be good at" after it has transformed.

You can evaluate the effectiveness of a capability and identify gaps and required improvement before committing to a specific solution. Specific solutions at this point are premature and can lead to chasing trends or the paths of your competitors, but both fail to identify the required competencies/abilities.

Specify Required Business Solution

The business solution must be a complete description of how the required business capabilities will be implemented in the transformation. Everything that must be created, enhanced, or removed needs to be part of the solution. This goes beyond technology and includes processes, policies, organization structures, work content, and locations. There can be no gaps or inconsistencies, and the new parts of the solution must be fully integrated into the existing solution. If the required business solution isn't defined in its entirety, then the business capabilities cannot be realized, and the transformation cannot be completed.

Specify Value Realization

The value objectives of a transformation quantify the purpose into tangible and intangible benefits. Value realization relates the value objectives to the required business capabilities—and their corresponding parts of the business solution. Without value realization, it is difficult to tell whether the transformation's purpose can be achieved through the solution. Also, if the solution is created and delivered incrementally, it will be difficult to know whether the value can be realized incrementally as well.

Specify the Delivery Sequence

The delivery is the aggregate of the business capabilities, business solution, and value objectives associated with the transformation. It is everything that must be fulfilled to achieve the purpose and scope of the transformation. If the purpose and scope cannot be achieved in a single delivery (likely for larger transformations), then a delivery sequence is required. The delivery sequence is the plan for executing the fulfillment of the scope. It should be obvious that, without a plan, there is no way to tell how long it will take to fulfill the scope, how much resource is required, or whether completion of some things depend on the completion of others.

Secure Required Resources for Leading/Executing

Project management discipline helps in estimating the number of team members required to complete the transformation delivery within the time frame and budget. However, it is also critical for the team members to have the skills and experience required to complete the work. The transformation must also have sufficient leadership (high enough in the company) to motivate the transformation and effectively carry out the delivery.

Transformation Execution

The reasons a company will fail the execution of its transformation are summarized as six primary challenges:

- insufficient program management rigor
- solution is overly complex/customized
- solution is improperly integrated
- business-solution change is insufficiently managed
- insufficient stakeholder communications
- ineffective or missing path to realize value

Instill Program Management Rigor

Program and project management concepts have been around for decades. There are best practices, templates, and techniques available through many sources. The Project Management Institute has published a body of knowledge on this subject and offers certifications as well.

It's hard to imagine that program management still needs to be called out explicitly as a challenge, but for the sake of completeness and given that a third of the reasons for failure were due to weak project management, it is included. For successful execution, business transformations require, at a minimum, scope change management, risk management, a program-governance structure and processes, a formal solution-delivery methodology/tools/processes, and rigorous tracking/evaluation/ management of the schedule, resources, and milestones.

Standardize Solutions

Complexity and customization increase the total life cycle cost of a solution and can negatively impact a solution's agility, flexibility, and scalability. Complex or customized solutions are not inherently bad or to be avoided at all cost, but they should be used appropriately. Complexity and customization become problems when it is unclear why they are proposed or there is no identifiable value over standard solutions. A solution-delivery methodology should at least include an assessment of complexity/customization to ensure it is considered in the execution of the transformation execution.

Integrate Solution

A solution that is integrated will be complete and flow contiguously among the components. It will not have missing or disjointed steps. The solution should be described completely during design. If the solution is delivered incrementally, it is possible to create an incomplete or disjointed intermediate state. Incomplete intermediate states may be acceptable, if only temporary, over some period. The solution-delivery methodology should include an assessment of integrated flow.

Manage Business-Solution Change

It's hard to imagine a business transformation without some form of change management. In this context, it means helping people overcome fear and resistance to change. There are many methodologies and approaches available including useful practices and insights into the nature of organizational change. If a business transformation does not (at a minimum) evaluate the degree of change resistance within the culture and take steps to reduce/manage the resistance to change, the business will not complete its transformation.

Communicate with Stakeholders

Stakeholder communications is typically a component of change management. However, as poor communications were a source of failure in the research, it's worthwhile to call it out separately. Communication becomes a challenge during the execution of a business transformation whenever the status of the transformation is not effectively shared with the stakeholders. This means either the content or frequency are inappropriate—or the entire audience has not been identified. Communication is also a challenge when there is no mechanism for stakeholders to provide feedback during execution. Feedback is critical to gauging change resistance, solution adoption, and blind spots.

Specify Path to Value

Recall that during design, value realization mapped the value objectives to the required business capabilities—and their corresponding parts of the business solution. "Path to value" is how the value is achieved and validated. It includes first identifying all the hurdles to achieving the business capabilities and value objectives and identifying mitigation strategies to overcome these hurdles. The hurdles and hurdle mitigations together form the path to value. Without an explicit path, there is no way to understand what prevents a value objective from being achieved—or what can be done about it should it occur.

Optimizing Phase Challenges and Goals

Optimizing phase challenges derail or impede the transformation's achievement and enhancement.

Transformation Achievement

The reasons a company will fail to achieve the purpose and scope of its transformation are summarized as two primary challenges:

- insufficient evaluation of achievement progress
- ineffective ability to overcome achievement hurdles

Measure/Evaluate Progress

Achieving the transformation means achieving the transformation's purpose, scope, and value objectives and deploying the required business capabilities and solutions. These are measurable throughout the course of the transformation execution. Achievement is at great risk without defining/ tracking/publishing corresponding metrics and creating a baseline assessment from which to compare the progress.

Overcome Value Hurdles

The path to realizing value is defined during the execution of the transformation and includes both the hurdles to value and a means to mitigate the hurdles. A company is severely challenged in achieving its transformation if it fails to overcome the hurdles. This occurs whenever the business neglects to assign and prioritize accountability for driving adoption of the business solution and realizing the value objectives—or it is sorely deficient in executing the hurdle mitigations.

Transformation Enhancement

The reasons a company will fail to enhance the achieved state of its transformation are summarized as two primary challenges:

- insufficient retention of business change/value
- ineffective incremental improvement

Retain Your Business Change/Value

The transformation effort is for naught if the business cannot retain the business changes and value achieved. This occurs when the business neglects to assign and prioritize accountability for retaining adoption of the business changes and value objectives. If accountability has been assigned, then resources will need to be allocated to retain the adoption and value. Business change adoption and value objective metrics must also be defined, tracked, and published to help retain the transformation.

Implement Incremental Improvement

The final challenge for consideration addresses the ability to incrementally improve the operating performance beyond the original business transformation. Incremental improvement is less disruptive than a business transformation. It is therefore in the company's best interest to pursue this course. Incremental improvement is jeopardized if the business either neglects to assign and prioritize accountability or neglects to commit resources and efforts for continuous improvement.

The twenty-three challenges condensing the reasons transformations fail are summarized in figure 45 (below).

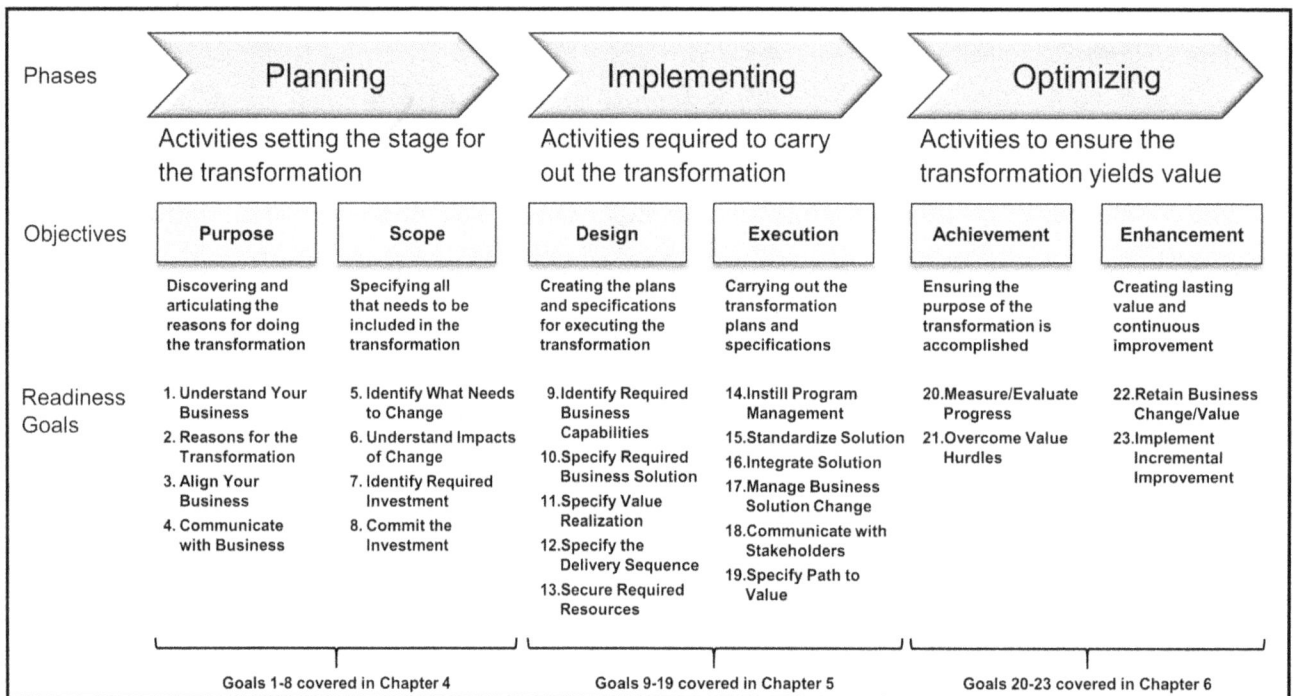

Phases	**Planning**		**Implementing**		**Optimizing**	
	Activities setting the stage for the transformation		Activities required to carry out the transformation		Activities to ensure the transformation yields value	
Objectives	**Purpose**	**Scope**	**Design**	**Execution**	**Achievement**	**Enhancement**
	Discovering and articulating the reasons for doing the transformation	Specifying all that needs to be included in the transformation	Creating the plans and specifications for executing the transformation	Carrying out the transformation plans and specifications	Ensuring the purpose of the transformation is accomplished	Creating lasting value and continuous improvement
Readiness Goals	1. Understand Your Business 2. Reasons for the Transformation 3. Align Your Business 4. Communicate with Business	5. Identify What Needs to Change 6. Understand Impacts of Change 7. Identify Required Investment 8. Commit the Investment	9. Identify Required Business Capabilities 10. Specify Required Business Solution 11. Specify Value Realization 12. Specify the Delivery Sequence 13. Secure Required Resources	14. Instill Program Management 15. Standardize Solution 16. Integrate Solution 17. Manage Business Solution Change 18. Communicate with Stakeholders 19. Specify Path to Value	20. Measure/Evaluate Progress 21. Overcome Value Hurdles	22. Retain Business Change/Value 23. Implement Incremental Improvement
	Goals 1-8 covered in Chapter 4		Goals 9-19 covered in Chapter 5		Goals 20-23 covered in Chapter 6	

Figure 45: Business Transformation Challenges Aligned with Life Cycle Phases and Objectives

Business Transformation Readiness

The twenty-three challenges spanning the three phases of a business transformation have something in common. In every case, the challenges indicate the company was not ready to begin the work within the phase, it didn't fully achieve the objectives of the phase, and it was not ready to begin subsequent work. In other words, the challenges are directly related to the company's readiness as it proceeds through the transformation.

Is there a way to ensure a company is ready? The answer, of course, is yes. Being ready during your business transformation requires two things as you progress: checking your state of readiness and (if necessary) taking steps to become ready. This is depicted in figure 46 (below).

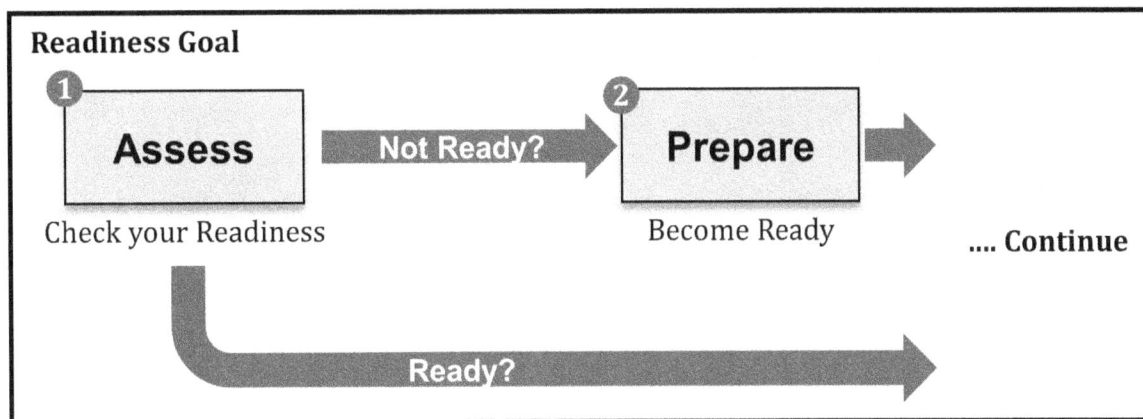

Figure 46: Business Transformation Readiness

The business transformation challenges were rephrased as goals. The purpose in doing that was to translate a business transformation challenge into a business transformation readiness goal. Business transformation readiness then means to complete all twenty-three readiness goals throughout the life cycle of the business transformation. The two activities—assess and prepare—shown in figure 46 can now be formalized as readiness assessments and readiness preparations. They will serve as gating activities and be distinguished from all other activities and deliverables in a business transformation. This helps to elevate their visibility and importance in addressing the challenges in a transformation.

Readiness Assessment

A readiness assessment defines a "standard of readiness" in addressing a transformation challenge and a method for evaluating "achievement toward that standard." Assessment standards and evaluation methods are defined and associated with each challenge, indicating the minimum degree of readiness required to address the challenge and achieve the readiness goal. This is depicted graphically in figure 47 (below).

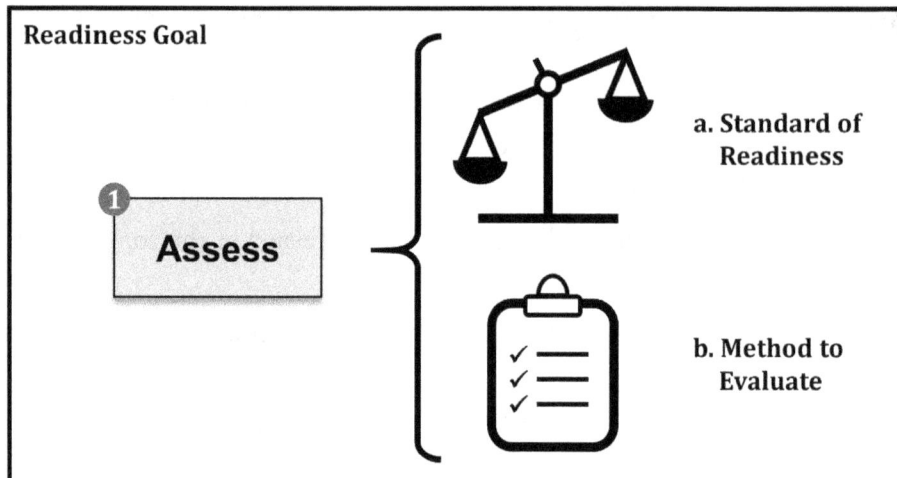

Figure 47: Business Transformation Readiness Assessment

Readiness Assessment Standards

Readiness assessment standards highlight the aspects most critical in overcoming a transformation challenge and attaining the readiness goal. As such, they must be uniquely defined for each readiness goal. This is illustrated schematically in figure 48 (below).

For example, consider readiness goal #1: Understand Your Business. This goal is in the "purpose" objective of the planning phase (figure 45). While there is a bit of an art in designing the best set of readiness assessment standards, it's not too difficult to convince yourself that you must at least know what your customers expect, know your competitor's performance, and know your own business performance. Therefore, the readiness assessment standards can be formally expressed as follows:

1. You know your customers' expectations.
2. You know your competitive environment.
3. You know your company's performance and capabilities with respect to your competitive environment.

If you know these, then you have attained readiness with respect to "Understand Your Business." The standards by themselves, indicate what is important in attaining the readiness goal, but they don't tell you how to evaluate whether you sufficiently understand your business. For that you'll also need assessment metrics.

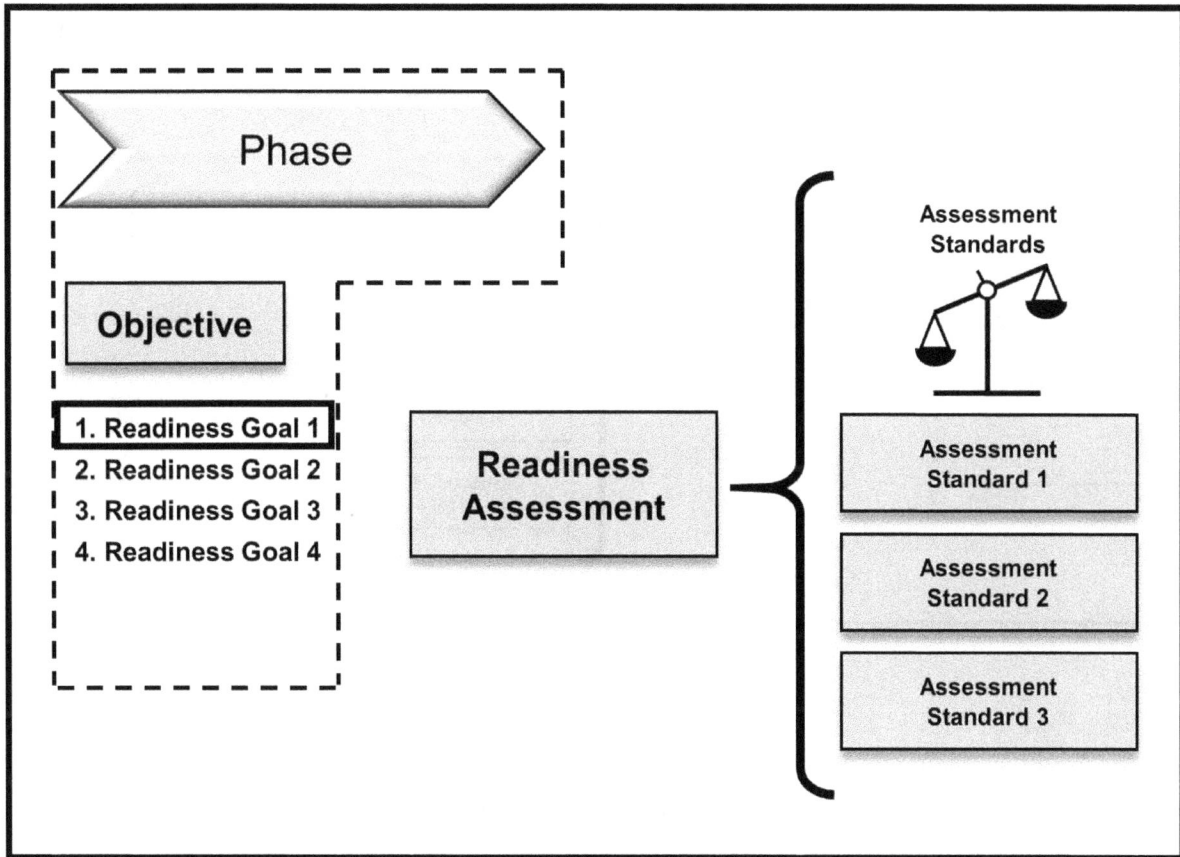

Figure 48:

Readiness Assessment Standards

Readiness Assessment Metrics

Readiness assessment metrics assist you in evaluating attainment of the standards of readiness for reach readiness goal. As such, they must be uniquely defined for each assessment standard in each readiness goal. This is illustrated schematically in figure 49 (below). The metrics are in the form of questions you can ask/answer to examine your company's readiness, and most importantly, to identify any gaps in your readiness.

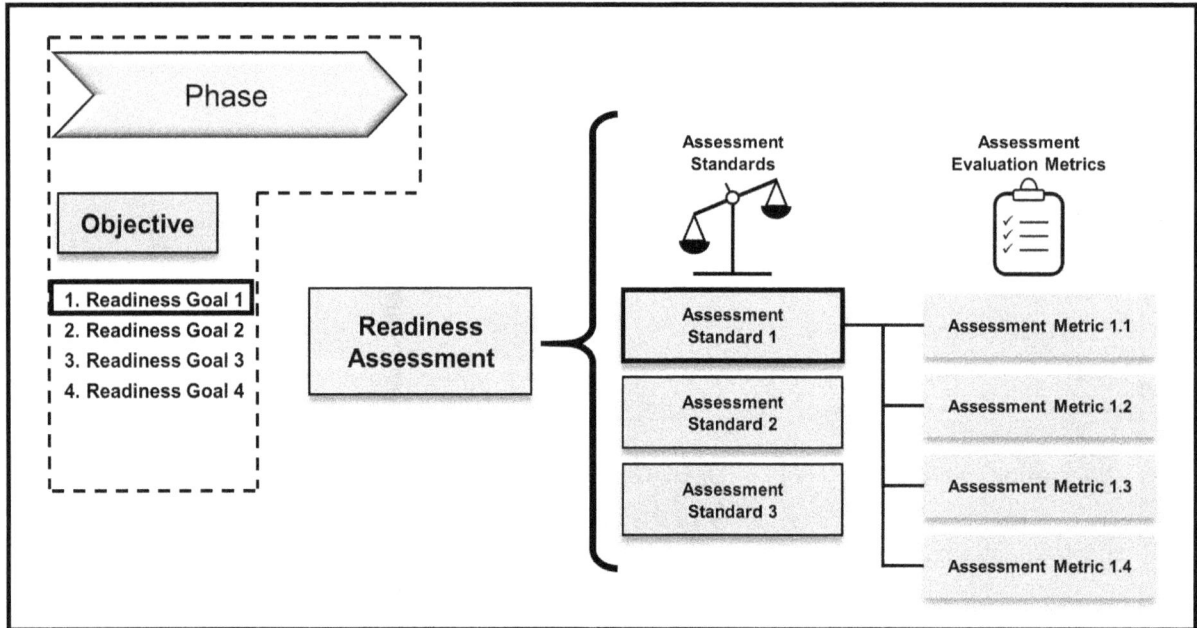

Figure 49: Readiness Assessment Metrics

For example, again consider readiness goal #1: Understand Your Business. The first readiness assessment standard was "You know your customers' expectations." The questions you could ask to evaluate whether you really know your customers' expectations might include the following:

1. Who are your key customers?
2. How do your customers want to engage you?
3. How well do you believe you meet your customers' expectations?
4. How well do your customers believe you meet their expectations?

There might be other questions you'd like to ask, but these are a minimum to attain the readiness standard. This example is illustrated in figure 50 (below) and shows the assessment standards and assessment evaluation metrics for the first standard.

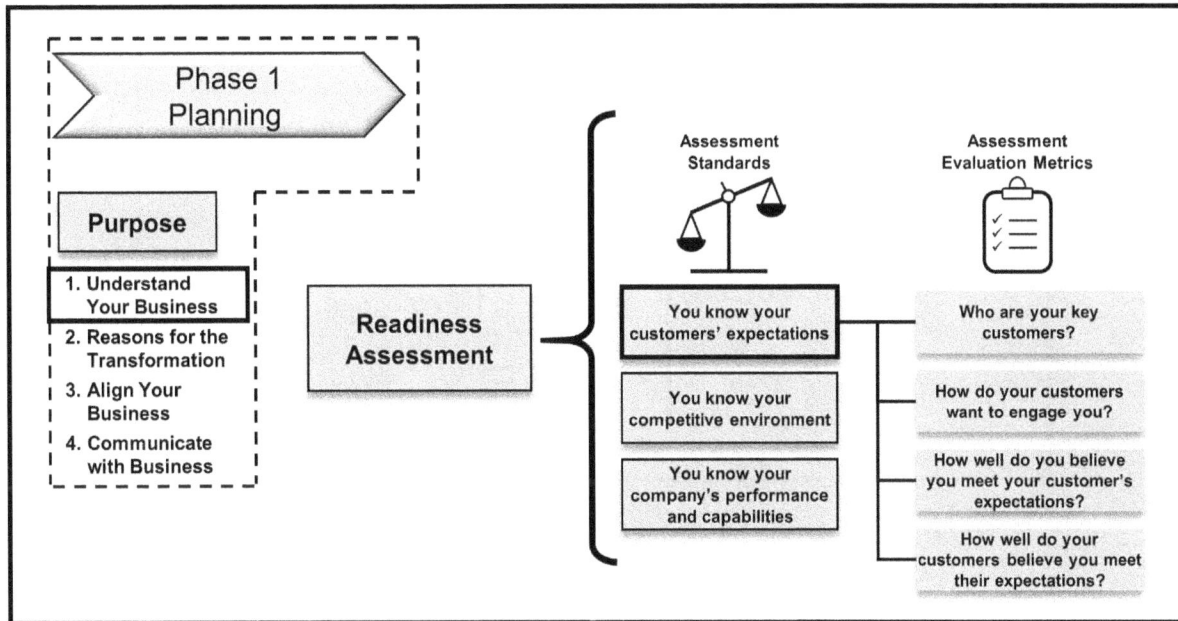

Figure 50: Readiness Assessment Example—Understand Your Business

Readiness Preparation

Readiness Preparation identifies "remedial actions" a company can take to help it attain the standards of readiness. If your company has not attained readiness, it must do something to become ready. You will not become ready with the passing of time. Inaction leads to paralysis, which can be as detrimental as moving ahead before you are ready. Action is required—specifically action that brings you to a state of readiness. Each readiness preparation specifies corresponding preparation actions for the company to take. If a company is both willing and able to carry out the preparation steps, then it will attain the assessment standard. Readiness preparations are arranged in the same way as readiness assessments. There is one readiness preparation for each readiness goal as shown in figure 51 (below).

Readiness Preparation Actions

Readiness preparation actions are designed specifically to satisfy the assessment standards. Once carried out, you will be able to conduct the readiness assessment and attain the readiness goal. As such, there is one readiness preparation action for each readiness assessment standard. This is illustrated schematically in figure 52 (below).

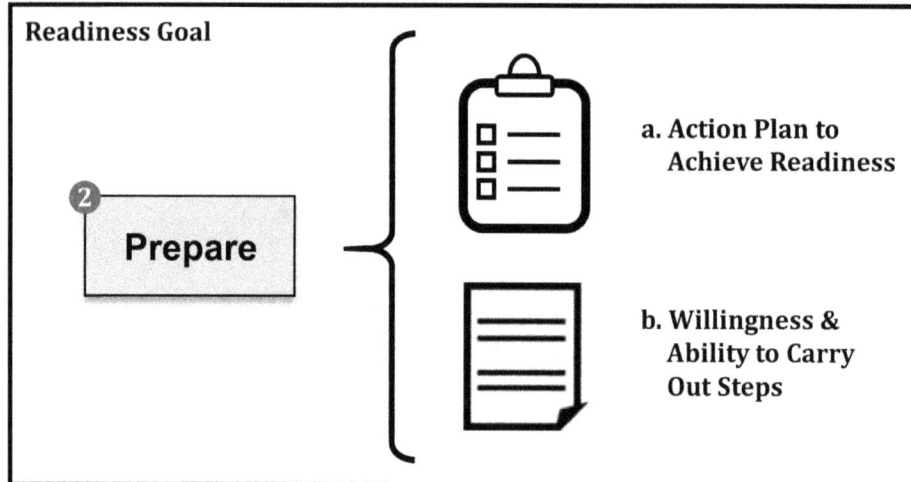

Figure 51: Business Transformation Readiness Preparation

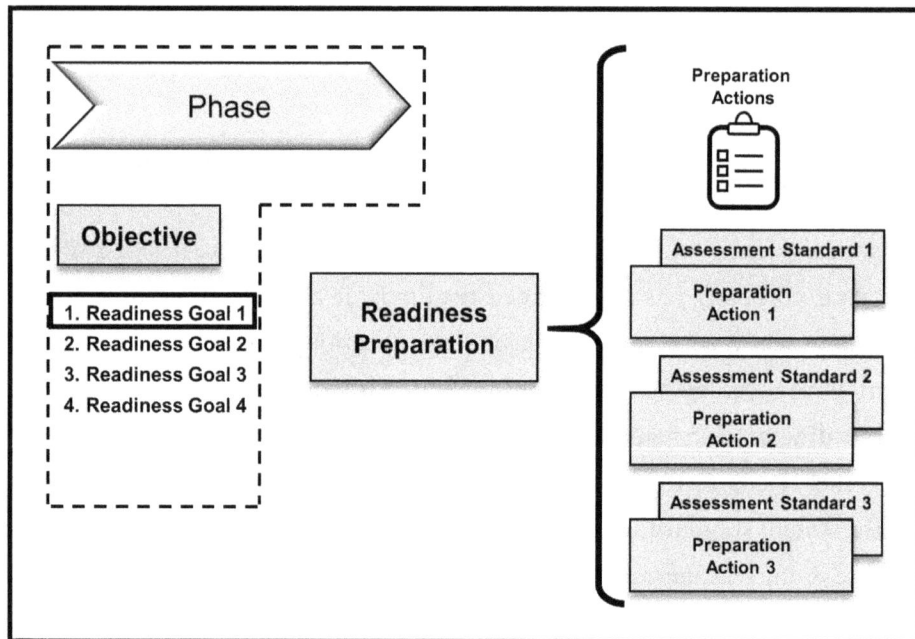

Figure 52: Readiness Preparation Actions

For example, consider again readiness goal #1: Understand Your Business. The readiness assessment standards were expressed as follows:

1. You know your customers' expectations.
2. You know your competitive environment.
3. You know your company's performance and capabilities with respect to your competitive environment.

The corresponding actions to ensure you attain these assessment standards are as follows:

1. You produce a customer service performance analysis of your company.
2. You produce an analysis of your competitors and their performance.
3. You produce an analysis of your performance.

If you complete these actions, then the next time you conduct the readiness assessment, you should attain the readiness goal. The actions by themselves indicate what is important to attain the standard, but they don't tell you how to attain the standard. For that, you'll need the preparation steps.

Readiness Preparation Steps

Readiness preparation steps assist you in carrying out the preparation actions for each readiness goal. As such, they must be uniquely defined for each assessment action in each readiness goal. This is illustrated schematically in figure 53 (below). The steps are in the form of artifacts you produce to carry out the preparation action and ultimately achieve the corresponding readiness standard.

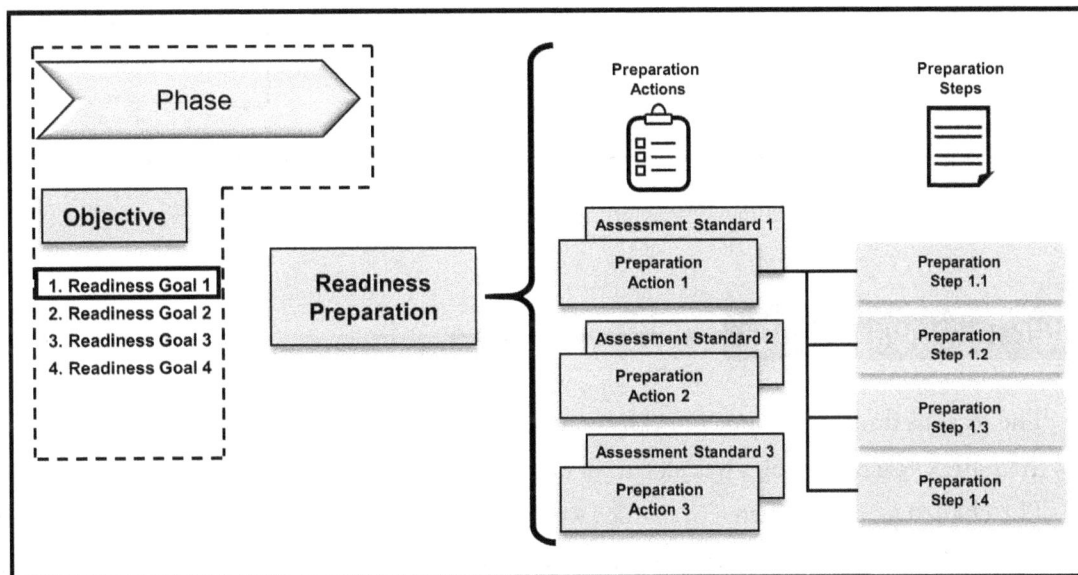

Figure 53: Readiness Preparation Deliverables

Continuing the example, consider readiness goal #1: Understand Your Business. The first readiness preparation action was "Produce a customer service performance analysis of your company." The steps you could take to carry out a customer service performance analysis include the following:

1. Identify relevant customers within your industry segment.
2. Conduct voice-of-the-customer (VOC) analysis.

3. Conduct VOC self-assessment.
4. Assess customer VOC responses.

There might be other steps you could take, but these are a minimum to carry out the preparation action and attain the readiness standard. This example is illustrated in figure 54 (below) and shows the preparation actions and the preparation steps for the first action.

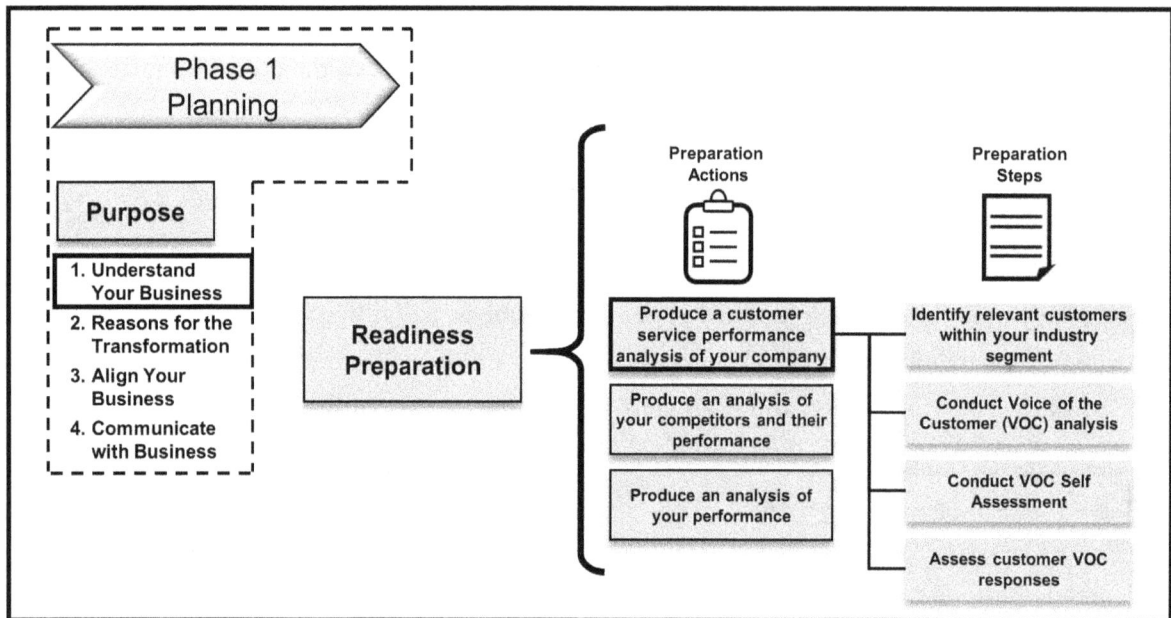

Figure 54: Readiness Preparation Example—Understand Your Business

Chapter Takeaway Points

- The reasons transformations fail can be attributed to twenty-three challenges throughout the three life cycle phases of a transformation.
- The challenges show where companies were not ready to begin the work within the phase or didn't fully achieve the objectives of the phase and were not ready to begin subsequent work.
- Business transformation readiness addresses the challenges in a transformation.
- Readiness consists of two activities: assessment and preparation.
- Readiness assessment defines a "standard of readiness" in addressing a challenge and a method for evaluating "achievement toward that standard."
- Readiness assessment standards highlight the aspects most critical in overcoming a transformation challenge and attaining the readiness goal.
- Readiness assessment metrics assist you in evaluating attainment of the standards of readiness for reach readiness goal.

- Readiness preparation identifies "remedial actions" a company can take to help it attain the standards of readiness.
- Readiness preparation actions are designed to satisfy the assessment standards.
- Readiness preparation steps assist you in carrying out the preparation actions for each readiness goal.

Chapter 4

PLANNING PHASE READINESS

All things are ready, if our mind be so.
—William Shakespeare

As stated earlier, the planning phase establishes the foundation for the transformation, defining the purpose, what it entails, why it is needed, and the value it will bring. Being ready in the planning phase means that you know exactly why your business needs to be transformed, you understand the magnitude of change you will experience, and you are prepared to undertake that change.

If you are not ready in the planning phase, you are not ready for a transformation. Knowing whether your company is ready for the transformation is valuable enough and allows you to avoid incurring unnecessary disruption and expense. However, readiness is more than just knowing whether you are ready—it also helps you to become ready.

If you are undertaking planning efforts, or considering them, you must already believe a transformation is necessary. Readiness will help you validate your belief and formally express it throughout your company.

This chapter presents readiness for the planning phase of a business transformation. It is organized in two sections; the first section covers readiness for the purpose objective, and the second section covers readiness for the scope objective. Each section will specify the readiness assessments and preparations for the respective readiness goals. The readiness goals for the purpose and scope objectives are shown in figure 55 (below).

Phase	Planning	
	Activities setting the stage for the transformation	
Objectives	**Purpose**	**Scope**
	Discovering and articulating the reasons for doing the transformation	Specifying all that needs to be included in the transformation
Readiness Goals	1. Understand Your Business	5. Identify What Needs to Change
	2. Reasons for the Transformation	6. Understand Impacts of Change
	3. Align Your Business	7. Identify Required Investment
	4. Communicate with Business	8. Commit the Investment

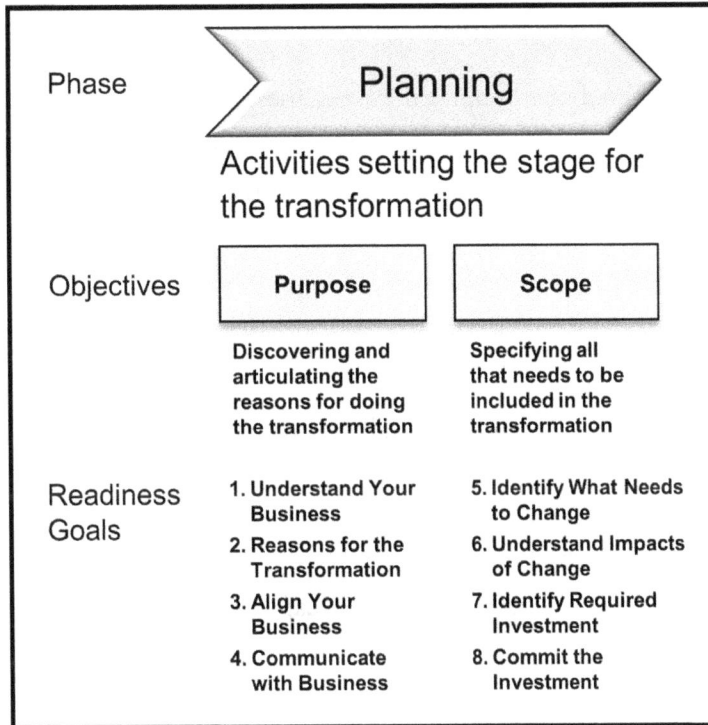

Figure 55: Planning Phase Readiness Goals

Purpose Readiness

The purpose of the planning phase of a business transformation is to discover and articulate the reasons for doing the transformation. Readiness of purpose is expressed through the attainment of the four readiness goals shown in figure 55 (above). Each of these readiness goals has an accompanying readiness assessment and readiness preparation. These are formally developed in the remainder of this section.

Goal #1: Understand Your Business

"Understand Your Business" means you understand your customers' expectations, understand the environment in which you compete, and understand your own capabilities and performance. If there is a reason to radically change something about your business, it will come from one or more of these three areas. For this reason, they will serve as the assessment standards for this readiness goal.

Readiness Assessment

A readiness assessment defined the "standard of readiness" and evaluated "achievement" toward that standard. This is facilitated through the specification of assessment standards and metrics. The standards highlight the aspects most critical to attaining the readiness goal. The metrics assist in evaluating attainment.

Readiness Assessment Standards

The readiness assessment standards can be formally expressed as follows:

1. You know your customers' expectations.
2. You know your competitive environment.
3. You know your company's performance and capabilities with respect to your competitive environment.

If you know these, then you have attained readiness for the Understand Your Business goal. If you don't, you will need to complete the readiness preparation described later in this section. The standards by themselves indicate what is important in attaining the goal, but they don't tell you how to evaluate whether you have attained the goal. For this, you'll need the assessment metrics.

Readiness Assessment Metrics

Each of the three readiness assessment standards have one or more corresponding assessment metrics to help you evaluate your attainment of the standard. The metrics are in the form of questions you can ask/answer to examine your company's readiness, and most importantly, identify any gaps in readiness. You can always ask additional questions, but if you can answer these at a minimum, you will demonstrate attainment of the standard.

> Standard 1: You know your customers' expectations.

An assessment of this standard is obtained by answering the following four questions:

a. Who are your key customers?
b. How do your key customers want to engage you with respect to the following?

- influencing products and services
- accessing knowledge of products and services

- finding/selecting products and services
- purchasing products and services
- fulfilling products and services
- billing/payment for products and services
- addressing inquiries and issues
- capturing and managing historical behavior

c. How well do you believe you meet your key customers' expectations with respect to the above?

d. How well do your key customers believe you meet their expectations with respect to the above?

➤ Standard 2: You know your competitive environment.

An assessment of this standard is obtained by answering the following five questions:

a. Who are your key competitors?

b. How well are your key competitors meeting their and your customers' expectations (from above)?

c. What are your key competitors' strengths and weaknesses?

- marketing
- sales/distribution channels
- customer experience
- products and services
- supply chain
- financial structure
- technology platforms
- business risk
- geographic structure
- business leadership
- talent management
- affiliations and relationships
- corporate culture/values

d. Why/how/where/when do the strengths of your key competitors pose a threat to your business?

e. Why/how/where/when do the weaknesses of your key competitors create a disadvantage for them?

➤ Standard 3: You know your company's performance and capabilities with respect to your competitive environment.

An assessment of this standard is obtained by answering the following three questions:

a. What are your company's strengths and weaknesses relative to the industry in which you operate?

- marketing
- sales/distribution channels
- customer experience
- products and services
- supply chain
- financial structure
- technology platforms
- business risk
- geographic structure
- business leadership
- talent management
- affiliations and relationships
- corporate culture/values

b. Which of your company's strengths will be assets during a transformation?
c. Which of your company's weaknesses will be liabilities during a transformation?

The complete readiness assessment for the goal "Understand Your Business" is shown in figure 56 (below).

Creating an Actionable Assessment

The readiness assessment summarized in figure 56 (below) can be made actionable by converting the standards and metrics into deliverables and then combining them with the corresponding activities for producing them. This creates a formal readiness assessment methodology for practitioners.

The deliverables are formalized responses to the assessment metrics, validating the questions that can be answered and highlighting those that cannot. The activities are formalized procedures for completing the deliverables. Templates for readiness assessments and preparations are provided in the companion guide to this book, available for download from X4MU.com/.

Readiness Assessment	#1: Understand Your Business		
Assessment Standards	1. You know your customers' expectations	2. You know your competitive environment	3. You know your company's performance and capabilities
Assessment Metrics	a. Who are your key customers?	a. Who are your key competitors?	a. What are your company's strengths and weaknesses relative to the industry in which you operate?
	b. How do your customers want to engage you?	b. How well are your competitors meeting customer expectations?	b. Which of your company's strengths will be assets during a transformation?
	c. How well do you believe you meet your customer's expectations?	c. What are your competitors strengths and weaknesses?	c. Which of your company's weaknesses will be liabilities during a transformation?
	d. How well do your customers believe you meet their expectations?	d. Why/how/where/when do the strengths of your competitors pose a threat to your business?	
		e. Why/how/where/when do the weaknesses of your competitors create a disadvantage for them?	

Figure 56: Readiness Assessment #1: Understand Your Business

Readiness Assessment Considerations

There are a few things to be aware of when completing this readiness assessment (and readiness assessments in general). The first is honesty. It makes no sense to take the time to complete an assessment if you aren't going to be forthright in answering the questions. For a quality assessment, you need an accurate understanding of your readiness.

The second is consistency. The degree of quality and completeness of the documented content must be consistent across the questions. Holding some questions to a higher degree of quality and others to a lower degree produces a misleading assessment.

Third is the time relevancy of the content. If the content is complete, but is old or obsolete, then you again end up with a misleading assessment. The content should be within a time frame that accurately depicts the environment in which you compete.

The final consideration is consensus across those conducting the assessment. The entire assessment team must agree with the assessment results. One of the goals of purpose readiness is to align the business leaders around the reason for the transformation. This is hardly possible if the assessment team does not agree on the results of the assessment.

Readiness Preparation

Recall that a readiness preparation identifies the "remedial actions" a company can take to help it attain the standards of readiness. If a company has failed to attain one or more of the assessment standards, it can carry out the remedial actions to bring it into a state of readiness.

A readiness preparation is structured to align with the corresponding readiness assessment (reference figure 57 below):

1. There is one readiness preparation for each readiness goal.
2. There is one preparation action for each assessment standard.
3. There is one preparation step for each assessment metric.

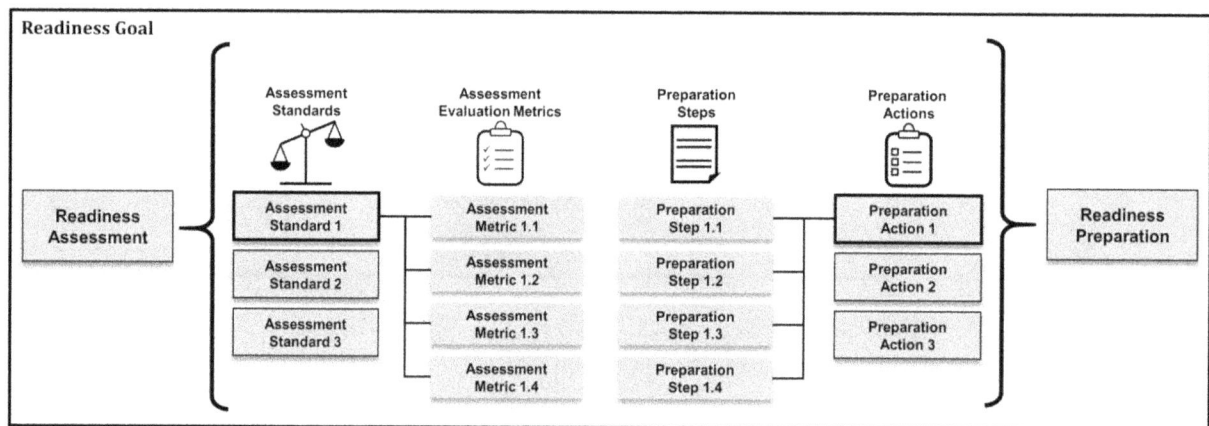

Figure 57: Readiness Preparation-Readiness Assessment Alignment

The preparation action is designed to help a company attain the corresponding assessment standard. Similarly, each preparation step is designed to help a company attain each assessment metric. Recall that the "Understand Your Business" readiness goal had three assessment standards:

1. You know your customers' expectations.
2. You know your competitive environment.
3. You know your company's performance and capabilities with respect to your competitive environment.

If your business is unable to attain these assessment standards, you will need to undertake preparation actions to remediate the gaps.

Readiness Preparation Actions

Each assessment standard requires a corresponding preparation action to help you attain that standard. The corresponding actions can be expressed as follows:

1. Produce a current-state customer service performance analysis of your company with respect to the customers in the industry segment you serve.
2. Produce a current-state analysis of your competitors and their performance with respect to the industry segment you serve.
3. Produce a current-state analysis of your performance with respect to the industry segment you serve.

The actions by themselves indicate what you can do to attain the corresponding standard, but they don't tell you how to attain it. For this, you'll need the preparation steps.

Readiness Preparation Steps

Every readiness assessment standard was assigned one or more metrics to facilitate evaluation. These metrics are used in designing the preparation steps. One preparation step is required for each assessment metric as shown in figure 57 (above):

➢ Action 1: Produce a current-state customer service performance analysis of your company with respect to the customers in the industry segment you serve.

Readiness was determined by answering the following four questions (i.e., readiness metrics), also shown in figure 56 (above):

a. Who are your key customers?
b. How do your key customers want to engage you with respect to the following?

- influencing products and services
- accessing knowledge of products and services
- finding/selecting products and services

c. How well do you meet your key customers' expectations with respect to the above?
d. How well do your key customers believe you meet their expectations with respect to the above?

Metric A: Who are your key customers?

For this metric, the preparation step is a list of customers representing relevant business demographics within your industry segment. For example, it could include your largest customers by annual sales, most loyal customers by spend/profitability, most recently acquired customers, or even customers with diminishing spend. The point is to know which of your customers have significant influence on the way you interact and operate your business. This step could be owned by sales and marketing or some other group that can carry out customer analytics from historical sales and credit records.

Metric B: How do your key customers want to engage you with respect to the following?

The preparation step has two parts. The first is to complete a voice-of-the-customer (VOC) analysis for a subset of the key customers defined above. The VOC should cover the engagement dimensions from the metric: influencing products and services, accessing knowledge of products and services, and finding/selecting products and services. When completed, the VOC provides valuable feedback from your key customers regarding the assessment of your performance.

This part of the preparation step could also be owned by sales and marketing. These teams can do the following:

1. Identify the key customers with a willingness to complete a VOC assessment.
2. Construct a VOC survey with questions to assess a customer's perspective on your company's performance and engagement, including the degree of importance they assign to a dimension, their expectations, preferences, and aversions.
3. Utilize internal/external channels, forums, and processes to capture the feedback and consolidate it into a VOC report.

The second part of the preparation step is to prepare a customer engagement journey line for a subset of key customers. The customer journey line is a visual representation of the activities a customer goes through before, during, and after engaging with your business. Journey lines are used to determine areas where the customer's experience can be improved.

This part of the preparation step could also be owned by sales and marketing. These teams can do the following:

1. Prepare list of key customers representing relevant business demographics and with a willingness to complete a customer journey line analysis.

2. Prepare a customer journey line inquiry identifying the activities a customer goes through in engaging with your business. It should also include the effort they expended on these activities.

3. Utilize interviews and forums to capture customer feedback and consolidate it into a journey line report.

Metric C: How well do you meet your key customers' expectations with respect to the above?

The preparation step consists of a self-assessment using the VOC developed for evaluating customer feedback. This can also be completed by sales and marketing. The completed VOC self-assessment provides your company with a frame of reference for customer engagement. This is useful in understanding whether you have the same perspectives as your key customers.

Metric D: How well do your key customers believe you meet their expectations with respect to the above?

The preparation step is a combination of the results of the completed VOC assessments and customer journey lines. This will reveal your customers' expectations, preferences, and aversions and help you to determine segmentation specifics, churn indicators, buying signals, purchasing influences, unmet market needs, new product ideas, missing features, perception, degree of satisfaction, and your company's reputation. You will also understand whether there are gaps in a customer's experience or whether your perspective is misaligned with your customer's perspective.

Sales and marketing should carry out this preparation step as well, which consists largely of analyzing the VOC and customer journey line data to identify areas of improvement.

➤ Action 2: Produce a current-state analysis of your competitors and their performance with respect to the industry segment you serve.

Readiness was determined by answering the following five questions (i.e., readiness metrics), also shown in figure 56:

a. Who are your key competitors?
b. How well are your key competitors meeting their and your customers' expectations?
c. What are your key competitors' strengths and weaknesses?

- marketing
- sales/distribution channels

d. Why/how/where/when do the strengths of your key competitors pose a threat to your business?

e. Why/how/where/when do the weaknesses of your key competitors create a disadvantage for them?

Metric A: Who are your key competitors?

The preparation step for this metric is a list of competitors representing the relevant business demographics within your industry segment and market segment. The industry segment competitors include those with the same or similar products and services, while the market segment competitors include those with the same or similar customer types. In considering both segments, you may find competitors offering substitute products/services or a different engagement experience. It is also useful to consider both industry segment and market segment competitors in different operating geographies.

The activities to produce this deliverable should be owned by sales and marketing and include researching and preparing competitor demographic information from sources such as industry registries, tradeshows, customer feedback, social networks, and internet searches.

Metric B: How well are your key competitors meeting their and your customers' expectations?

This metric examines how well your competitors meet customer engagement dimensions such as influencing products and services, accessing knowledge of products and services, and finding/selecting products and services. The preparation step is an extension the VOC analysis using a subset of your key competitors. If you plan to use a VOC analysis to gauge your customer's perspective of your competitors, it is best to include the key competitors at the same time you request the VOC on your own business. This will minimize the impact on your customer's time and provide a side-by-side comparison between you and your competitors.

The activities to produce this deliverable should be owned by sales and marketing. These teams will identify the key competitors to include in the VOC assessment and manage the analysis as described above.

Metric C: What are your key competitors' strengths and weaknesses?

The preparation step for this metric requires an attribute framework to assess strengths and weaknesses of a business. The framework should evaluate the various areas of a business including marketing, sales/distribution channels, customer experience, products and services, supply chain, financial structure, technology platforms, business risk, geographic structure, business leadership, talent management, affiliations and relationships, and corporate culture/values.

The activities to produce this deliverable should also be owned by sales and marketing. These teams will identify the key competitors to include in the strengths/weaknesses assessment and utilize the results from the VOC and other sources to prepare a strengths/weaknesses report. This report becomes the source data for determining competitor impact on your business.

Metric D: Why/how/where/when do the strengths of your key competitors pose a threat to your business?

The key competitor strengths/weaknesses report (above) is used in producing this preparation step. The sales and marketing teams determine which of your competitor's strengths pose a strategic or tactical threat to your business. The results are consolidated across all key competitors in the form of competitive threat report.

Metric E: Why/how/where/when do the weaknesses of your key competitors create a disadvantage for them?

The key competitor strengths/weaknesses report (above) is also used to produce this preparation step. The sales and marketing teams determine which of your competitor's weaknesses pose a strategic or tactical disadvantage to their respective businesses. The results are consolidated across all key competitors in the form of a competitor weaknesses report.

➤ Action 3: Produce a current state analysis of your performance with respect to the industry segment you serve.

Readiness was determined by answering the following three questions (i.e., readiness metrics), also shown in figure 56.

a. What are your company's strengths and weaknesses relative to the industry in which you operate?
b. Which of your company's strengths will be assets during a transformation?
c. Which of your company's weaknesses will be liabilities during a transformation?

Metric A: What are your company's strengths and weaknesses relative to the industry in which you operate?

The preparation step for this metric requires the attribute framework used above (with your competitors) to assess the strengths and weaknesses of your business. The activities to produce this step should again be owned by sales and marketing. These teams will utilize results of the attribute framework (self-analysis mode), together with internal business performance, leadership perspectives, and other sources to prepare a strengths/weaknesses evaluation of your company. This evaluation becomes the source data for determining how your business will handle a transformation.

Metric B: Which of your company's strengths will be assets during a transformation?

The strengths/weaknesses self-assessment report (above) is used to produce this preparation step. The sales and marketing teams determine which of your company's strengths can be leveraged as an asset for your company during a business transformation. Sales and marketing consolidates the results into a business transformation asset report.

Metric C: Which of your company's weaknesses will be liabilities during a transformation?

The strengths/weaknesses self-assessment report (above) is also used to produce this preparation step. The sales and marketing teams determine which of your company's weaknesses will create a liability for your company during a business transformation. Sales and marketing consolidates the results into a business transformation liabilities report.

The complete readiness preparation for the goal "Understand Your Business" is shown in figure 58 (below).

Creating an Actionable Preparation

The readiness preparation summarized in figure 58 (below) can be made actionable by converting the actions and steps into deliverables and then combining them with the corresponding activities for producing them. This creates a formal readiness preparation methodology for practitioners.

Actions correspond to assessment standards, and steps correspond to readiness metrics. One deliverable is assigned to each preparation step and contains content required for attaining the corresponding assessment metric. Activities are formalized procedures for completing the deliverables. Templates for readiness assessments and preparations are provided in the companion guide to this book, available for download from X4MU.com/.

Readiness Preparation	#1: Understand Your Business		
Preparation Actions	**1. Produce a current state customer service performance analysis of your company**	**2. Produce a current state analysis of your competitors and their performance**	**3. Produce a current state analysis of your performance**
Preparation Steps	a. List your customers representing relevant business demographics within your industry segment	a. List your competitors representing the relevant business demographics within your industry and market segments	a. Complete attribute assessment of strengths and weaknesses of your business
	b. Voice of the Customer (VOC) Analysis Customer Engagement Journey Line	b. Extend Voice of the Customer (VOC) Analysis for a subset of your competitors	b. Determine which of your company's strengths can be leveraged as an asset during a transformation
	c. Voice of the Customer (VOC) Analysis Self-Assessment	c. Complete attribute assessment of strengths and weaknesses of your competitors	c. Determine which of your company's weaknesses will create a liability during a transformation
	d. Voice of the Customer (VOC) Analysis Customer Assessment Customer Journey Line Assessment	d. Determine which of your competitor's strengths pose a strategic or tactical threat to your business	
		e. Determine which of your competitor's weaknesses pose a strategic or tactical disadvantage to their respective businesses	

Figure 58: Readiness Preparation #1: Understand Your Business

Readiness Preparation Considerations

In completing this readiness preparation, there are a few things to be aware of to ensure you obtain quality input. Sales and marketing are the recommended owners for the readiness goal (Understand Your Business). You may choose to assign this to a different group within your business. If you do, ensure the group can be objective in assessing customer expectations, your competitive environment, and your company's performance and capabilities. The rest of the considerations are specific to each preparation action.

Customer Expectations

Ensure you select a good cross section of customers and include those who have been dissatisfied as well as those who are satisfied. You need critical feedback during your VOC.

Customer journey lines require a significant amount of time from your customers. Customers may only be willing to invest time in completing a journey line if you are going to commit to improving their engagement experience. It may help to include a question on the VOC to gauge a customer's interest in a journey line exercise.

You need to be brutally honest with your VOC self-assessment. It should be checked against what your customers are telling you. Disparities in the evaluations should be noted and used to improve future self-assessments.

Competitive Environment

Ensure you select representative competitors from both industry and market segments to provide insights into potentially emerging competition and substitute products. As mentioned previously, you can include these competitors on your VOC to evaluate your customers' perspectives on how well they are doing. This allows efficient use of your customers' time and will give you a differential comparison to your competitors

Not all information on your competitors will be available, especially if they are private companies. You will need to seek alternative sources, including your customers, social media reviews, or secret shopper services, to evaluate competitor strengths and weaknesses.

While not all your competitor's strengths pose a threat to your business, don't underestimate the importance of those strengths to your customers.

Finally, your competitors may be undergoing transformations of their own. Even though a weakness creates a competitive disadvantage for them today, it does not mean it will last indefinitely.

Your Company's Performance and Capabilities

Your self-assessment needs to be as objective and accurate as possible. It may help to get perspectives from different departments within your company. The goal is to understand where you will experience challenges during your transformation and where your company's strengths will help you during your transformation.

Goal #2: Define the Reason for the Transformation

Define the Reason for the Transformation is arguably the key readiness goal for the entire planning phase. Attaining this goal means you understand why you need to transform your business, and the reason is both aligned with your company's mission and produces a compelling next state with lasting value. These will serve as the assessment standards for this readiness goal.

Readiness Assessment

Readiness Assessment Standards

The readiness assessment standards can be formally expressed as follows:

1. You understand the reason for your transformation.
2. Your reason is aligned with your company's mission.
3. Your reason produces a compelling next state with lasting value.

If you know these, then you have attained readiness with respect to "Define the Reason for the Transformation." If you don't, you will need to complete the readiness preparation described later in this section. As with all the readiness assessments, metrics are defined to evaluate your attainment of these standards.

Readiness Assessment Metrics

The metrics are again in the form of questions you can answer to examine your company's readiness, and most importantly, identify the gaps in your understanding.

➢ Standard 1: You understand the reason for your transformation.

An assessment of this standard is provided by answering the following three questions:

a. Do you know what is motivating your company to transform its business?
b. Have you created a formal statement of purpose for the transformation including (reason/direction/goals/objectives)?
c. Is the statement of purpose clear and without ambiguity?

➢ Standard 2: Your reason is aligned with your company's mission.

An assessment of this standard is provided by answering the following three questions:

a. Does your reason follow logically from the current state of your business?
b. Is it reasonable to get to the next state from the current state?
c. Is the next state on the path of your mission?

> Standard 3: Your reason produces a compelling next state with lasting value.

An assessment of this standard is provided by answering the following three questions:

a. Does the reason create a compelling next state?
b. Does the next state create lasting value for your company?
c. Does the statement of purpose express the value to the company?

The complete readiness assessment for the goal "Identify the Reason for the Transformation" is shown in figure 59 (below).

Readiness Assessment	#2: Identify the Reason for the Transformation		
Assessment Standards	1. You understand the reason for your transformation	2. Your reason is aligned with your company's mission	3. Your reason produces a compelling next state with lasting value
Assessment Metrics	a. Do you know what is motivating your company to transform its business?	a. Does your reason follow logically from the current state of your business?	a. Does the reason create a compelling next state?
	b. Have you created a formal Statement of Purpose for the transformation?	b. Is it reasonable to get to the next state from the current state?	b. Does the next state create lasting value for your company?
	c. Is the Statement of Purpose clear and without ambiguity?	c. Is the next state on the path of your mission?	c. Does the Statement of Purpose express the Value to the company?

Figure 59: Readiness Assessment #2: Identify the Reason for the Transformation

Creating an Actionable Assessment

As in the case of readiness goal #1 (and all the remaining readiness goals), the readiness assessment summarized in figure 59 (above) can be made actionable by converting the standards and metrics into deliverables and then combining them with the corresponding activities for producing them. Templates for readiness assessments and preparations are provided in the companion guide to this book.

Readiness Assessment Considerations

There is one critical item to be aware of—in addition to the general readiness assessment considerations. When completing the metric "Do you know what is motivating your company to transform its business," it is crucial to disregard poorly defined motivators. The poorly defined motivators include "Be more innovative," "Management differentiation," and "Everyone is doing it." Poorly defined motivators fail to capture an objective business reason to undertake the transformation. A business should also avoid considering motivators that appear to reactively follow another company's transformation or reactively follow a technology trend.

Readiness Preparation

The readiness assessment standards for "Define the Reason for the Transformation" were defined as follows:

1. You understand the reason for your transformation.
2. Your reason is aligned with your company's mission.
3. Your reason produces a compelling next state with lasting value.

If your business is unable to attain these readiness assessment standards, you will need to undertake preparation actions to remediate the gaps.

Readiness Preparation Actions

The actions you can take to help you identify why you need to transform your business to a new state with lasting value are formally expressed as follows:

1. Produce a transformation statement of purpose.
2. Align your statement of purpose within the context of your company's purpose.
3. Produce a formal statement of value for your transformation.

By taking these actions, you ensure your business can attain the corresponding standards. The preparation steps presented next will guide you in completing these actions.

Readiness Preparation Steps

Every readiness assessment standard was assigned one or more metrics to facilitate evaluation. These metrics are now used in designing the preparation steps. One preparation step is required for each assessment metric.

➢ Action 1: Produce a transformation statement of purpose.

Readiness was determined by answering the following three questions (i.e., readiness metrics), also shown in figure 59 (above):

a. Do you know what is motivating your company to transform its business?
b. Have you created a formal statement of purpose for the transformation?
c. Is the statement of purpose clear and without ambiguity?

Metric A: Do you know what is motivating your company to transform its business?

For this metric, the preparation step is the business transformation statement of motivation. The executive team owns this step. It is produced by first reviewing the analyses from "Goal #1: Understand Your Business" to identify gaps in customer expectations, strategic/tactical threats from your competitors, and weaknesses in your business performance and capabilities. The executive team then uses figure 2: Business Transformation Motivators to determine whether the transformation is motivated by factors in the competitive environment, external environment, internal environment, or some combination. Finally, the executive team identifies and prioritizes the motivators that address the gaps in customer expectations, strategic/tactical threats from your competitors, and weaknesses in your business performance and capabilities.

Metric B: Have you created a formal statement of purpose for the transformation?

For this metric, the preparation step is the business transformation statement of purpose—the reason for taking on a transformation. It should be stated using clear and concise language as it will be used in communications throughout the transformation. The executive team uses the prioritized set of motivators from the statement of motivation (metric A above) to draft a "statement of purpose" for the business transformation. This should be on the form: "To improve the competitive position of our business, we will undertake a business transformation to address <list of prioritized motivators>."

Metric C: Is the statement of purpose clear and without ambiguity?

This metric is a quality check on your statement of purpose. The preparation step is a business transformation confirmation of clarity. The executive team reviews the prioritized set of motivators and statement of purpose, providing their feedback. They may not agree all motivators should be addressed at this time, but you still need them to confirm their understanding of the statement of purpose. It must be clear within your executive team before reviewing with a broader audience.

> ➤ Action 2: Align your statement of purpose within the context of your company's purpose.

Readiness was determined by answering the following three questions (i.e., readiness metrics), also shown in figure 59 (above):

    a.   Does your reason follow logically from the current state of your business?
    b.   Is it reasonable to get to the next state from the current state?
    c.   Is the next state on the path of your mission?

Metric A: Does your reason follow logically from the current state of your business?

For this metric, the preparation step is a statement of purpose validation. The executive team is the owner. To ensure your statement of purpose is logically connected to your current state, the executive team identifies data from the findings in "Goal #1: Understand Your Business" that align with the motivators in the statement of purpose. A table or matrix can be used to correlate the motivators in your statement of purpose with gaps in customer expectations, strategic/tactical threats from your competitors, and weaknesses in your business performance and capabilities. This demonstrates the legitimacy of the transformation using the sources for your motivators.

Metric B: Is it reasonable to get to the next state from the current state?

This metric is the first test of reasonableness for your statement of purpose. The preparation step is a statement of purpose feasibility. It is produced by projecting a future state of the business where all motivators have been addressed. The executive team reviews this future state to determine whether it is realistic and attainable from the current state. The findings in "Goal #1: Understand Your Business" can be used to determine if it is reasonable to reach the future state from the current state. If the future state is unrealistic or unreasonable to attain, the executive team will need to adjust the statement of purpose accordingly.

Metric C: Is the next state on the path of your mission?

This metric is the second test of reasonableness for your statement of purpose. The preparation step is the statement of purpose congruence. It is produced by comparing the motivations in your statement of purpose with the company's mission and purpose. Misalignment between the purpose of your transformation and the purpose of your company creates confusion within your business and difficulty in making decisions during the transformation. The executive team must ensure the future state is consistent with the company's mission and purpose. If it is not, the statement of purpose must be adjusted until it aligns with the company's mission and purpose.

> Action 3: Produce a formal statement of value for your transformation.

Readiness was determined by answering the following three questions (i.e., readiness metrics), also shown in figure 59 (above):

a. Does the reason create a compelling next state?
b. Does the next state create lasting value for your company?
c. Does the statement of purpose express the value to the company?

Metric A: Does the reason create a compelling next state?

These last three preparation steps for the readiness goal "Define the Reason for the Transformation" pertain to identifying the business value resulting from the transformation. For this first metric, the preparation step is to produce a transformation vision statement. The vision statement is a formal version of the future state. The executive team uses the statement of purpose and knowledge of your current state to draft a transformation vision statement conveying what your company will look like once the motivators are addressed. The executive team then evaluates the vision statement to ensure it creates a sense of excitement for your business. In other words, it should be worthwhile to address the motivators.

Metric B: Does the next state create lasting value for your company?

The preparation step for this metric is to produce the transformation value proposition. The value proposition articulates the payoff from undertaking the business transformation. The executive team uses the transformation vision statement and knowledge of the motivators to identify the value created when the vision state is achieved. The value should be quantified so it clearly expresses what will be achieved and demonstrates the sustainability within your business. Once the future state is achieved, you do not want to slide back to the current state.

Metric C: Does the statement of purpose express the value to the company?

The final preparation step is a formal statement of purpose/value. The executive team summarizes the transformation value proposition into a value statement. The value statement is then appended onto the statement of purpose to create a composite statement of purpose/value. This should be of the form: "To improve the competitive position of our business, we will undertake a business transformation to address <list of prioritized motivators>, which will produce <value statement>."

The complete readiness preparation for the goal "Identify the Reason for the Transformation" is shown in figure 60 (below).

Readiness Preparation	#2: Identify the Reason for the Transformation		
Preparation Actions	1. Produce a Transformation Statement of Purpose	2. Align your Statement of Purpose within the context of your Company's Purpose	3. Produce a formal Statement of Value for your Transformation
Preparation Steps	a. Business Transformation Statement of Motivation	a. Statement of Purpose Validation	a. Transformation Vision Statement
	b. Business Transformation Statement of Purpose	b. Statement of Purpose Feasibility	b. Transformation Value Proposition
	c. Business Transformation Confirmation of Clarity	c. Statement of Purpose Congruence	c. Statement of Purpose/Value

Figure 60: Readiness Preparation #2: Identify the Reason for the Transformation

Creating an Actionable Preparation

As in the case of readiness goal #1 (and all the remaining readiness goals), the readiness preparation summarized in figure 60 (above) can be made actionable by converting the actions and steps into deliverables and then combining them with the corresponding activities for producing them. Templates for readiness assessments and preparations are provided in the companion guide to this book.

Readiness Preparation Considerations

There are several things to be aware of as you work through the action and preparation steps for "Define the Reason for the Transformation." They are specific to each preparation action.

Transformation Statement of Purpose/Value

Your transformation may require a combination of competitive, external, and internal motivators. While this is certainly possible, the complexity is much greater. You may wish to consider a sequence of smaller transformations to reduce transformational change impact.

You may also discover that your motivation consists of one of the "poorly defined motivators" discussed earlier: "Be More Innovative," "Management Differentiation," and "Everyone is Doing It." Resist the urge to include these as your motivators. They make it difficult to create a compelling future state and quantify the business value of your transformation.

Align Your Statement of Purpose

Ensure your motivators are traced back to actual findings from the "Understand Your Business" analyses; otherwise, you run the risk of creating poorly defined motivators for your business. The reason you undertake a transformation must be grounded in the realities of your business and not the desires of a person or group.

As you assemble your statement of motivation, it is possible to create a unique market solution that does not currently exist but is impossible for your business to attain. You need to use the information produced during "Understand Your Business" to determine whether your business can achieve the resulting future state.

You may find your future sate is inconsistent with your company's current mission and purpose, yet it is as a desirable/valuable end state. If this is the case, then the company mission and purpose need to be adjusted to accommodate the transformation motivators. It is challenging to move in the direction of a future state in opposition to the company's mission and purpose. That future state will not be compelling, and the change impacts will be more difficult to manage.

Statement of Value

To verify the transformation vision statement does indeed create a compelling future state, you can solicit feedback from a test group of leaders within your business. The vision must be clear to everyone in the business once it is broadly communicated.

Finally, ensure you have quantified the value in your value proposition statement. Avoid generalities like improves, reduces, and increases without hard numbers behind them. Quantifiable values will be used in later phases to ensure the transformation is successful, the change is adopted, and the value is achieved.

Goal #3: Align the Business Leaders around the Reason

Once you have a clear understanding of the reason for undertaking a business transformation, it is imperative that all business leaders are in alignment. Transformations impact the entire business. Without alignment among those responsible for leading the change, achievement of the purpose/value is at great risk. This means your executive team must understand, agree with, and be committed to carrying out the transformation. These will serve as the readiness standards for assessing this goal.

Readiness Assessment Standards

The readiness assessment standards can be formally expressed as follows:

1. You have identified all stakeholders.
2. All stakeholders understand the statement of purpose/value of the business transformation.
3. All stakeholders are committed to carrying out the business transformation.

If you know these, then you have attained readiness with respect to "Align the Business Leaders around the Reason" for your transformation. If you don't, you will need to complete the readiness preparation described later in this chapter. As with all the other readiness assessments, metrics are defined to evaluate your attainment of these standards.

Readiness Assessment Metrics

The metrics are in the usual form of questions you can answer to examine your company's readiness, and most importantly, identify the gaps in your understanding.

➤ Standard 1: You have identified all stakeholders.

An assessment of readiness is provided by answering the following two questions:

a. Have you identified all the stakeholders in achieving your business transformation?
b. Do you know which ones will lead the transformation, which ones will execute the transformation, and which ones will experience the impacts of the transformation?

➤ Standard 2: All stakeholders understand the statement of purpose/value of the business transformation.

An assessment of readiness is provided by answering the following two questions:

a. Have you reviewed the statement of purpose/value with all stakeholders?
b. Have you ensured all stakeholders have a clear understanding of the statement of purpose/ value?

> ➤ Standard 3: All stakeholders are committed to carrying out the business transformation.

An assessment of readiness is provided by answering the following two questions:

a. Have you identified all statement of purpose/value misalignments among the stakeholders?
b. Have you reconciled all misalignments among the stakeholders and ensured commitment?

The complete readiness assessment for the goal "Align the Business around the Reason" is shown in figure 61 (below).

Readiness Assessment	#3: Align the Business Leaders Around the Reason		
Assessment Standards	1. You have identified all stakeholders	2. All stakeholders understand the Statement of Purpose/Value of the Business Transformation	3. All stakeholders are committed to carrying out the business transformation
Assessment Metrics	a. Have you identified all the stakeholders in achieving your Business Transformation?	a. Have you reviewed the Statement of Purpose/Value with all stakeholders?	a. Have you identified all Statement of Purpose/Value misalignments among the stakeholders?
	b. Do you know which ones will lead the transformation, which ones will execute the transformation, and which ones will experience the impacts of the transformation?	b. Have you ensured all stakeholders have a clear understanding of the Statement of Purpose/Value?	b. Have you reconciled all misalignments among the stakeholders and ensured commitment?

Figure 61: Readiness Assessment #3: Align the Business Leaders around the Reason

Create an Actionable Assessment

The readiness assessment summarized in figure 61 (above) can be made actionable by converting the standards and metrics into deliverables and then combining them with the corresponding activities for producing them. Templates for readiness assessments and preparations are provided in the companion guide to this book.

Readiness Assessment Considerations

There is one critical item to be aware of in addition to the general readiness assessment considerations. When evaluating the metric "Have you identified all statement of purpose/value misalignments among the business leader stakeholders," you need to be aware of when executives aren't clear on the statement of purpose/value, when they aren't being honest about their misalignment, or when they are reluctant to express their misalignment (this happens frequently with executives who are new in their roles or new to organizations).

Readiness Preparation

The readiness assessment standards for "Align the Business Leaders around the Reason" were defined as follows:

1. You have identified all stakeholders.
2. All stakeholders understand the statement of purpose/value of the business transformation.
3. All stakeholders are committed to carrying out the business transformation.

If your business is unable to attain these readiness assessment standards, you will need to undertake preparation actions to remediate the gaps.

Readiness Preparation Actions

The actions you can take to help you align your stakeholders around the reasons you need to transform your business to a new state with lasting value are formally expressed as follows:

1. Identify the stakeholders of the business transformation.
2. Ensure stakeholders understand the statement of purpose/value.
3. Secure stakeholder commitment the statement of purpose/value.

By taking these actions, you ensure your business can attain the corresponding standards. The preparation steps presented next will guide you in completing these actions.

Readiness Preparation Steps

Every readiness assessment standard was assigned one or more metrics to facilitate evaluation. These metrics are now used in designing the preparation steps. One preparation step is required for each assessment metric.

➤ Action 1: Identify the stakeholders of the business transformation.

Readiness was determined by answering the following two questions (i.e., readiness metrics), also shown in figure 61 (above):

a. Have you identified all the stakeholders in achieving your business transformation?

b. Do you know which ones will lead the transformation, which ones will execute the transformation, and which ones will experience the impacts of the transformation?

Metric A: Have you identified all the stakeholders in achieving your business transformation?

The preparation step is the business transformation stakeholder list. To prepare this list, the executive team identifies people inside and outside of the organization who will be critical in leading the transformational change and ensuring the purpose and value are realized. Stakeholders will review business transformation communications and high-level work products, identify risks, challenges, and issues, and assist in their resolution. The stakeholders will be leveraged throughout the transformation whenever evaluation or action is required.

Metric B: Do you know which ones will lead the transformation, which ones will execute the transformation, and which ones will experience the impacts of the transformation?

Business transformation stakeholders will take on specific roles during the transformation. Some stakeholders may take on multiple roles. For example, some stakeholders may be required to lead portions of the transformation, and others may need to implement portions. Still others will be required to adopt the transformational changes. The preparation step for this metric is the stakeholder role assignment. The executive team assigns the most appropriate role(s) to each stakeholder and ensures the stakeholder is capable of and willing to take on their role in the transformation.

➤ Action 2: Ensure stakeholders understand the statement of purpose/value.

Readiness was determined by answering the following two questions (i.e., readiness metrics), also shown in figure 61 (above):

a. Have you reviewed the statement of purpose/value with all stakeholders?

b. Have you ensured all stakeholders have a clear understanding of the statement of purpose/ value?

Metric A: Have you reviewed the statement of purpose/value with all business leader stakeholders?

For this metric, the preparation step is the stakeholder statement of purpose/value communication. The executive team prepares business transformation statement of purpose/value communications suitable for internal and external stakeholders.

Metric B: Have you ensured all business leader stakeholders have a clear understanding of the statement of purpose/value?

The preparation step here is the stakeholder statement of purpose/value acknowledgment—a formal indication that all stakeholders have received and understood the purpose and value of the transformation. The executive team reviews the business transformation statement of purpose/value communications with internal and external stakeholders and obtains an acknowledgment of understanding from all stakeholders. The degree of formality in the acknowledgment depends on the stakeholder group and the complexity of the statement of purpose/value for your transformation.

➤ Action 3: Secure stakeholder commitment the statement of purpose/value.

Readiness was determined by answering the following two questions (i.e., readiness metrics), also shown in figure 61 (above):

a. Have you identified all statement of purpose/value misalignments among the stakeholders?
b. Have you reconciled all misalignments among the stakeholders and ensured commitment?

Metric A: Have you identified all statement of purpose/value misalignments among the stakeholders?

This metric goes beyond a simple acknowledgment of understanding and seeks to understand concerns or disagreements from your stakeholders. The preparation step is the stakeholder reconciliation plan. The executive team solicits feedback from the stakeholders on the business transformation statement of purpose/value. The executive team then identifies areas of misalignment among the stakeholders, including disagreements and concerns with elements of the statement of purpose/scope. The executive team consolidates the misalignments into a reconciliation plan.

Metric B: Have you reconciled all misalignments among the stakeholders and ensured commitment?

The preparation step is the stakeholder commitment confirmation, which means the transformation statement of purpose/value has been accepted and will be supported by your stakeholders.

The executive team will work with stakeholders to reconcile the misalignments identified in the stakeholder reconciliation plan. Reconciliation includes additional clarification/explanation or may imply some minor adjustments to the transformation's purpose or value. Your stakeholders may have insights that your executive team does not have. This is the time to hear them out and assess whether these insights pose a risk to your transformation. You will need to have your stakeholders fully committed before moving forward.

The complete readiness preparation for the goal "Align the Business Leaders around the Reason" is shown in figure 62 (below).

Readiness Preparation	#3: Align the Business Leaders Around the Reason		
Preparation Actions	1. Identify the Stakeholders of the Business Transformation	2. Ensure Stakeholders Understand the Statement of Purpose/Value	3. Secure Stakeholder Commitment the Statement of Purpose/Value
Preparation Steps	a. Business Transformation Stakeholder List	a. Stakeholder Statement of Purpose/Value Communication	a. Stakeholder Reconciliation Plan
	b. Stakeholder Role Assignment	b. Stakeholder Statement of Purpose/Value Acknowledgement	b. Stakeholder Commitment Confirmation

Figure 62: Readiness Preparation #3: Align the Business Leaders around the Reason

Creating an Actionable Preparation

The readiness preparation summarized in figure 62 (above) can be made actionable by converting the actions and steps into deliverables and then combining them with the corresponding activities for producing them. Templates for readiness assessments and preparations are provided in the companion guide to this book.

Readiness Preparation Considerations

There are several things to be aware of as you work through the action and preparation steps for "Align the Business Leaders around the Reason." They are specific to each preparation action.

Identify the Stakeholders of Your Business Transformation

It is helpful to be as complete as possible in identifying your stakeholders. They are critical in helping to realize the purpose and value of the transformation. If you have missed a stakeholder, it will become apparent as you begin implementing the changes. You'll encounter passive or active resistance to the change—or delayed concerns about why something will not work. Your stakeholders can help you identify whether additions are needed.

The leader roles must be assigned only to those stakeholders with the skills, capacity, and enthusiasm to lead transformational change. They are not always employees with formal management roles; they can also be informal or de facto leaders within the organization.

Nearly everyone will be impacted by the transformation and will need to adopt some elements of change. However, the adopter stakeholder roles are influential employees who can identify areas of concern as well as work supportively to overcome the concerns.

Ensure Stakeholders Understand the Statement of Purpose/Value

You may need to communicate the statement of purpose/value live to your stakeholders (e.g., in person, video/conference call) to ensure they understand it. They do not need to provide feedback at this point, and you may not wish to entertain feedback in a group setting. The stakeholders must have an opportunity at some point to express their feedback—positive and critical—and have it addressed.

Secure Stakeholder Commitment to the Statement of Purpose/Value

Your stakeholders must be fully committed before moving forward. If you can't get their commitment, you'll need to gauge their importance in the transformation and potentially consider substitutions.

It can be difficult to assess whether a stakeholder is fully committed. Personalities vary as do the way in which people reveal their concerns. They may commit at this time but exhibit resistance to change later. You will need to identify that and address it when it occurs.

In extreme instances, a misalignment may be valid and require rework of your statement of purpose/value. When this is completed, your statement of purpose/value will need to be revalidated. The readiness preparation for the goal "Identify the Reason for the Transformation" will have to be revisited as appropriate.

Goal #4: Communicate the Reason throughout Your Business

Communication is important throughout all three phases of a business transformation. It is one of the tools for mitigating the impacts of transformational change. During the early stages of a transformation, communication helps in creating excitement as well as addressing rumors and other potentially negative perceptions. Your business needs to prepare a version of the statement of purpose/value that is appropriate for a general audience and ensure that it is communicated throughout the organization. These will serve as the readiness standards for assessing this goal.

Readiness Assessment

Readiness Assessment Standards

The readiness assessment standards are formally expressed as follows:

1. You have prepared a version of the transformation statement of purpose/value suitable for general business communications.
2. You have communicated the transformation statement of purpose/value within your business.

If you know these, then you have attained readiness with respect to "Communicate the Reason throughout Your Business." If you don't, then you will need to complete the readiness preparation described later in this chapter. As with all the other readiness assessments, metrics are defined to evaluate your attainment of these standards.

Readiness Assessment Metrics

The metrics are again in the form of questions you can answer to examine your company's readiness, and most importantly, identify the gaps in your understanding.

➤ Standard 1: You have prepared a version of the transformation statement of purpose/value suitable for general business communications.

An assessment of readiness is provided by answering the following three questions:

a. Have you created internal and external versions of the statement of purpose for a wide range of communication?
b. Have you positioned the statement of purpose/value in the context of your business purpose and mission?
c. Have you created a business transformation communication package?

➤ Standard 2: You have communicated the transformation statement of purpose/value within your business.

An assessment of readiness is provided by answering the following four questions:

a. Have you communicated the business transformation communication package throughout your company?
b. Do you have a way to receive feedback on the business transformation communications?

c. Do you have a way to address feedback on the business transformation communications?

d. Have you addressed feedback on the business transformation communications?

The complete readiness assessment for the goal "Communicate the Reason throughout Your Business" is shown in figure 63 (below).

Readiness Assessment	#4: Communicate the Reason Throughout Your Business	
Assessment Standards	1. You have prepared a version of the Transformation Statement of Purpose/Value suitable for general business communications	2. You have communicated the Transformation Statement of Purpose/Value within your business
Assessment Metrics	a. Have you created Internal and External versions of the Statement of Purpose for wide range communication?	a. Have you communicated the Business Transformation Communication Package throughout your company?
	b. Have you positioned the Statement of Purpose/Value in the context of your business purpose and mission?	b. Do you have a way to receive feedback on the Business Transformation Communications?
	c. Have you created a Business Transformation Communication Package?	c. Do you have a way to address feedback on the Business Transformation Communications?
		d. Have you addressed feedback on the Business Transformation Communications?

Figure 63: Readiness Assessment #4: Communicate the Reason throughout Your Business

Create an Actionable Assessment

The readiness assessment summarized in figure 63 (above) can be made actionable by converting the standards and metrics into deliverables and then combining them with the corresponding activities for producing them. Templates for readiness assessments and preparations are provided in the companion guide to this book.

Readiness Assessment Considerations

There is one critical item to be aware of, in addition to the general readiness assessment considerations. When completing the metric "Have you addressed feedback on the business transformation communications," you need to be sure the feedback was effectively addressed. In other words, if questions/concerns were raised around the transformation statement of purpose/value, your responses need to answer the questions and address the concerns. This first communication experience sets a positive tone and precedent with your business.

Readiness Preparation

The readiness assessment standards for "Communicate the Reason throughout Your Business" were defined as follows:

1. You have prepared a version of the transformation statement of purpose/value suitable for general business communications.
2. You have communicated the transformation statement of purpose/value within your business.

If your business is unable to attain these readiness assessment standards, you will need to undertake preparation actions to remediate the gaps.

Readiness Preparation Actions

The actions you can take to help you communicate the reasons why you need to transform your business to a new state with lasting value are formally expressed as follows:

1. Prepare statement of purpose/scope communication.
2. Deliver statement of purpose/scope communication.

By taking these actions, you ensure your business can attain the corresponding standards. The preparation steps presented next will guide you in completing these actions.

Readiness Preparation Steps

Every readiness assessment standard was assigned one or more metrics to facilitate evaluation. These metrics are now used in designing the preparation steps. One preparation step is required for each assessment metric.

➤ Action 1: Prepare statement of purpose/scope communication.

Readiness was determined by answering the following three questions (i.e., readiness metrics), also shown in figure 63 (above):

a. Have you created internal and external versions of the statement of purpose for a wide range of communication?

b. Have you positioned the statement of purpose/value in the context of your business strategy, future state, and mission?

c. Have you created a business transformation communication package?

Metric A: Have you created internal and external versions of the statement of purpose for a wide range of communication?

The preparation step is the statement of purpose/value general communications. The executive team prepares business transformation statement of purpose/value communications suitable for the general internal and external business audience (i.e., not the stakeholders). These can simply be variants of the stakeholder communications.

Metric B: Have you positioned the statement of purpose/value in the context of your business purpose and mission?

This metric ensures consistency between the statement of purpose/value and your company's purpose and mission. The preparation step is the statement of purpose/value in business purpose and mission context. The executive team uses the material prepared earlier to align statement of purpose/value with the company purpose and mission to prepare a version for a wider range of communications.

Metric C: Have you created a business transformation communication package?

This preparation step is the business transformation communication package. The executive team prepares a final communication package for the business transformation, including the statement of purpose/scope and company purpose and mission alignment.

➤ Action 2: Deliver statement of purpose/scope communication.

Readiness was determined by answering the following four questions (i.e., readiness metrics), also shown in figure 63 (above):

a. Have you communicated the business transformation communication package throughout your company?

b. Do you have a way to receive feedback on the business transformation communications?

c. Do you have a way to address feedback on the business transformation communications?

d. Have you addressed feedback on the business transformation communications?

Metric A: Have you communicated the business transformation communication package throughout your company?

The preparation step is the business transformation communication delivery acknowledgment. The executive team distributes the business transformation communication package to the general internal and external audiences with instructions to review and provide both positive and critical feedback.

Metric B: Do you have a way to receive feedback on the business transformation communications?

The preparation step is the business transformation communication feedback mechanism. The executive team has a mechanism set up to receive feedback on the business transformation communication package from internal and external audiences. This can include live group forums, email, or written feedback.

Metric C: Do you have a way to address feedback on the business transformation communications?

The preparation step is the business transformation communication response mechanism. The executive team has a mechanism set up to respond to feedback on the business transformation communication package from internal and external audiences. Again, this can include live group forums, email, or written feedback. The executive team reviews the feedback and prepares responses for internal and external audiences.

Metric D: Have you addressed feedback on the business transformation communications?

The preparation step is the business transformation communication response acknowledgment. The executive team distributes responses to the feedback on the business transformation communication package to internal and external audiences—soliciting acknowledgment of the responses. The acknowledgments are reviewed by the executive team. At this point, there should be no unresolved critical feedback of the business transformation communication.

The complete readiness preparation for the goal "Communicate the Reason throughout the Business" is shown in figure 64 (below).

Readiness Preparation	#4: Communicate the Reason Throughout Your Business	
Preparation Actions	1. Prepare Statement of Purpose/Scope Communication	2. Deliver Statement of Purpose/Scope Communication
Preparation Steps	a. Statement of Purpose/Value General Communications	a. Business Transformation Communication Delivery Acknowledgement
	b. Statement of Purpose/Value in Business Purpose and Mission Context	b. Business Transformation Communication Feedback Mechanism
	c. Business Transformation Communication Package	c. Business Transformation Communication Response Mechanism
		d. Business Transformation Communication Response Acknowledgement.

Figure 64: Readiness Preparation #4: Communicate the Reason throughout Your Business

Creating an Actionable Preparation

The readiness preparation summarized in figure 64 (above) can be made actionable by converting the actions and steps into deliverables and then combining them with the corresponding activities for producing them. Templates for readiness assessments and preparations are provided in the companion guide to this book.

Readiness Preparation Considerations

There are several things to be aware of as you work through the action and preparation steps for "Communicate the Reason throughout the Business." They are specific to each preparation action.

Prepare Statement of Purpose/Scope Communication

Elements of the statement of purpose/value may contain confidential information or information you are not ready to share with a broader audience. You may need several versions of communications. Furthermore, what you share internally may be branded/phrased differently than what you share externally. At this point, the stakeholders should already be committed. They can be used to help prepare the general audience communications.

Deliver Statement of Purpose/Scope Communication

It is important to share the business transformation statement of purpose/value in a genuine way. This is one of the earlier change management activities and helps establish a culture of openness and honesty, which is required for a successful transformation.

Ensure that you take feedback seriously and address it in a form that can be retained and referenced throughout the transformation (e.g., frequently asked questions). Not everyone will provide feedback, but most are interested in the feedback and your responses.

Scope Readiness

The scope objective in the planning phase of a business transformation is to identify and express the extent to which your business will be transformed. Readiness of scope is expressed through the attainment of four readiness goals (see figure 55):

1. Identify what needs to change.
2. Understand the impact of the change.
3. Identify the investment required to change.
4. Commit the required investment.

Each of these readiness goals has an accompanying readiness assessment and readiness preparation. These are defined and presented in detail in the remainder of this section.

Goal #5: Identify What Needs to Change

Identify What Needs to Change means being able to articulate what must change in your business to achieve the purpose/value of your transformation and then aligning your stakeholders around this change. These will serve as the readiness standards for assessing your grasp of the change in your business and, if needed, for remediating readiness gaps.

Readiness Assessment

Readiness Assessment Standards

The readiness assessment standards can be formally expressed as follows:

1. You know what needs to change in your business to achieve the transformation.
2. You have a statement of transformation scope.
3. Your stakeholders are aligned around the statement of transformation scope.

If you know these, you have attained readiness with respect to "Identify What Needs to Change." If you don't, you will need to complete the readiness preparation described later. As with all the readiness assessments, metrics are defined to evaluate your attainment of these standards.

Readiness Assessment Metrics

The metrics are again in the form of questions you can answer to examine your company's readiness, and most importantly, identify the gaps in your understanding.

➢ Standard 1: You know what needs to change in your business to achieve the transformation.

An assessment of readiness is provided by answering the following two questions:

a. Have you identified everything in your business that needs to change to achieve your transformation?
b. Have you assigned a priority and sequence to the set of changes?

➢ Standard 2: You have a statement of transformation scope.

An assessment of readiness is provided by answering the following question:

• Have you prepared a formal statement of transformation scope?

➢ Standard 3: Your stakeholders are aligned around the statement of transformation scope.

An assessment of readiness is provided by answering the following two questions:

a. Have you reviewed the statement of transformation scope with all stakeholders for validation and commitment?
b. Do you have validation and commitment?

The complete readiness assessment for the goal "Identify What Needs to Change" is shown in figure 65 (below).

Readiness Assessment	#5: Identify What Needs to Change		
Assessment Standards	1. You know what needs to change in your business to achieve the transformation	2. You have a Statement of Transformation Scope	3. Your stakeholders are aligned around the Statement of Transformation Scope
Assessment Metrics	a. Have you identified EVERYTHING in your business that needs to change to achieve your transformation?	Have you prepared a formal statement of transformation scope?	a. Have you reviewed the statement of transformation scope with all stakeholders for validation and commitment?
	b. Have you assigned a priority and sequence to the set of changes?		b. Do you have validation and commitment?

Figure 65: Readiness Assessment #5: Identify What Needs to Change

Creating an Actionable Assessment

The readiness assessment summarized in figure 65 (above) can be made actionable by converting the standards and metrics into deliverables and then combining them with the corresponding activities for producing them. Templates for readiness assessments and preparations are provided in the companion guide to this book.

Readiness Assessment Considerations

When considering what needs to change in your business to achieve your transformation, it's critical to identify the activities and relationships you need to stop as well as those you need to start. The stops are often overlooked but can represent significant change in your business.

The statement of transformation scope is intended to be a high-level scope—enough to understand the large components of change driving value and cost. Scope will be revisited in more detail during the implementing phase.

Finally, it is critical for your executive team to be aligned with respect to the changes required to achieve the purpose/value of your transformation. At this point, the executive team may start to realize the extent to which the changes impact their functional areas. This could materialize as passive or active disagreement around the scope. It is important to understand whether this is happening and to address it quickly.

Readiness Preparation

The readiness assessment standards for "Identify What Needs to Change" were defined as follows:

1. You know what needs to change in your business to achieve the transformation.
2. You have a statement of transformation scope.
3. Your stakeholders are aligned around the statement of transformation scope.

If your business is unable to attain these readiness assessment standards, you will need to undertake preparation actions to remediate the gaps.

Readiness Preparation Actions

The actions you can take to help you identify what needs to change in your business to achieve your business transformation are formally expressed as follows:

1. Prepare inventory of business changes.
2. Prepare statement of transformation scope.
3. Secure stakeholder commitment to the statement of transformation scope.

By taking these actions, you ensure your business can attain the corresponding standards. The preparation steps presented next will guide you in completing these actions.

Readiness Preparation Steps

Every readiness assessment standard was assigned one or more metrics to facilitate evaluation. These metrics are now used in designing the preparation steps. One preparation step is required for each assessment metric.

➤ Action 1: Prepare inventory of business changes.

Readiness was determined by answering the following two questions (i.e., readiness metrics), also shown in figure 65 (above):

a. Have you identified everything in your business that needs to change to achieve your transformation, including what needs to stop as well as start?
b. Have you assigned a priority and sequence to the set of changes?

Metric A: Have you identified everything in your business that needs to change to achieve your transformation, including what needs to stop as well as start?

The preparation step is the statement of business change. To produce this, the executive team first reviews the motivators for the transformation declared in the statement of purpose/value. This was created earlier in this chapter in the section "Define the Reason for the Transformation." The complete set of motivators are shown again in figure 66 (below). In chapter 1, the transformation motivators were mapped to the set of common business changes. This is shown again in figure 67 (below). The dark circles indicate the business changes most likely to occur during a transformation for each of the motivators. The potential changes your business can expect during your transformation are indicated by the set of business changes across all your transformation's motivators.

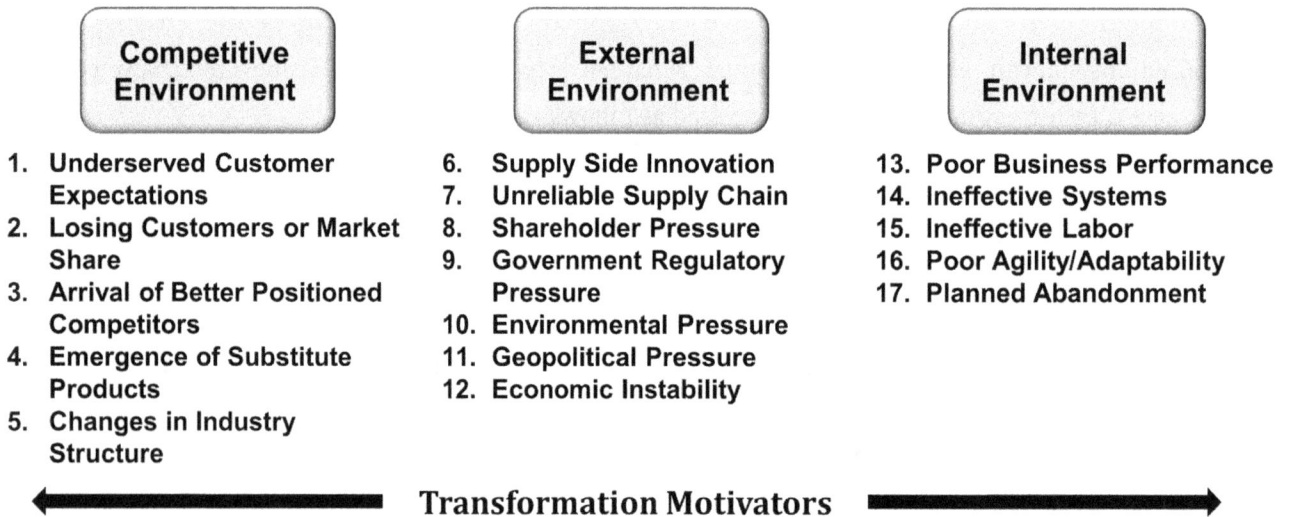

Competitive Environment

1. Underserved Customer Expectations
2. Losing Customers or Market Share
3. Arrival of Better Positioned Competitors
4. Emergence of Substitute Products
5. Changes in Industry Structure

External Environment

6. Supply Side Innovation
7. Unreliable Supply Chain
8. Shareholder Pressure
9. Government Regulatory Pressure
10. Environmental Pressure
11. Geopolitical Pressure
12. Economic Instability

Internal Environment

13. Poor Business Performance
14. Ineffective Systems
15. Ineffective Labor
16. Poor Agility/Adaptability
17. Planned Abandonment

◀━━━━━━ **Transformation Motivators** ━━━━━━▶

Figure 66: Business Transformation Motivators

Transformation Motivators (Reasons for your Transformation)	1. Product Scope	2. Service Scope	3. Industry/Market Served	4. Customer Experience	5. Technology Platform	6. Cost Structure	7. Ownership Structure	8. Internal Organization	9. Sales/Distribution Channel	10. Core Capabilities Definition	11. Outsourcing & Insourcing	12. Risk Profile	13. Regulatory Profile	14. Geographic Structure	15. Corporate Culture/Values
Competitive Environment															
1. Underserved Customer Expectations	●	●	●	●	●					●	●				
2. Losing Customers or Market Share	●	●	●	●		●				●					
3. Arrival of Better Positioned Competitors	●	●	●	●	●	●					●				
4. Emergence of Substitute Products	●	●	●	●							●				
5. Changes in Industry Structure		●			●	●	●	●			●			●	
External Environment															
6. Supply Side Innovation	●	●		●	●	●					●				
7. Unreliable Supply Chain	●	●			●	●					●	●	●	●	
8. Shareholder Pressure						●	●				●		●	●	●
9. Government Regulatory Pressure	●		●						●		●		●	●	
10. Environmental Pressure											●	●	●	●	●
11. Geopolitical Pressure											●	●	●	●	●
12. Economic Instability	●	●	●			●	●				●	●		●	
Internal Environment															
13. Poor Business Performance	●	●	●	●	●	●	●	●	●	●	●				
14. Ineffective Systems					●	●				●	●	●		●	
15. Ineffective Labor					●	●		●			●		●	●	●
16. Poor Agility/Adaptability					●	●		●		●	●				●
17. Planned Abandonment	●	●	●			●				●	●	●	●	●	

Figure 67: Transformation Motivators Mapped to Common Business Changes

For example, suppose a statement of purpose/value contained the following transformation motivators:

- underserved customer expectations
- losing customers or market share
- ineffective systems

This could be the case if your business used outdated technology for engaging your customers. The set of potential business changes[3] associated with these motivators is shown in figure 68 (below).

---

[3] Note: These are potential business changes. The actual changes will depend on the nature of your transformation.

The

Transformation Motivators (Reasons for your Transformation)	1. Product Scope	2. Service Scope	3. Industry/Market Served	4. Customer Experience	5. Technology Platform	6. Cost Structure	7. Ownership Structure	8. Internal Organization	9. Sales/Distribution Channel	10. Core Capabilities Definition	11. Outsourcing & Insourcing	12. Risk Profile	13. Regulatory Profile	14. Geographic Structure	15. Corporate Culture/Values
Competitive Environment															
1. Underserved Customer Expectations	●	●	●	●	●				●	●					
2. Losing Customers or Market Share	●	●	●	●		●			●						
3. Arrival of Better Positioned Competitors															
4. Emergence of Substitute Products															
5. Changes in Industry Structure															
External Environment															
6. Supply Side Innovation															
7. Unreliable Supply Chain															
8. Shareholder Pressure															
9. Government Regulatory Pressure															
10. Environmental Pressure															
11. Geopolitical Pressure															
12. Economic Instability															
Internal Environment															
13. Poor Business Performance															
14. Ineffective Systems					●	●					●	●	●	●	
15. Ineffective Labor															
16. Poor Agility/Adaptability															
17. Planned Abandonment															

Figure 68: Business Transformation Change Map Example

The executive team then uses the business transformation change map to create a statement of business change for your business transformation: "To address the motivations for our business transformation <insert list of motivators>, we will need make changes in the following areas <insert map of changes>."

Continuing the example from above, the statement of business change would be:

What are the motivations for our business transformation?

- underserved customer expectations
- losing customers or market share
- ineffective systems

We will need make changes in the following areas:

- product scope
- service scope
- industry/market served
- customer experience

- technology platform
- cost structure
- sales/distribution channel
- core capabilities definition
- outsourcing and insourcing
- risk profile
- geographic structure

Metric B: Have you assigned a priority and sequence to the set of changes?

The preparation step is the business change priority and sequence plan. To produce this, the executive team reviews the statement of business change to identify which of the changes consist of "starts" and which consist of "stops." Starts means the change introduces something new, while stops means the change terminates an existing activity, relationship, or asset. The executive team then uses knowledge of their business and the start/stop changes to assign a priority (high/low) and relative ordering to the changes. The business change priority and ordering can be captured in the business change priority and sequence plan template shown in figure 69 (below). You may need to iterate a few times on priority and ordering to produce a reasonable sequence—one that reflects dependencies and differences in business value.

Business Change	Starts (Yes/No)	Stops (Yes/No)	Priority (High/Low)	Sequence (1, 2, 3)
1. Product Scope				
2. Service Scope				
3. Industry/Market Served				
4. Customer Experience				
5. Technology Platform				
6. Cost Structure				
7. Ownership Structure				
8. Internal Organization				
9. Sales/Distribution Channel				
10. Core Capabilities Definition				
11. Outsourcing & Insourcing				
12. Risk Profile				
13. Regulatory Profile				
14. Geographic Structure				
15. Corporate Culture/Values				

Figure 69: Change Priority and Sequence Plan Template

Continuing the example, suppose the transformation was driven by the need to service customers digitally, which is frequently the case for retailers. The change priority and sequence are shown in figure 70 (below) and capture the introduction of an online sales channel. In this example, note the following:

- Some of the business changes were not required—they have no in both starts and stops.
- Technology has both a start (new transactional ecommerce site) and a stop (retirement of old information-only website).
- Some of the changes can be introduced before others, but many must occur together within the sequence

Business Change	Starts (Yes/No)	Stops (Yes/No)	Priority (High/Low)	Sequence (1, 2, 3)
1. Product Scope	No	No		
2. Service Scope	No	No		
3. Industry/Market Served	Yes	No	Low	2
4. Customer Experience	Yes	Yes	High	1
5. Technology Platform	Yes	Yes	High	1
6. Cost Structure	Yes	No	Low	1
7. Ownership Structure				
8. Internal Organization				
9. Sales/Distribution Channel	Yes	No	High	1
10. Core Capabilities Definition	Yes	No	High	1
11. Outsourcing & Insourcing	No	No		
12. Risk Profile	Yes	No	Low	2
13. Regulatory Profile				
14. Geographic Structure	No	No		
15. Corporate Culture/Values				

Figure 70: Change Priority and Sequence Plan Example

The three steps used to prepare the inventory of business changes are shown as a flow diagram in figure 71 (below).

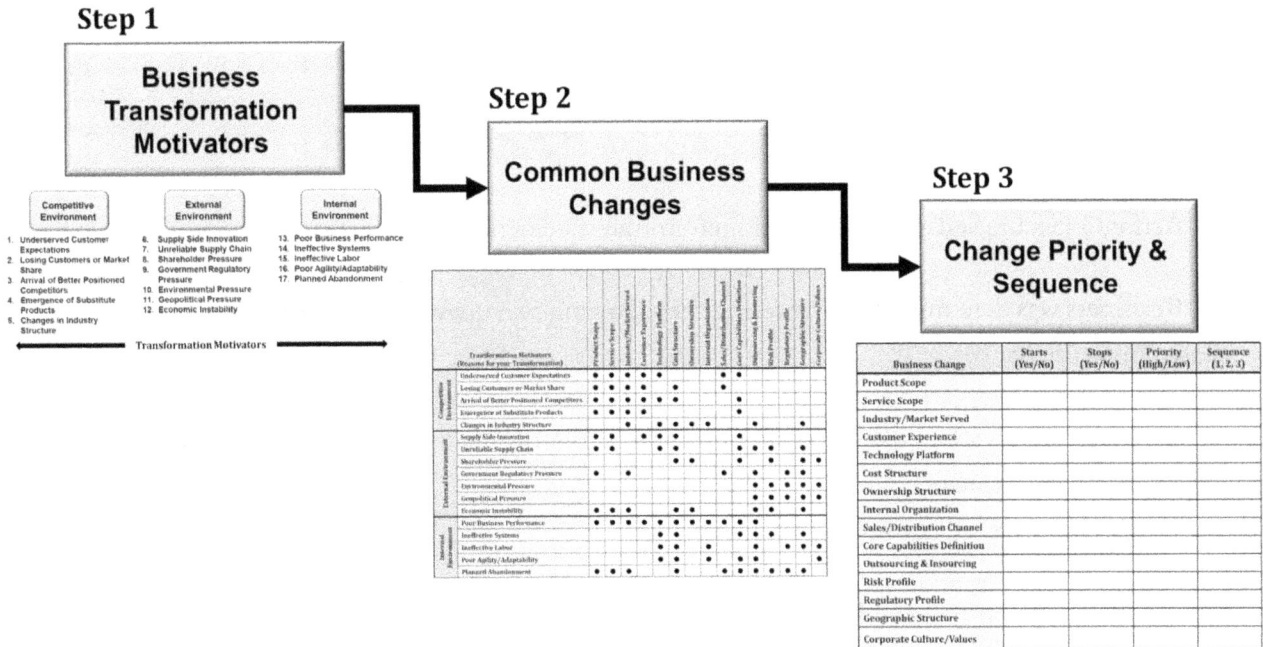

Figure 71: Overview of Deliverables for Inventory of Business Changes

➤ Action 2: Prepare statement of transformation scope.

Readiness was determined by answering the single question (i.e., readiness metric), also shown in figure 65.

Metric: Have you prepared a formal statement of transformation scope?

The preparation step is the statement of transformation scope. To produce this, the executive team uses the statement of business change and the business change priority and sequence plan (produced above) to create a formal statement of transformation scope: "To achieve the purpose and value of our business transformation, we will undertake the following scope of business changes <insert your prioritized and sequenced business changes>."

From the example above, the statement of transformation scope would then be:

To achieve the purpose and value of our business transformation, we will undertake the following scope of business changes:

• Priority 1 Changes:

   o adds and discontinues to our customer experience

   o adds and discontinues to our technology platform

   o adds to our sales channel

   o adds to our core capabilities

- Priority 2 Changes:

  o adds to our market served
  o adds to reduce our risk profile

➢ Action 3: Secure stakeholder commitment to the statement of transformation scope.

Readiness was determined by answering the following two questions (i.e., readiness metrics), also shown in figure 65:

a. Have you reviewed the statement of transformation scope with all stakeholders for validation and commitment?
b. Do you have validation and commitment?

Metric A: Have you reviewed the statement of transformation scope with all stakeholders for validation and commitment?

The preparation step is the stakeholder statement of transformation scope communication. The executive team uses the statement of transformation scope to prepare communications suitable for internal and external stakeholders.

Metric B: Do you have validation and commitment?

The preparation step is the stakeholder statement of transformation scope acknowledgment. The executive team reviews statement of transformation scope communications with internal and external stakeholders and ensures these communications are understood by all stakeholders. The executive team then creates an acknowledgment of this communication by all stakeholders

The complete readiness preparation for the goal "Identify What Needs to Change" is shown in figure 72 (below).

Readiness Preparation	#5: Identify What Needs to Change		
Preparation Actions	1. Prepare Inventory of Business Changes	2. Prepare Statement of Transformation Scope	3. Secure Stakeholder Commitment to the Statement of Transformation Scope
Preparation Steps	a. Statement of Business Change	Statement of Transformation Scope	a. Stakeholder Statement of Transformation Scope Communication
	b. Business Change Priority & Sequence Plan		b. Stakeholder Statement of Transformation Scope Acknowledgement

Figure 72: Readiness Preparation #5: Identify What Needs to Change

Creating an Actionable Preparation

The readiness preparation summarized in figure 72 (above) can be made actionable by converting the actions and steps into deliverables and then combining them with the corresponding activities for producing them. Templates for readiness assessments and preparations are provided in the companion guide to this book.

Readiness Preparation Considerations

Prepare Inventory of Business Changes

As you develop your inventory of business changes, there are several things to consider. First, this is a very high-level set of business changes. They will be developed in more detail through the remainder of scope readiness and into implementation readiness. Furthermore, the motivators shown in figure 67 (above) are mapped to all potential common business changes that could occur. You will need to determine which ones will occur in your business transformation. This depends on the nature of your business and what you are trying to accomplish in your transformation.

Second, as you identify the priority and sequence of your changes—reference figure 69 (above)— you can group the changes into primary and secondary priorities. Primary priorities will be addressed sequentially before the secondary priorities, but you can also create a sequence within each priority group. The transformation is not complete until the changes in all priorities and sequences have been implemented. You may need to make some choices during implementation. Prioritization and sequencing of the changes supports these choices and allows you to delay the changes that depend on the completion of earlier changes.

Secure Stakeholder Commitment to the Statement of Transformation Scope

It is critical your executive team and stakeholders align around the changes required to achieve the purpose/value of your transformation. As your executives and stakeholders begin to realize how the changes impact their functional areas, you may see passive or active disagreement with the statement of transformation scope. It is important to understand if this is happening and address the disagreements now. Resist the urge to change the scope of your transformation based on negative reactions to the accompanying changes from your executives and stakeholders.

Goal #6: Understand the Impact of the Change

"Understand the Impact of the Change" means being able to articulate the impact of the change on your business and understanding whether your business is ready to undertake the change. These will serve as the readiness standards for assessing your grasp of the change impacts and if needed, for remediating your readiness gaps.

Readiness Assessment

Readiness Assessment Standards

The readiness assessment standards are formally expressed as follows:

1. You understand the impact of the change scope on your business.
2. Your business is ready to undertake the change scope.

If you know these, then you have attained readiness with respect to "Understand the Impact of the Change." If you don't, you will need to complete the readiness preparation described later. As with all the readiness assessments, metrics are defined to evaluate your attainment of these standards.

Readiness Assessment Metrics

The metrics (represented as questions) examine your company's readiness and allow you to identify the gaps in your understanding.

➢ Standard 1: You understand the impact of the change scope on your business.

An assessment of readiness is provided by answering the following two questions:

a. Have you identified the business impacts of all the changes required for the transformation?
b. Have you expressed the magnitude of the impact to your business in a statement of transformation impact?

➢ Standard 2: Your business is ready to undertake the Change Scope

An assessment of readiness is provided by answering the following two sets of questions:

a. Do you know which of the changes will be difficult for your business to enact or adopt? Is your business ready to begin implementing the changes?

b. If not, what is required to occur or be in place to commence with change implementation and adoption? Can your business address all open change implementation/adoption readiness gaps prior to investment?

The complete readiness assessment for the goal "Understand the Impact of the Change" is shown in figure 73 (below).

Readiness Assessment	#6: Understand the Impact of the Change	
Assessment Standards	1. You understand the impact of the Change Scope on your business	2. Your business is ready to undertake the Change Scope
Assessment Metrics	a. Have you identified the business impacts of all the changes required for the transformation?	a. Do you know which of the changes will be difficult for your business to enact or adopt? Is your business ready to begin implementing the changes?
	b. Have you expressed the magnitude of the impact to your business - in a Statement of Transformation Impact?	b. If not, what is required to occur or be in place to commence with change implementation and adoption? Can your business address all open change implementation/adoption readiness gaps prior to investment?

Figure 73: Readiness Assessment #6: Understand the Impact of the Change

Creating an Actionable Assessment

The readiness assessment summarized in figure 73 (above) can be made actionable by converting the standards and metrics into deliverables and then combining them with the corresponding activities for producing them. Templates for readiness assessments and preparations are provided in the companion guide to this book.

Readiness Assessment Considerations

It is important to understand all the business impacts resulting from the scope of change for your transformation. This includes business assets that may be difficult to develop or acquire and business liabilities that may be difficult or costly to eliminate.

Arguably, the most critical assessment you will undertake is to evaluate whether your business is ready to begin the transformation. Is your business ready to address all the changes and change impacts? If you are not ready to begin, it is important to understand why you're not ready and whether you can ever be ready. A partial transformation does not achieve the purpose/value of the transformation. If you are not ready, do not move forward.

Readiness Preparation

The readiness assessment standards for "Understand the Impact of the Change" were defined as follows:

1. You understand the impact of the change scope on your business.
2. Your business is ready to undertake the change scope.

If your business is unable to attain these readiness assessment standards, you will need to undertake the following preparation actions to remediate the gaps.

Readiness Preparation Actions

The actions you can take to help you understand the impact of the changes on your business to achieve your transformation are formally expressed as follows:

1. Prepare a statement of transformation impact.
2. Assess your readiness to begin the transformation.

By taking these actions, you ensure your business can attain the corresponding standards. The deliverables and activities presented next will guide you in completing these actions.

Readiness Preparation Steps

Every readiness assessment standard was assigned one or more metrics to facilitate evaluation. These metrics are now used in designing the preparation steps. One preparation step is required for each assessment metric.

➢ Action 1: Prepare statement of transformation impact.

Readiness was determined by answering the following two questions (i.e., readiness metrics), also shown in figure 73 (above):

a. Have you identified the business impacts of all the changes required for the transformation?
b. Have you expressed the magnitude of the impact to your business—in a statement of transformation impact?

Metric A: Have you identified the business impacts of all the changes required for the transformation?

The preparation step includes a change impact profile and transformation change impact matrix. As shown in figure 74 (below), the change impact profile is used in the creation of the transformation change impact matrix.

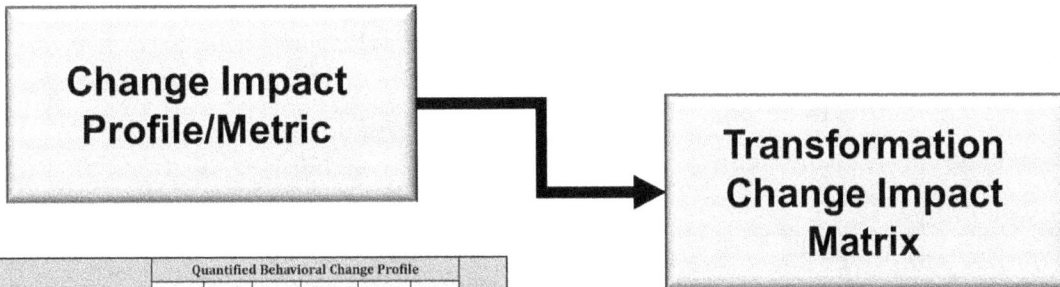

#	Business Changes	Quantified Behavioral Change Profile						Total
		What	How	Who	Where	When	Why	
1	Product Scope	5	5	5	5	0	0	20
2	Service Scope	10	10	5	5	0	5	35
3	Industry/Market Served	5	5	10	5	5	10	40
4	Customer Experience	10	10	10	0	0	10	40
5	Technology Re-Platform	10	10	5	0	0	5	30
6	Cost Restructure	10	10	10	5	0	10	45
7	Ownership Restructure	5	5	10	10	5	10	45
8	Internal Reorganization	0	5	10	5	5	10	35
9	Sales/Distribution Channel	10	10	10	10	5	10	55
10	Core Capabilities Redefinition	10	10	5	5	5	10	45
11	Outsourcing & Insourcing	5	10	10	10	5	10	50
12	Risk Profile	5	10	5	5	5	5	35
13	Regulatory Profile	10	10	5	5	5	5	40
14	Geographic Structure	5	5	10	10	5	5	40
15	Corporate Culture/Values	5	10	10	0	0	10	35
	Total Behavioral Change Impact	105	125	120	80	45	115	590

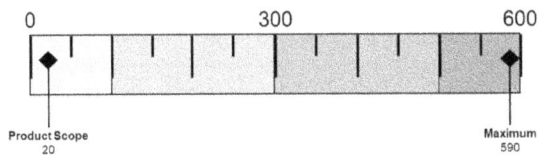

Figure 74: Change Impact Profile and Transformation Change Impact Matrix

The change impact profile was introduced in chapter 1. To produce the change impact profile for your transformation, the executive team adjusts the generalized change impact profile, shown again in figure 75 (below), using the specific changes for your company's transformation. The changes for your transformation are outlined in your statement of transformation scope (produced earlier in this chapter for readiness goal #5: Identify What Needs to Change).

#	Business Changes	Quantified Change Impact Profile						Total
		What	How	Who	Where	When	Why	
1	Product Scope	5	5	5	5	0	0	20
2	Service Scope	10	10	5	5	0	5	35
3	Industry/Market Served	5	5	10	5	5	10	40
4	Customer Experience	10	10	10	0	0	10	40
5	Technology Platform	10	10	5	0	0	5	30
6	Cost Structure	10	10	10	5	0	10	45
7	Ownership Structure	5	5	10	10	5	10	45
8	Internal Organization	0	5	10	5	5	10	35
9	Sales/Distribution Channel	10	10	10	10	5	10	55
10	Core Capabilities Definition	10	10	5	5	5	10	45
11	Outsourcing & Insourcing	5	10	10	10	5	10	50
12	Risk Profile	5	10	5	5	5	5	35
13	Regulatory Profile	10	10	5	5	5	5	40
14	Geographic Structure	5	5	10	10	5	5	40
15	Corporate Culture/Values	5	10	10	0	0	10	35
	Total Change Impact	105	125	120	80	45	115	590

● "10" Significant Change Impact   ◖ "5" Moderate Change Impact   ○ "0" Minimal Change Impact

Figure 75: Change Impact Profile

Continuing the earlier example, recall the statement of transformation scope was "to achieve the purpose and value of our business transformation, we will undertake the following scope of business changes."

- Priority 1 Changes:

  o adds and discontinues to our customer experience
  o adds and discontinues to our technology platform

○ adds to our sales channel

○ adds to our core capabilities

• Priority 2 Changes:

○ adds to our market served

○ adds to reduce our risk profile

Applying the priority 1 and priority 2 changes to the generalized change impact profile results in the specific change impact profile for the transformation—shown in figure 76 (below). The change impact metric is 245 as illustrated in figure 77 (below).

#	Business Changes	Quantified Change Impact Profile						
		What	How	Who	Where	When	Why	Total
1	Product Scope							
2	Service Scope							
3	Industry/Market Served	5	5	10	5	5	10	40
4	Customer Experience	10	10	10	0	0	10	40
5	Technology Platform	10	10	5	0	0	5	30
6	Cost Structure							
7	Ownership Structure							
8	Internal Organization							
9	Sales/Distribution Channel	10	10	10	10	5	10	55
10	Core Capabilities Definition	10	10	5	5	5	10	45
11	Outsourcing & Insourcing							
12	Risk Profile	5	10	5	5	5	5	35
13	Regulatory Profile							
14	Geographic Structure							
15	Corporate Culture/Values							
	Total Change Impact	50	55	45	25	20	50	245

Figure 76: Change Impact Profile Example

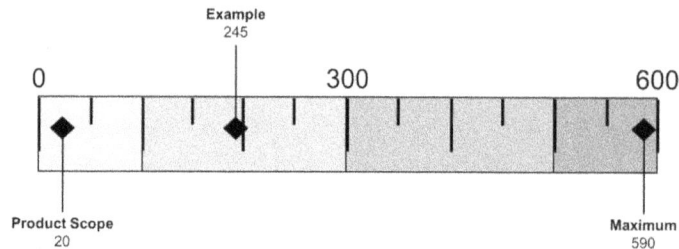

Figure 77: Change Impact Metric Example

The second part of this preparation step is the transformation change impact matrix. Whereas the change impact profile quantifies the total change impact of your transformation, the transformation change impact matrix specifies the nature of each impact. It specifies the impact to each dimension (column) of the change impact profile for each business change (row) in the profile. Hence, it is a matrix. The nature of the change impact is unique to each dimension and business change.

What Change Impacts

The what dimension represents the content or the deliverables of a business. It includes the products and services a business offers to its customers as well as the intermediate products and services used in producing the commercial offering. Impacts to the what dimension include the following:

- adding new products/services
- modifying existing products/services
- eliminating existing products/services
- combining existing products/services
- splitting existing products/services

The nature of the impact is also influenced by the business change. For example, if the business change is "service scope," then you must identify any of the above five impacts occurring as a result of changing your "service scope." Similarly, if the business change is "industry/market served," then you must identify any of the above five impacts occurring as a result of changing your "industry/market served." This continues for each of the business changes in your change impact profile.

How Change Impacts

The how dimension represents methods, policies, or procedures used to perform work by a business. It includes methods/policies/procedures used in producing work content and deliverables as well as those used in the administration of the business. Impacts to the how dimension include the following:

- adding new methods, policies, or procedures
- modifying existing methods, policies, or procedures
- eliminating existing methods, policies, or procedures

Again, the nature of the impact is also influenced by the business change. So, you must identify any of the three impacts (above) occurring for each business change in your change impact profile.

Who Change Impacts

The who dimension represents the relationships through which work is performed by a business. It includes internal, reporting, customer, supplier, regulatory and other external entity relationships. Impacts to the who dimension include the following:

- adding new relationships with entities engaged during the performance of work
- modifying existing relationships with entities engaged during the performance of work
- eliminating existing relationships with entities engaged during the performance of work

The nature of the impact is also influenced by the business change. So, you must identify any of the three impacts (above) occurring for each business change in your change impact profile.

Where Change Impacts

The where dimension represents the locations at which work is performed by a business. It includes offices, workspaces, customer and supplier sites, and other external entity sites. Impacts to the where dimension include the following:

- adding new locations where work is conducted
- modifying existing locations where work is conducted
- eliminating existing locations where work is conducted

You must then identify any of the three impacts (above) occurring for each business change in your change impact profile.

When Change Impacts

The when dimension represents the time at which work is performed by a business. It includes the start/stop time of business activities as well as patterns or cycles of activity. Impacts to the when dimension include the following:

- adding new timing, cycles, or patterns for work activities
- modifying existing timing, cycles, or patterns for work activities
- eliminating existing timing, cycles, or patterns for work activities

You must then identify any of the three impacts (above) occurring for each business change in your change impact profile.

Why Change Impacts

The why dimension represents the reason work is performed by a business. It includes the purpose or motivation for performing a business activity. Impacts to the why dimension include the following:

- adding a new reason work activity is performed by the business
- modifying a reason work activity is performed by the business
- eliminating a reason work activity is performed by the business

You must then identify any of the three impacts (above) occurring for each business change in your change impact profile. A template for capturing the change impacts influenced by each dimension (column) of the change impact profile and each business change (row) in the profile is shown in figure 78 (below).

		What	How	Who	Where	When	Why
		Content & Deliverables	Methods & Procedures	Relationships	Locations	Timing & Cycles	Purpose & Motivation
#	Business Changes	Changes to work content or the deliverables for the job that must be done	Changes to work methods, policies or procedures	Changes to work relationships including internal, reporting, customer, supplier, regulatory, etc.	Changes to work location including workspaces, offices, customers and suppliers	Changes to the timing (start/stop) or cycles of work	Changes to work purpose, reason or motivation
1	Product Scope	[ ] Add New [ ] Discontinue [ ] Modify [ ] Combine [ ] Split Product Scope Induced Products or Services	[ ] Add New [ ] Discontinue [ ] Modify Product Scope Induced Sourcing, Production, Selling, Marketing, Fulfillment, Financial or Business Support <Method, Policy, or Procedure>	[ ] Add New [ ] Discontinue [ ] Modify Product Scope Induced Relationship <Internal, Reporting, Customer, Supplier, Regulatory Agency>	[ ] Add New [ ] Discontinue [ ] Modify Product Scope Induced Location <Workspaces, Offices, Customers, Suppliers>	[ ] Add New [ ] Discontinue [ ] Modify Product Scope Induced Timing or Cycles {Not Common}	[ ] Add New [ ] Discontinue [ ] Modify Product Scope Induced Purpose or Motivation {Not Common}
2	Service Scope	[ ] Add New [ ] Discontinue [ ] Modify [ ] Combine [ ] Split Service Scope Induced Products or Services	[ ] Add New [ ] Discontinue [ ] Modify Service Scope Induced Sourcing, Production, Selling, Marketing, Fulfillment, Financial or Business Support <Method, Policy, or Procedure>	[ ] Add New [ ] Discontinue [ ] Modify Service Scope Induced Relationship <Internal, Reporting, Customer, Supplier, Regulatory Agency>	[ ] Add New [ ] Discontinue [ ] Modify Service Scope Induced Location <Workspaces, Offices, Customers, Suppliers>	[ ] Add New [ ] Discontinue [ ] Modify Service Scope Induced Timing or Cycles {Not Common}	[ ] Add New [ ] Discontinue [ ] Modify Service Scope Induced Purpose or Motivation
·	·	·	·	·	·	·	·

Figure 78: Transformation Change Impact Matrix Excerpt

To produce the transformation change impact matrix, the executive team completes the transformation change impact matrix template by reviewing all business changes in the change impact profile and iterating across all the change impact dimensions—what, how, and who. The method is shown in figure 79 (below).

For example, consider the product scope business change and the what change impact profile dimension. The change impact pertains to changes to the content and deliverables of the business— that is, the products and services. If your business transformation requires adding new products whenever you have a product scope change, then you would check the "add new" change impact. Or, if your business transformation requires discontinuing products, then you would check the "discontinue" change impact and proceed similarly for the other change impacts.

Now consider the how change impact profile dimension. The change impact pertains to changes to the methods and procedures of the business: sourcing, production, selling, marketing, fulfillment, financial, or business support methods, policies, or procedures. If your business transformation requires adding new methods, policies, or procedures whenever you have a product scope change, then you would check the "add new" change impact. Similarly, if your business transformation requires discontinuing methods, policies, or procedures, then you would check the "discontinue" change impact.

Iterate →

#	Business Changes	What	How	Who
		Content & Deliverables	**Methods & Procedures**	**Relationships**
		Changes to work content or the deliverables for the job that must be done	Changes to work methods, policies or procedures	Changes to work relationships including internal, reporting, customer, supplier, regulatory, etc.
1	**Product Scope**	[ ] Add New [ ] Discontinue [ ] Modify [ ] Combine [ ] Split Product Scope Induced Products or Services	[ ] Add New [ ] Discontinue [ ] Modify Product Scope Induced Sourcing, Production, Selling, Marketing, Fulfillment, Financial or Business Support <Method, Policy, or Procedure>	[ ] Add New [ ] Discontinue [ ] Modify Product Scope Induced Relationship <Internal, Reporting, Customer, Supplier, Regulatory Agency>
2	**Service Scope**	[ ] Add New [ ] Discontinue [ ] Modify [ ] Combine [ ] Split Service Scope Induced Products or Services	[ ] Add New [ ] Discontinue [ ] Modify Service Scope Induced Sourcing, Production, Selling, Marketing, Fulfillment, Financial or Business Support <Method, Policy, or Procedure>	[ ] Add New [ ] Discontinue [ ] Modify Service Scope Induced Relationship <Internal, Reporting, Customer, Supplier, Regulatory Agency>

All Changes ↓

Figure 79: Change Impact Matrix Completion

You will continue this process until you've considered all your business changes. Furthermore, if you incorporate the prioritization and sequence information from your change priority and sequence plan, you can obtain a prioritized sequence of change impacts for your business transformation. All the change impacts must eventually be addressed and absorbed during your transformation.

Metric B: Have you expressed the magnitude of the impact to your business—in a statement of transformation impact?

The preparation step for this metric is the statement of transformation impact. To produce this, the executive team uses the transformation change impact matrix (developed above) to create a formal statement of transformation impact: "To complete the scope of changes for our business transformation, we will address and absorb the following business change impacts <insert your prioritized and sequenced business change impacts>."

➤ Action 2: Assess readiness to begin transformation.

Readiness was determined by answering the following two sets of questions (i.e., readiness metrics), also shown in figure 73.

    a. Do you know which of the changes will be difficult for your business to enact or adopt? Is your business ready to begin implementing the changes?
    b. If not, what is required to occur or be in place to commence with change implementation and adoption? Can your business address all open change implementation/adoption readiness gaps prior to investment?

Metric A: Do you know which of the changes will be difficult for your business to enact or adopt? Is your business ready to begin implementing the changes?

The preparation step for this metric is the transformation change readiness assessment. This is one of the most important preparation steps as it determines how much effort you will need to expend to prepare your business for the change impacts incurred during the transformation. The effort expended will then drive the total investment required to implement your transformation.

Transformation Change Readiness

To evaluate your company's readiness to begin implementing the transformational change, you need to understand whether any of the change impacts pose a "gap" in readiness. There are two distinct types of readiness gaps: willingness gaps and ability gaps.

Willingness captures the degree of consent or inclination toward addressing a change impact. You can denote a willingness gap as either a reluctance or an uncertainty. Reluctance indicates a stronger gap in willingness than uncertainty.

Ability captures the degree of qualification to address a change impact. You can denote an ability gap as a missing competency, license/permission, or resource. Transformation change readiness means the willingness and ability gaps are known and can be resolved prior to starting your transformation or as you begin implementing. Figure 80 (below) illustrates the relationship between the two types of transformation readiness gaps and change impacts.

Change Impact	Transformation Readiness	
	Willingness Gaps	**Ability Gaps**
[ ] Add New	[ ] Reluctance [ ] Uncertainty	[ ] Competency [ ] License/Permission [ ] Resource
[ ] Discontinue	[ ] Reluctance [ ] Uncertainty	[ ] Competency [ ] License/Permission [ ] Resource
[ ] Modify	[ ] Reluctance [ ] Uncertainty	[ ] Competency [ ] License/Permission [ ] Resource

Figure 80: Transformation Change Readiness Gaps

Change readiness gaps can be captured for all change impacts by extending the transformation change impact matrix from figure 78 to include the willingness gaps and ability gaps illustrated in figure 80 (above). This becomes the transformation change readiness assessment template as shown in figure 81 (below).

| # | Business Changes | What | | | How | | | ... |
| | | Content & Deliverables | Transformation Readiness Assessment | | Methods & Procedures | Transformation Readiness Assessment | | ... |
		Changes to work content or the deliverables for the job that must be done	Willingness Gaps	Ability Gaps	Changes to work methods, policies or procedures	Willingness Gaps	Ability Gaps	...
1	Product Scope	[ ] Add New [ ] Discontinue [ ] Modify [ ] Combine [ ] Split Product Scope Induced Products or Services	[ ] Reluctance [ ] Uncertainty	[ ] Competency [ ] License/Permission [ ] Resource	[ ] Add New [ ] Discontinue [ ] Modify Product Scope Induced Sourcing, Production, Selling, Marketing, Fulfillment, Financial or Business Support <Method, Policy, or Procedure>	[ ] Reluctance [ ] Uncertainty	[ ] Competency [ ] License/Permission [ ] Resource	...
2	Service Scope	[ ] Add New [ ] Discontinue [ ] Modify [ ] Combine [ ] Split Service Scope Induced Products or Services	[ ] Reluctance [ ] Uncertainty	[ ] Competency [ ] License/Permission [ ] Resource	[ ] Add New [ ] Discontinue [ ] Modify Service Scope Induced Sourcing, Production, Selling, Marketing, Fulfillment, Financial or Business Support <Method, Policy, or Procedure>	[ ] Reluctance [ ] Uncertainty	[ ] Competency [ ] License/Permission [ ] Resource	...

Figure 81: Transformation Change Readiness Assessment Template

To produce the transformation change readiness assessment, the executive team first creates a transformation change readiness assessment template by extending the transformation change impact matrix shown in figure 81 (above). The transformation change readiness template allows you to identify gaps in your company's readiness to address the change impacts of your transformation.

Metric B: If not, what is required to occur or be in place to commence with change implementation and adoption? Can your business address all open change implementation/ adoption readiness gaps prior to investment?

The presentation step for this metric is the transformation change readiness gap closure. This important preparation step determines how the readiness gaps will be addressed. Once you understand your gaps in readiness, you need to determine how to close the gaps—and then close them.

Readiness Gap Closure

The method used to close a gap in readiness depends on the type of gap: willingness or ability. A willingness gap is closed using either incentives or disincentives to address the reluctance or uncertainty. You will need to determine which method is used to close each gap.

An ability gap is closed by acquiring or developing the missing competencies, licenses/permissions, and resources—or by resequencing business changes to alleviate the impact of the gap. Again, you will need to determine which method is used to close each gap.

Figure 82 (below) illustrates the relationship between change impacts, change readiness gap types and change readiness gap closure methods.

Change Impact	Willingness Gaps		Ability Gaps	
	Readiness Gaps	Gap Closure	Readiness Gaps	Gap Closure
[ ] Add New	[ ] Reluctance [ ] Uncertainty	[ ] Incentives [ ] Disincentives	[ ] Competency [ ] License/Permission [ ] Resource	[ ] Acquire [ ] Develop [ ] Re-Sequence
[ ] Discontinue	[ ] Reluctance [ ] Uncertainty	[ ] Incentives [ ] Disincentives	[ ] Competency [ ] License/Permission [ ] Resource	[ ] Acquire [ ] Develop [ ] Re-Sequence
[ ] Modify	[ ] Reluctance [ ] Uncertainty	[ ] Incentives [ ] Disincentives	[ ] Competency [ ] License/Permission [ ] Resource	[ ] Acquire [ ] Develop [ ] Re-Sequence

Figure 82: Transformation Change Readiness Gap Closure

To produce this deliverable, the executive team first creates a transformation change readiness gap closure template by extending the transformation change readiness assessment as shown in figure 83 (below).

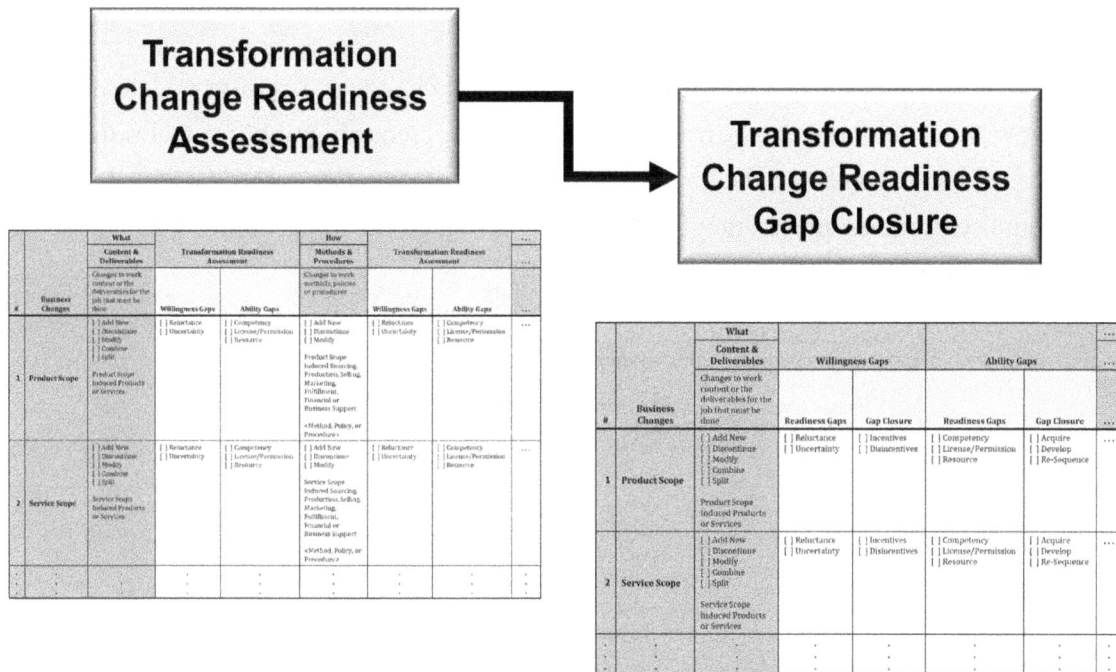

Figure 83: Extending the Change Readiness Assessment into a Change Readiness Gap

Closure

The transformation change readiness gap closure template (reference figure 84 below) allows you to identify the chosen closure method for each gap in your company's change readiness.

#	Business Changes	What		Willingness Gaps		Ability Gaps		...
		Content & Deliverables						...
		Changes to work content or the deliverables for the job that must be done	Readiness Gaps	Gap Closure	Readiness Gaps	Gap Closure	...
1	Product Scope	[ ] Add New [ ] Discontinue [ ] Modify [ ] Combine [ ] Split Product Scope Induced Products or Services	[ ] Reluctance [ ] Uncertainty	[ ] Incentives [ ] Disincentives	[ ] Competency [ ] License/Permission [ ] Resource	[ ] Acquire [ ] Develop [ ] Re-Sequence	...
2	Service Scope	[ ] Add New [ ] Discontinue [ ] Modify [ ] Combine [ ] Split Service Scope Induced Products or Services	[ ] Reluctance [ ] Uncertainty	[ ] Incentives [ ] Disincentives	[ ] Competency [ ] License/Permission [ ] Resource	[ ] Acquire [ ] Develop [ ] Re-Sequence	...
.	.	.	.	.	.	.	.

Figure 84: Transformation Change Readiness Gap Closure Template

The executive team can then review the transformation change gap closure to determine when your business can close all the change readiness gaps. The gaps requiring significant closure will need to be addressed before you begin the implementing phase.

The complete readiness preparation for the goal "Understand the Impact of the Change" is shown in figure 85 (below).

Readiness Preparation	#6: Understand the Impact of the Change	
Preparation Actions	1. Prepare Statement of Transformation Impact	2. Assess Readiness to Begin Transformation
Preparation Steps	a. Change Impact Profile and Transformation Change Impact Matrix	a. Transformation Change Readiness Assessment
	b. Statement of Transformation Impact	b. Transformation Change Readiness Gap Closure

Figure 85: Readiness Preparation #6: Understand the Impact of the Change

Creating an Actionable Preparation

The readiness preparation summarized in figure 85 (above) can be made actionable by converting the actions and steps into deliverables and then combining them with the corresponding activities for producing them. Templates for readiness assessments and preparations are provided in the companion guide to this book.

Readiness Preparation Considerations

Prepare Statement of Transformation Impact

The change impact profile identifies the set of all possible changes that can occur during a business transformation. You filter the set based on your motivators to arrive at something that characterizes your transformation. However, you must still review the list carefully to determine whether all changes are relevant to your transformation. If some are not required, then discard them from your list.

The accompanying change impact metric is intended to provide an indication of the magnitude of change in your transformation. It is useful in understanding the level of change your organization will undergo, relative to the transformations of other businesses. If your transformation is close to the high end of the spectrum, you should expect significant change impact.

The transformation change impact matrix will take considerable time and focus to complete. You must not skip through this step as it identifies the specific impacts from the changes in your transformation. By answering the questions across all the behavioral change dimensions, you will uncover secondary impacts related to the primary changes. Also, it is equally important to understand what must be discontinued as it is what must be added or modified. The things that must stop are frequently in strategic opposition to the additions. Furthermore, you may be able to recover their operational cost, which can then be used to fund the additions.

Assess Readiness to Begin Transformation

The transformation change readiness assessment provides crucial insight into whether your business is ready to begin tackling the change impacts of your transformation. You must honestly identify the willingness and ability gaps for each of the change impacts. You should not be concerned that you have gaps. If your business needs a transformation, it is quite likely you have gaps. At this point, you need to understand where the gaps are, the type of gaps you have, and whether they are critical to close before you begin the transformation.

Do not underestimate the readiness gaps. If they go unresolved, your transformation begins at a disadvantage that eventually must be addressed. If the gaps are ignored, you will expend more time and money to address them during the transformation. The analyses produced in preparing for the goal "Understanding Your Business" can help you determine whether your assets help you overcome the gaps.

If you are not ready to begin, it is important to understand why you're not ready and whether you can ever be ready. At this point, you have a couple of options for continuing with the transformation. The first is to determine whether you can achieve sufficient purpose and value by descoping the transformation in a way that reduces the readiness gaps. If this is not possible, you can undertake interim efforts or scope resequencing to address the gaps.

Finally, the transformation change readiness gap closure indicates the type of resolution to your gaps—but not the specific resolution. Specific resolutions will need to be identified during the implementation phase.

Goal #7: Identify the Investment Required to Change

"Identify the Investment Required to Change" means being able to articulate the investment in resources and time required to enact the changes and adopt the change impacts of your business transformation—and then determine whether the investment is justified by the purpose and value of the transformation. These will serve as the readiness standards for assessing your grasp of the investment and, if needed, for remediating your readiness gaps.

Readiness Assessment

Readiness Assessment Standards

The readiness assessment standards are formally expressed as follows:

1. You understand the investment in time and resources to enact the transformation.
2. Your transformation purpose and value justify the required investment.

If you know these, then you have attained readiness with respect to "Identify the Investment Required to Change." If you don't, you will need to complete the readiness preparation described later. As with all the readiness assessments, metrics are defined to evaluate your attainment of these standards.

Readiness Assessment Metrics

The metrics (represented as questions) examine your company's readiness and allow you to identify the gaps in your understanding.

➢ Standard 1: You understand the investment in time and resources to enact the transformation.

An assessment of readiness is provided by answering the following two questions:

a. Have you estimated the time and resources required to enact the changes and absorb the change impacts?

b. Have you estimated the time and resources required to close the change readiness gaps?

➢ Standard 2: Your transformation purpose and value justify the required investment

An assessment of readiness is provided by answering the following two questions:

a. Have you prepared a business justification for the investment in enacting and absorbing your transformation's changes?

b. Is the transformation investment justified by the transformation purpose and value?

The complete readiness assessment for the goal "Identify the Investment Required to Change" is shown in figure 86 (below).

Readiness Assessment	#7: Identify the Investment Required to Change	
Assessment Standards	1. You understand the investment in time and resources to enact the transformation	2. Your transformation purpose and value justify the required investment
Assessment Metrics	a. Have you estimated the time and resources required to enact the changes and absorb the change impacts?	a. Have you prepared a business justification for the investment in enacting and absorbing your transformation's changes?
	b. Have you estimated the time and resources required to close the change readiness gaps?	b. Is the transformation investment justified by the transformation purpose and value?

Figure 86: Readiness Assessment #7: Identify the Investment Required to Change

Creating an Actionable Assessment

The readiness assessment summarized in figure 86 (above) can be made actionable by converting the standards and metrics into deliverables and then combining them with the corresponding activities for producing them.

Readiness Assessment Considerations

The business transformation investment is an estimate. You do not need to be detailed—and you cannot be detailed at this point—but you do need to be realistic and ensure the resources required to manage change impacts have not been underestimated or avoided altogether.

You may discover your transformation purpose/value does not justify the required investment. It is possible your estimate of the scope, investment, or value are inaccurate. However, your business may be at the point where it requires an investment just to survive—even if the cost is higher than expected or warranted.

Readiness Preparation

The readiness assessment standards for "Identifying the Investment Required to Change" were defined as follows:

1. You understand the investment in time and resources to enact the transformation.
2. Your transformation purpose and value justify the required investment.

Once again, if your business is unable to attain these readiness assessment standards, you will need to undertake the following preparation actions to remediate the gaps.

Readiness Preparation Actions

The actions you can take to help you understand the investment required to enact your transformation and whether the investment is justified are formally expressed as follows:

1. Prepare a statement of transformation investment.
2. Prepare a statement of business justification.

By taking these actions, you ensure your business can attain the corresponding standards. The deliverables and activities presented next will guide you in completing these actions.

Readiness Preparation Steps

Every readiness assessment standard was assigned one or more metrics to facilitate evaluation. These metrics are now used in designing the preparation steps. One preparation step is required for each assessment metric.

➤ Action 1: Prepare a statement of transformation investment.

Readiness was determined by answering the following two questions (i.e., readiness metrics), also shown in figure 86 (above):

    a. Have you estimated the time and resources required to enact the changes and absorb the change impacts?
    b. Have you estimated the time and resources required to close the change readiness gaps?

Metric A: Have you estimated the time and resources required to enact the changes and absorb the change impacts?

Metric B: Have you estimated the time and resources required to close the change readiness gaps?

The preparation steps for metric A and metric B will be considered together as the methods to produce them are similar. Metric A's preparation step is the change impact implementation investment and metric B's preparation step is the readiness gap closure investment. Together, they form the statement of business transformation investment. To produce this, the executive team must identify the resources and time required to implement and absorb all change impacts and close all the transformation change readiness gaps. The investment components are shown schematically in figure 87 (below).

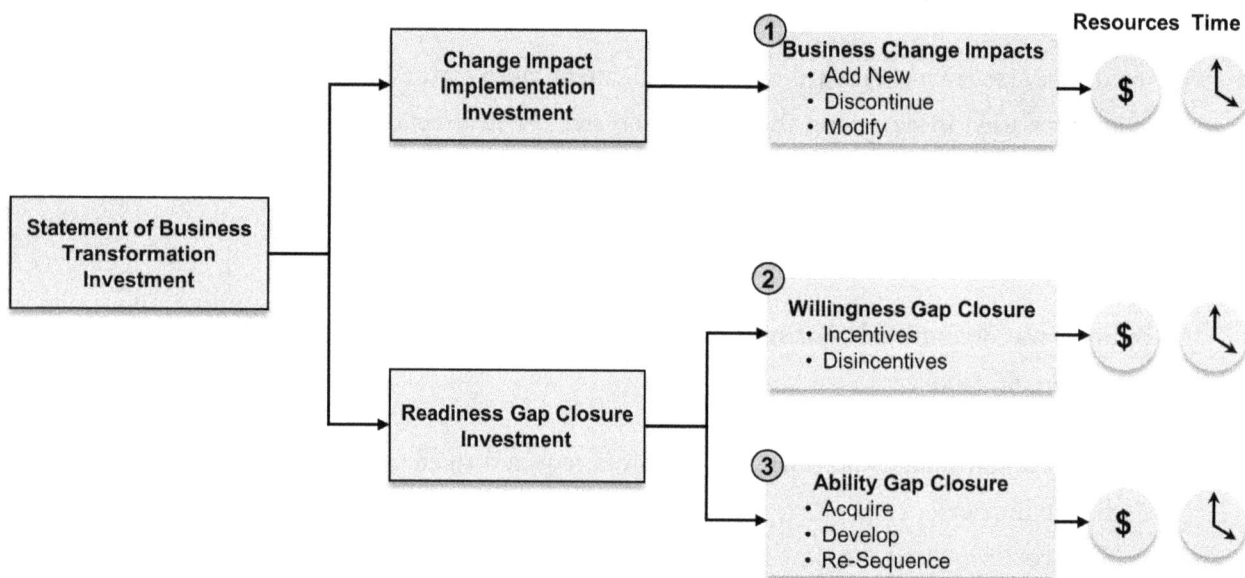

Figure 87: Statement of Business Transformation Investment

The investment components, shown in the numbered circles (above), are estimates that will be used to determine whether your transformation is justified. Change impacts were identified in the transformation change impact matrix and comprise investment component 1. The transformation readiness gap closure helps you identify the investment required to close the willingness and ability gaps—components 2 and 3. You will have to use your knowledge of similar activities to come up with a reasonable estimate for the resources and time. Once you have estimates for the change impacts and gap closure activities, you can sum across the entire set to produce the total business transformation investment.

➢ Action 2: Prepare statement of business justification.

Readiness was determined by answering the following two questions (i.e., readiness metrics), also shown in figure 86 (above):

a. Have you prepared a business justification for the investment in enacting and absorbing your transformation's changes?

b. Is the transformation investment justified by the transformation purpose and value?

Metric A: Have you prepared a business justification for the investment in enacting and absorbing your transformation's changes?

The preparation step is the business transformation justification. To produce this, the executive team compares the value of the business transformation to the total investment required. This is shown schematically in figure 88 (below).

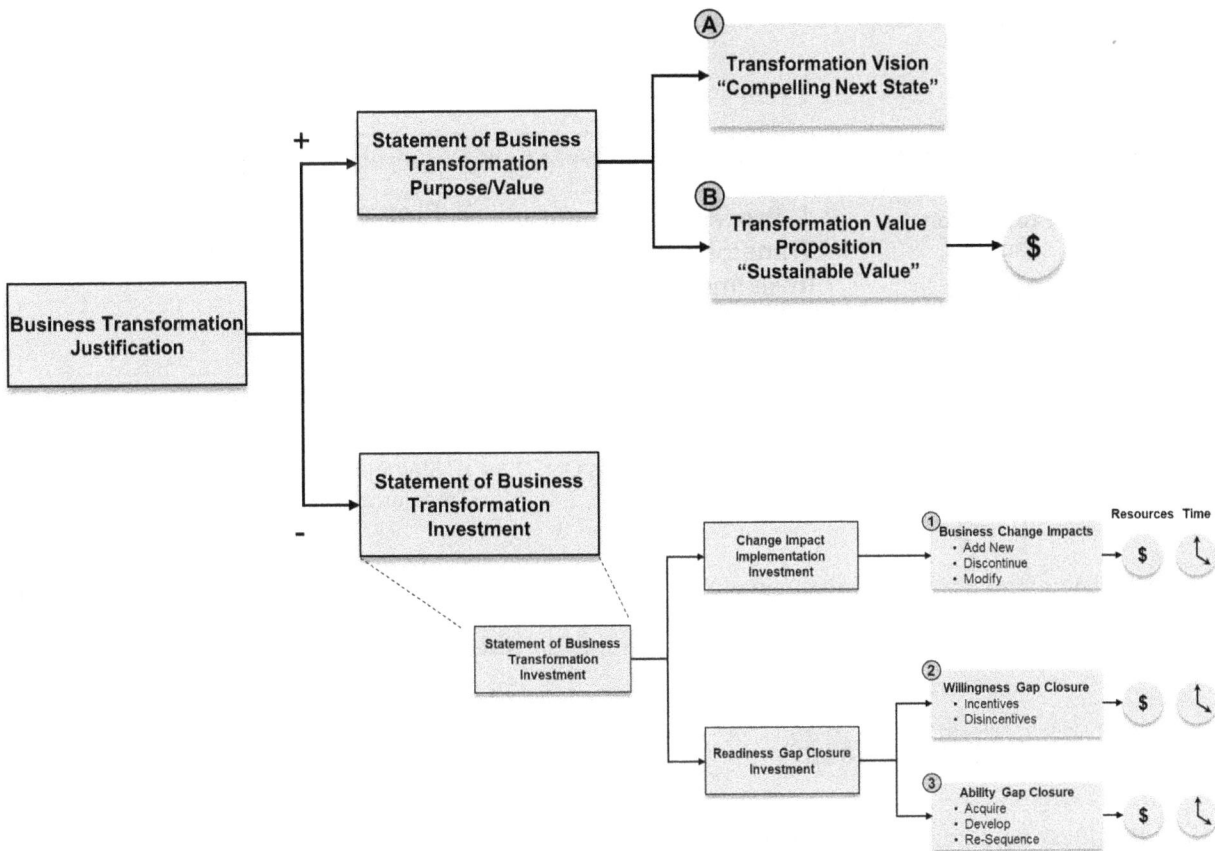

Figure 88: Statement of Business Transformation Justification

The value components are represented by the transformation vision and transformation value proposition—the circles with "A" and "B," respectively. These come directly from the statement of purpose/value developed earlier in this chapter. The statement of business transformation investment was produced above. The value components and investment components come together to form the statement of business justification: "The investment of <insert your resource estimates> in resources and <insert your time estimates> in duration to complete our business transformation will bring about <insert your value statement>."

Metric B: Is the transformation investment justified by the transformation purpose and value?

The preparation step is the statement of transformation justification. To produce this, the executive team assesses the statement of business justification to determine whether the transformation investment is justified by the value it brings to your business. If the transformation's value does not justify the investment, the executive team must determine whether it is due to inaccuracies in estimating scope, cost, or value, or whether the transformation is in fact unreasonably defined.

The complete readiness preparation for the goal "Understand the Impact of the Change" is shown in figure 89 (below).

Readiness Preparation	#7: Identify the Investment Required to Change	
Preparation Actions	1. Prepare Statement of Transformation Investment	2. Prepare Statement of Business Justification
Preparation Steps	a. Change Impact Implementation Investment	a. Business Transformation Justification
	b. Change Readiness Gap Closure Investment	b. Statement of Business Transformation Justification

Figure 89: Readiness Preparation #7: Identify the Investment Required to Change

Creating an Actionable Preparation

The readiness preparation summarized in figure 89 (above) can be made actionable by converting the actions and steps into deliverables and then combining them with the corresponding activities for producing them. Templates for readiness assessments and preparations are provided in the companion guide to this book.

Readiness Preparation Considerations

Prepare Statement of Transformation Investment

As mentioned earlier, the business transformation investment is a first pass estimate. You do not need to be detailed—and you cannot be at this point—but do not underestimate or avoid including the cost to manage change impacts. Your transformation will fail if your business is not able to operate in the transformed environment. Sufficient time and effort are required to address all the change impacts.

You may need professional help to calculate the investments in time and resources. There are many competent companies that can produce a usable estimate of time and resources to complete your transformation.

Prepare a Statement of Business Justification

It is possible your transformation's purpose/value does not justify the required investment. This can result from inaccuracies in scope, cost, or value. You can do additional work to improve the accuracy of your estimates, but your transformation may still be unjustified. It is possible you are at the point where a business survival investment is required—even if the cost is higher than warranted. You know your company's performance and capabilities with respect to your competitive environment. The findings from goal #1: Understand Your Business can help you conclude whether you should move forward with the transformation, adjust the scope until you get to the point of justification, or abandon the transformation at this time.

Goal #8: Commit the Required Investment

"Commit the Required Investment" means being both able and willing to invest in the changes and absorb the change impacts of your business transformation. These will serve as the readiness standards for assessing your grasp of the investment and if needed, for remediating your readiness gaps.

Readiness Assessment

Readiness Assessment Standards

The readiness assessment standards are formally expressed as follows:

1. Your business is able to invest in the changes and absorb the change impacts.
2. Your business is willing to commit the investment in the changes and change impacts.

If you know these, then you have attained readiness with respect to "Commit the Required Investment." If you don't, you will need to complete the readiness preparation described later. As with all the readiness assessments, metrics are defined to evaluate your attainment of these standards.

Readiness Assessment Metrics

The metrics (represented as questions) examine your company's readiness and allow you to identify the gaps in your understanding.

➢ Standard 1: Your business is able to invest in the changes and absorb the change impacts.

   a. Do you have access to funding and resources to enact and absorb the changes?
   b. If not, what is required to secure funding and resources, and when will you be able to secure them?

➢ Standard 2: Your business is willing to commit the investment in the changes and change impacts.

   a. Have you secured commitment from all stakeholders to prioritize the investment in the transformation changes?
   b. If not, have you identified what is required to secure commitment, and are you able to proceed?

The complete readiness assessment for the goal "Commit to the Required Investment" is shown in figure 90 (below).

Readiness Assessment	#8: Commit the Required Investment	
Assessment Standards	1. Your business is able to invest in the changes and absorb the change impacts	2. Your business is willing to commit the investment in the changes and change impacts
Assessment Metrics	a. Do you have access to funding and resources to enact and absorb the changes?	a. Have you secured commitment from all stakeholders to prioritize the investment in the transformation changes?
	b. If not, what is required to secure funding and resources, and when will you be able to secure them?	b. If not, have you identified what is required to secure commitment, and are you able to proceed?

Figure 90: Readiness Assessment #8: Commit the Required Investment

Creating an Actionable Assessment

The readiness assessment summarized in figure 90 (above) can be made actionable by converting the standards and metrics into deliverables and then combining them with the corresponding activities for

producing them. Templates for readiness assessments and preparations are provided in the companion guide to this book.

Readiness Assessment Considerations

It is important to secure commitment to the entire transformation investment before starting any of the spend. Otherwise, you risk halting the transformation at some point, which causes restart delays and expense, increasing the total transformation investment.

Lastly, it is crucial to understand the events or circumstances that could derail your willingness to commit the investment in your transformation. If they should occur, what are you prepared to do to preserve the momentum?

Readiness Preparation

The readiness assessment standards for committing the required investment were defined as follows:

1. Your business is able to invest in the changes and absorb the change impacts.
2. Your business is willing to commit the investment in the changes and change impacts.

If your business is unable to attain these readiness assessment standards, you will need to undertake the following preparation actions to remediate the gaps.

Readiness Preparation Actions

The actions you can take to help you evaluate your company's ability and willingness to commit to the investment in your business transformation are formally expressed as follows:

1. Secure your transformation investment.
2. Commit to your transformation investment.

By taking these actions, you ensure your business can attain the corresponding standards. The deliverables and activities presented next will guide you in completing these actions.

Readiness Preparation Steps

Every readiness assessment standard was assigned one or more metrics to facilitate evaluation. These metrics are now used in designing the preparation steps. One preparation step is required for each assessment metric.

➢ Action 1: Secure your transformation investment.

Readiness was determined by answering the following two questions (i.e., readiness metrics), also shown in figure 90 (above):

   a. Do you have access to funding and resources to enact and absorb the changes?
   b. If not, what is required to secure funding and resources, and when will you be able to secure them?

Metric A: Do you have access to funding and resources to enact and absorb the changes?

The preparation step is the transformation investment assurance document. To produce this, the executive team must identify potential funding sources for the business transformation investment. The statement of business justification can be used to help secure the investment funding.

Metric B: If not, what is required to secure funding and resources, and when will you be able to secure them?

No new preparation step is required. Rather, the executive team must ensure investment funding is available at sufficient levels and throughout the period required to carry out the transformation.

➢ Action 2: Commit to your transformation investment.

Readiness was determined by answering the following two questions (i.e., readiness metrics), also shown in figure 90 (above):

   a. Have you secured commitment from all stakeholders to prioritize the investment in the transformation changes?
   b. If not, have you identified what is required to secure commitment, and are you able to proceed?

Metric A: Have you secured commitment from all stakeholders to prioritize the investment in the transformation changes?

The preparation step is the transformation investment commitment, which consists of obtaining commitment from stakeholders to make the investment in resources/effort and the time frame required to achieve the purpose/scope of the transformation. To secure commitment, the executive team can use a variety of previously created scope readiness preparation documents as follows:

- The statement of transformation impact is used to convey the specific impacts of the behavioral changes, as well as the prioritized sequence in which they must be addressed and absorbed.
- The transformation change readiness assessment is used to convey the gaps in readiness that must be addressed prior to undertaking the change impacts of the transformation.
- The transformation change readiness gap closure is used to convey the means to close gaps in readiness prior to beginning your business transformation.
- The statement of transformation investment is used to convey the time and resources required to enact the changes and absorb the change impacts and the time and resources required to close all readiness gaps prior to starting the transformation.
- The statement of transformation justification is used to convey that the transformation investment is indeed justified by the value it brings to your business.
- The transformation investment assurance is used to convey that the investment funding is available at sufficient levels and throughout the period required to carry out the transformation.

Metric B: If not, have you identified what is required to secure commitment, and are you able to proceed?

The preparation step is a formal transformation investment commitment contingency plan. This is the final step in validating commitment from your stakeholders to proceed with the transformation. To produce this, the executive team first requests feedback, questions, and concerns around the list of transformation investment commitment items from above. The executive team then

- works with stakeholders to address feedback/questions/concerns;
- secures commitment from all stakeholders and produces a final transformation investment commitment;
- prepares a business transformation commitment communication for the transformation, including excerpts from the statement of transformation impact, the transformation change

readiness assessment, the transformation change readiness gap closure, the statement of transformation justification, and the transformation investment assurance; and

- distributes the business transformation commitment communication to the general internal and external audiences—at this point, the business transformation is official, and the business is under transformational change.

The complete readiness preparation for the goal "Commit the Required Investment" is shown in figure 91 (below).

Readiness Preparation	#8: Commit the Required Investment	
Preparation Actions	1. Secure Your Transformation Investment	2. Commit to Your Transformation Investment
Preparation Steps	a. Transformation Investment Assurance document	a. Transformation Investment Commitment
	b. No new step required	b. Transformation Investment Commitment Contingencies

Figure 91: Readiness Preparation #8: Commit the Required Investment

Creating an Actionable Preparation

The readiness preparation summarized in figure 91 (above) can be made actionable by converting the actions and steps into deliverables and then combining them with the corresponding activities for producing them. Templates for readiness assessments and preparations are provided in the companion guide to this book.

Readiness Preparation Considerations

Secure Your Transformation Investment

As mentioned in the considerations under the readiness assessment, it is important to secure commitment to the entire investment before starting any of the spend. If you suspect there are circumstances or conditions that could impact the investment, it is better to address them at this point. Otherwise, you risk halting the transformation, causing restart delays and expense, and increasing the total transformation investment.

Commit to Your Transformation Investment

At this point in the planning phase, stakeholder feedback should be positive, questions should be of the nature of clarifications, and concerns should be primarily around addressing personal impacts from the change. However, it is important to think about the events or circumstances that could derail your willingness to commit the investment. There are external factors beyond your control. Which of these could have an impact? If there are controllable events with the potential to derail your commitment, a transformation may not be the most important investment your business can make.

Chapter Takeaway Points

- We defined the four readiness goals for the purpose objective—understand your business, define the reason for the transformation, align the business leaders around the reason, communicate the reason throughout your business.
- We defined the four readiness goals for the scope objective—identify what needs to change, understand the impact of the change, identify the investment required to change, commit the required investment.
- We defined readiness assessment standards and metrics for each of the readiness goals.
- We defined readiness preparations actions and steps for each of the readiness goals.
- Preparation actions directly addressed assessment standards, and preparation steps directly addressed assessment metrics.
- We described how to make the readiness assessment and preparation actionable and identified items for consideration during a transformation.
- The business transformation motivators developed in chapter 1: "Why Business Transformations Are Necessary," were used in the readiness preparation for goal #2: "Define the Reason for the Transformation"
- The common business changes developed in chapter 1, "Business Changes Initiated during a Transformation," were used in the readiness preparation for goal #5: "Identify What Needs to Change."
- The change impact profile developed in chapter 1, "Business Impacts Induced during a Transformation," was used in the readiness preparation for goal #6: "Understand the Impact of the Change."
- The transformation change readiness assessment was developed to identify gaps in your readiness to determine how much effort you will need to expend to prepare your business for the change impacts incurred during your transformation.

- The transformation change readiness gap closure was developed to determine how the readiness gaps will be addressed.
- A method was presented to help you identify the total investment to address the changes and change impacts in your transformation and close the gaps in readiness.
- A method was presented to help you prepare a business justification for your transformation.

Chapter 5

IMPLEMENTING PHASE READINESS

Without execution, "vision" is just another word for hallucination.
—Mark V. Hurd

The implementing phase is where the transformational change activities are carried out to achieve the purpose and scope defined in the planning phase. The changes must be specified in detail and completed in entirety. The change impacts must be managed and completely absorbed within your business. If not, the value of the transformation and even existing operations are at risk. No one wants a transformation to become a hallucination.

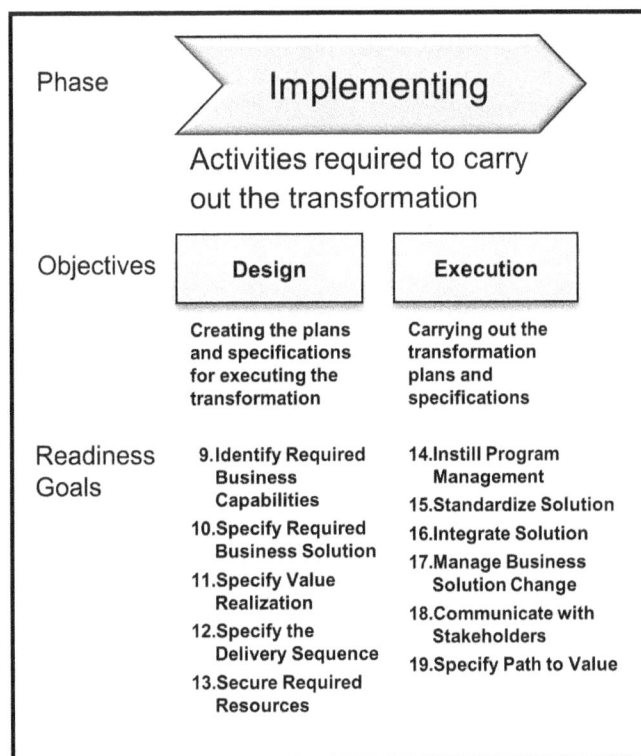

Phase	**Implementing**	
	Activities required to carry out the transformation	
Objectives	**Design**	**Execution**
	Creating the plans and specifications for executing the transformation	Carrying out the transformation plans and specifications
Readiness Goals	9. Identify Required Business Capabilities 10. Specify Required Business Solution 11. Specify Value Realization 12. Specify the Delivery Sequence 13. Secure Required Resources	14. Instill Program Management 15. Standardize Solution 16. Integrate Solution 17. Manage Business Solution Change 18. Communicate with Stakeholders 19. Specify Path to Value

Figure 92: Implementing Phase Readiness Goals

This chapter introduces readiness for the implementing phase of a business transformation. It is organized in two sections; the first section covers readiness for the design objective, and the second covers readiness for the execution objective. Each section will specify the readiness assessments and readiness preparations for the respective readiness goals. The readiness goals for the design and execution objectives are shown again in figure 92 (below).

Design Readiness

Design in the implementing phase of a business transformation is an elaboration of the plans and specifications for the scope of change identified during the planning phase. Readiness of design is expressed through the attainment of the five readiness goals shown in figure 92 (above). Each of these readiness goals has specific readiness assessments and readiness preparations—formally developed in the remainder of this section.

Goal #9: Identify Required Business Capabilities

Identify Required Business Capabilities means you understand the competencies and abilities your company needs to carry out business. Capabilities are skills, physical assets, or relationships that provide your business with a commercial advantage. Business capabilities provide a way to represent what your company "needs to be good at" after it has transformed.

Examples of business capabilities include product engineering and manufacturing, a mobile transactional website, a comprehensive distribution network, or the right to sell products and services in a foreign country.

Business capabilities provide a bridge between a company's vision/strategy and the implementation of that vision/strategy. They describe the what of the business as opposed to the how and promote a shared understanding of the business operating model. The Open Group has created an introduction to business capability modeling. There are also many commercially available modeling tools that provide tutorials on business capability modeling concepts embedded within the tools.

While in-depth instruction on business capability modeling is beyond the scope of this book, a few guidelines are helpful in producing a business capability model that facilitates business transformation readiness.

- Business capabilities can be expressed hierarchically and arranged as a tree. There is no limit to the number of levels in the hierarchy, but trees beyond three levels can become cumbersome and difficult to comprehend.
- The business capability model should provide a complete description of the business. The top level of the model should contain seven to ten business capabilities to cover the entire scope of the business. The lower levels can contain fewer business capabilities.
- The business capabilities should be mutually exclusive, and their scopes should not overlap.
- The child-level business capabilities should completely describe their parent.
- Business capabilities should not imply an organizational structure, a solution method, or a degree of quality.

The business capability model is supposed to be a stable representation of your business. However, when companies undergo a transformation, quite often their business capabilities will change. New capabilities may be acquired, and existing capabilities may be enhanced or retired. You can evaluate the effectiveness of a capability and identify gaps and required improvements before committing to a specific solution. Specific solutions at this point are premature and can lead to chasing trends or the paths of your competitors, which fail to identify the competencies/abilities required for your business.

Business capabilities are used throughout the implementing phase and are essential in designing and executing the business solution, value realization, and delivery sequence.

Example: Let Us Eat Cakes

The business capabilities model for Let Us Eat Cakes can be described with seven first-level business capabilities and thirty-four second-level business capabilities as shown in figure 93 (below).

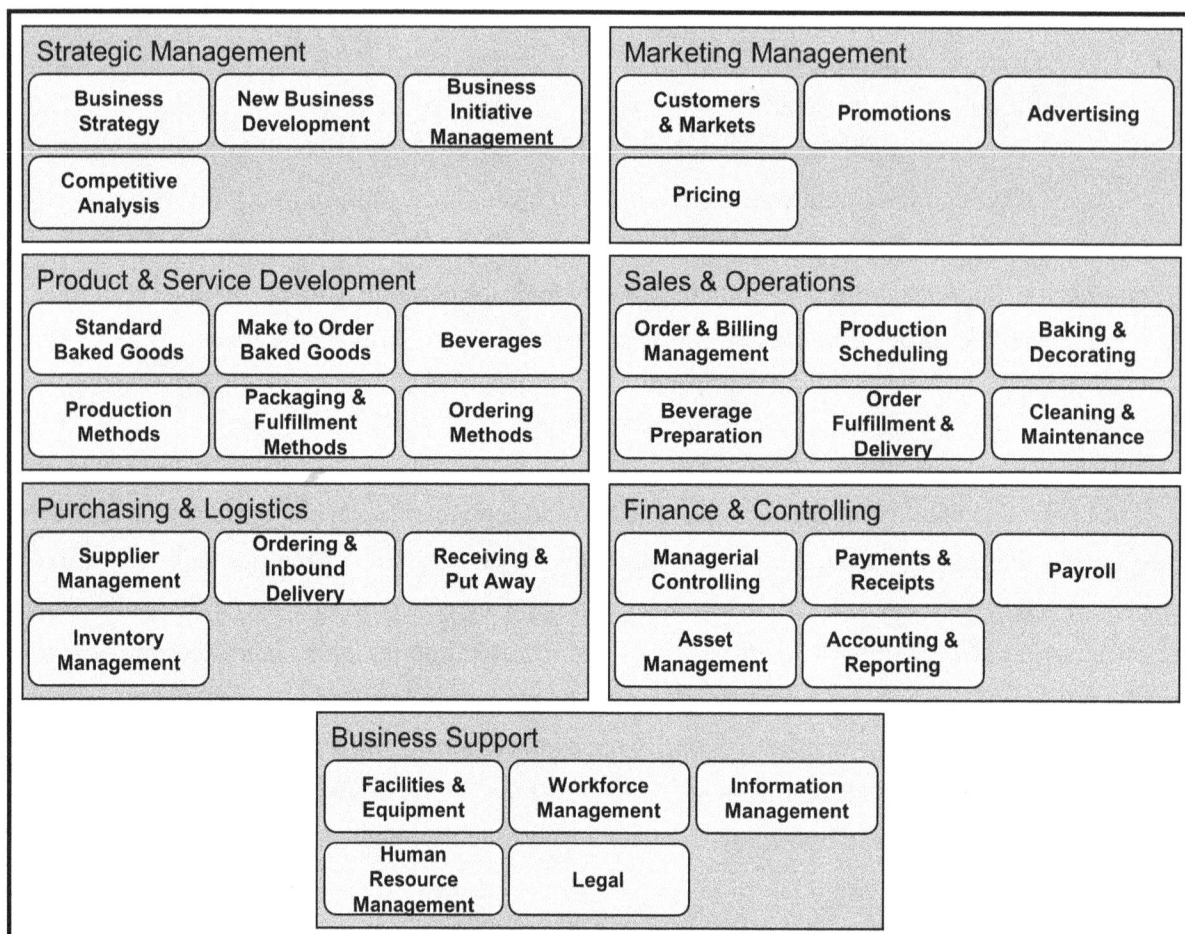

Figure 93: Let Us Eat Cakes Top Level Business Capabilities Model

The first-level capabilities cover the entire business operation including the following:

- strategic management
- marketing management
- product and service development
- sales and operations
- purchasing and logistics
- finance and controlling
- business support

Each first-level capability contains between four and six child capabilities. Level 3 for sales and operations is shown in figure 94 (below). Sales and operations is comprised of six level 2 business capabilities and twenty-three level 3 business capabilities. Even a small bakery like Let Us Eat Cakes will have more than one hundred level 3 business capabilities. Level 3 conveys the competencies Let Us Eat Cakes must possess to deliver value within their competitive environment. The Let Us Eat

Cakes business transformation may require enhancing some of these capabilities and adding new ones to support the transformation purpose and value.

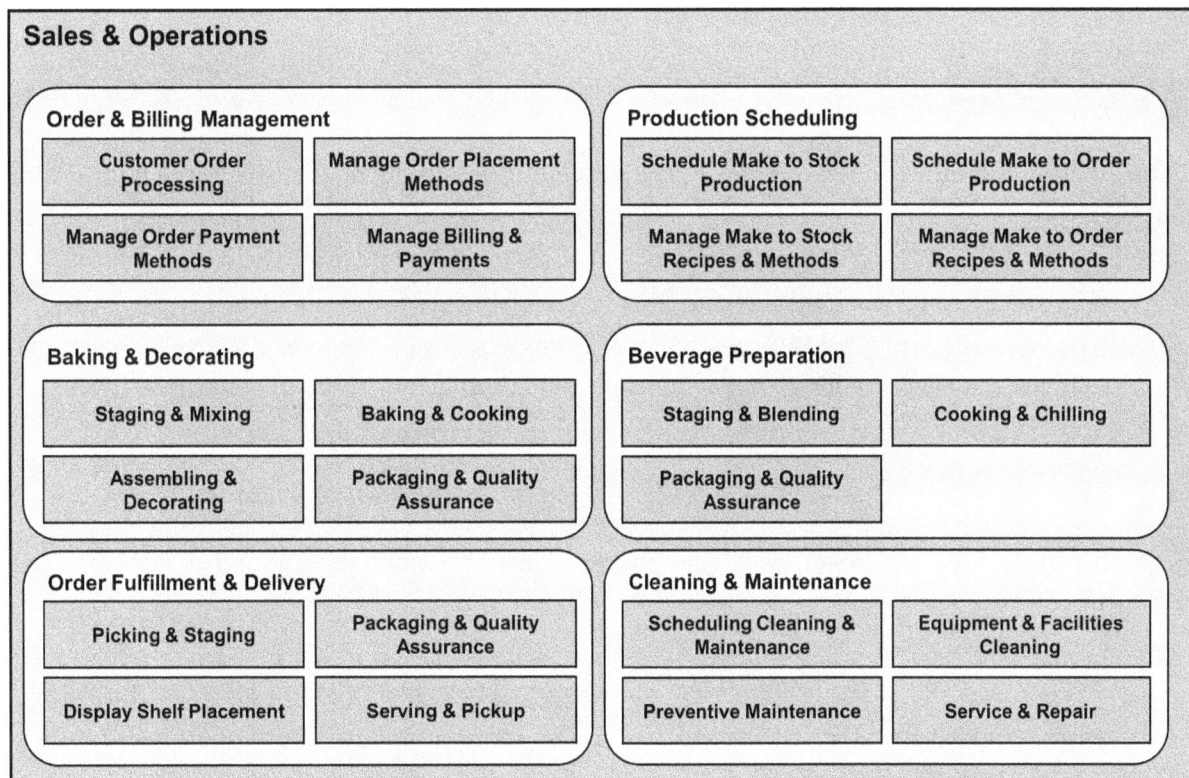

Sales & Operations

Order & Billing Management
Customer Order Processing	Manage Order Placement Methods
Manage Order Payment Methods	Manage Billing & Payments

Production Scheduling
Schedule Make to Stock Production	Schedule Make to Order Production
Manage Make to Stock Recipes & Methods	Manage Make to Order Recipes & Methods

Baking & Decorating
Staging & Mixing	Baking & Cooking
Assembling & Decorating	Packaging & Quality Assurance

Beverage Preparation
Staging & Blending	Cooking & Chilling
Packaging & Quality Assurance	

Order Fulfillment & Delivery
Picking & Staging	Packaging & Quality Assurance
Display Shelf Placement	Serving & Pickup

Cleaning & Maintenance
Scheduling Cleaning & Maintenance	Equipment & Facilities Cleaning
Preventive Maintenance	Service & Repair

Figure 94: Let Us Eat Cakes Level 2 Sales and Operations Business Capabilities Model

Readiness Assessment

As with the readiness goals introduced in chapter 5, a readiness assessment defines the "standard of readiness" and evaluates "achievement" toward that standard.

Readiness Assessment Standards

The readiness assessment standards are formally expressed as follows:

1. You have documented your current-state business capabilities.
2. You have documented the business capability changes required to support your business transformation.

If you know these, then you have attained readiness with respect to "Identify Required Business Capabilities." If you don't, you will need to complete the readiness preparation described later. As with all the readiness assessments, metrics are defined to evaluate your attainment of these standards.

Readiness Assessment Metrics

These metrics examine your company's readiness and allow you to identify the gaps in your understanding.

➢ Standard 1: You have documented your current-state business capabilities.

    a. Do you know what your company must be good at to deliver value to customers?

    b. Do you know your strengths/weaknesses with respect to your capabilities?

    c. Which capabilities, if any, are underutilized?

➢ Standard 2: You have documented the business capability changes required to support your business transformation.

    a. Have you identified the net new capabilities required to support your business transformation?

    b. Have you identified the existing capabilities that must be enhanced to support your business transformation?

    c. Have you identified the existing capabilities that must be discontinued to support your business transformation?

The complete readiness assessment for the goal "Identify Required Business Capabilities" is shown in figure 95 (below).

Readiness Assessment	#9: Identify Required Business Capabilities	
Assessment Standards	1. You have documented your current state business capabilities	2. You have documented the business capability changes required to support your business transformation
Assessment Metrics	a. Do you know what your company must be good at to deliver value to customers?	a. Have you identified the net new capabilities required to support your business transformation?
	b. Do you know your strengths/weaknesses with respect to your capabilities?	b. Have you identified the existing capabilities that must be enhanced to support your business transformation?
	c. Which capabilities, if any, are underutilized?	c. Have you identified the existing capabilities that must be discontinued to support your business transformation?

Figure 95: Readiness Assessment #9: Identify Required Business Capabilities

Creating an Actionable Assessment

The readiness assessment summarized in figure 95 (above) can be made actionable by converting the standards and metrics into deliverables and then combining them with the corresponding activities for producing them. Templates for readiness assessments and preparations are provided in the companion guide to this book.

Readiness Assessment Considerations

As you carry out the readiness assessment for this goal, there are a few considerations to keep in mind. First, identifying what your company needs to be good at can be subjective. Different companies will choose to service their customers in unique ways. If your business has a competitive advantage, does it overcompensate for missing competencies that would otherwise augment that advantage? You can use the results of voice-of-the-customer studies to help identify the gaps.

If you have underutilized capabilities, it is necessary to understand why they are underutilized. Underutilized capabilities can represent untapped assets. However, they can also represent unnecessary legacies consuming valuable resources to maintain them.

Finally, as you identify new business capabilities or enhancements to existing capabilities, you must look beyond the technologies and physical assets. Business capabilities should not represent solutions or implementations.

Readiness Preparation

The readiness assessment standards for identifying the required business capabilities were defined as follows:

1. You have documented your current-state business capabilities.
2. You have documented the business capability changes required to support your business transformation.

If your business is unable to attain these readiness assessment standards, then you will need to undertake the following preparation actions to remediate the gaps.

Readiness Preparation Actions

The actions you can take to help you understand the competencies and abilities your company needs to carry out business are formally expressed as follows:

1. Prepare a current-state business capabilities model.
2. Prepare a future-state business capabilities model.

By taking these actions, you ensure your business can attain the corresponding standards. The deliverables and activities presented next will guide you in completing these actions.

Readiness Preparation Steps

Every readiness assessment standard was assigned one or more metrics to facilitate evaluation. These metrics are now used in designing the preparation steps. One preparation step is required for each assessment metric.

➢ Action 1: Prepare a current-state business capabilities model.

Readiness was determined by answering the following three questions (i.e., readiness metrics), also shown in figure 95 (above):

182

a. Do you know what your company must be good at to deliver value to customers?

b. Do you know your strengths/weaknesses with respect to your capabilities?

c. Which capabilities, if any, are underutilized?

Metric A: Do you know what your company must be good at to deliver value to customers?

The preparation step is to create a business capabilities model. To produce this, the executive team reviews the company's value-proposition statements to identify the values created for customers. Each of these values depends on one or more operational competencies. The values and operational competencies are candidates for the business capabilities. The business capabilities are then arranged in a hierarchical tree following the guidelines.

Metric B: Do you know your strengths/weaknesses with respect to your capabilities?

The preparation step consists of annotating your business capabilities model to indicate whether a business capability is a strength or weakness. The executive team can use information from Goal #1: Understand Your Business to assess your company's level of competency with each business capability. A simple annotation scheme (e.g., green/yellow/red) can be used to indicate strength/acceptable/weakness, respectively, for each capability.

Metric C: Which capabilities, if any, are underutilized?

The preparation step consists of annotating your business capabilities model to indicate whether a business capability is underutilized in delivering value. The executive team can again use the information from Goal #1: Understand Your Business to identify competencies that are underutilized (or not utilized at all). A simple annotation scheme (e.g., blue box) can be used to indicate an underutilized/unutilized capability.

The current-state business capabilities model is an aggregate of the three preparation steps for action 1.

➢ Action 2: Prepare a future-state business capabilities model.

Readiness was determined by answering the following three questions (i.e., readiness metrics), also shown in figure 95 (above):

a. Have you identified the net new capabilities required to support your business transformation?

b. Have you identified the existing capabilities that must be enhanced to support your business transformation?

c. Have you identified the existing capabilities that must be discontinued to support your business transformation?

Metric A: Have you identified the net new capabilities required to support your business transformation?

The preparation step is to identify the net new capabilities required to support your business transformation. To carry out this step, the executive team reviews the transformation statement of value produced in Goal #2: Define the Reason for the Transformation, to identify new business values introduced through the transformation. The executive team then reviews the statement of transformation impact and change impact matrix produced in Goal #6: Understand Impacts of Change to identify new capabilities required to complete the transformation. Finally, the new capabilities are added to the current-state business capabilities model (produced via action 1, above).

Metric B: Have you identified the existing capabilities that must be enhanced to support your business transformation?

The preparation step is to identify the existing capabilities that must be enhanced to support your business transformation. To carry out this step, the executive team reviews the transformation statement of value produced in Goal #2: Define the Reason for the Transformation, to identify existing business values modified by the transformation. The executive team then reviews the statement of transformation impact and change impact matrix produced in Goal #6: Understand Impacts of Change, to identify existing capabilities that must be enhanced to complete the transformation. Finally, the existing capabilities that must be enhanced are annotated in the current-state business capabilities model.

Metric C: Have you identified the existing capabilities that must be discontinued to support your business transformation?

The preparation step is to identify the existing capabilities that must be discontinued to support your business transformation. The executive team carries out this step by first reviewing the transformation statement of value produced in Goal #2: Define the Reason for the Transformation to identify existing business values discontinued through the transformation. The executive team then reviews the statement of transformation impact and change impact matrix produced in Goal #6: Understand Impacts of Change, to identify existing capabilities that must be discontinued to complete the transformation. Finally, the existing capabilities that must be discontinued are annotated in the current-state business capabilities model.

The future-state business capabilities model is an aggregate of the three preparation steps for action 2. The complete readiness preparation for the goal "Identify Required Business Capabilities" is shown in figure 96 (below).

Readiness Preparation	#9: Identify Required Business Capabilities	
Preparation Actions	1. Prepare a Current State Business Capabilities Model	2. Prepare a Future State Business Capabilities Model
Preparation Steps	a. Create a business capabilities model framework	a. Identify the net new capabilities required to support your business transformation
	b. Annotate your business capabilities model to indicate whether a business capability is a strength or weakness	b. Identify the existing capabilities that must be enhanced to support your business transformation
	c. Annotate your business capabilities model to indicate whether a business capability is underutilized in delivering value	c. Identify the existing capabilities that must be discontinued to support your business transformation

Figure 96: Readiness Preparation #9: Identify the Required Business Capabilities

Creating an Actionable Preparation

The readiness preparation summarized in figure 96 (above) can be made actionable by converting the actions and steps into deliverables and then combining them with the corresponding activities for producing them. Templates for readiness assessments and preparations are provided in the companion guide to this book.

Readiness Preparation Considerations

There are several things to be aware of as you work through the action and preparation steps for "Identify Required Business Capabilities."

Prepare a Current-State Business Capabilities Model

As you prepare your s business capabilities model, ensure you are following the guidelines. Resist the temptation to include too much detail. While the detail may be useful to specific functional groups, if you create a model beyond three levels, it will become a process model or functional model. You may find it useful to engage an outside consulting firm to help you prepare your business capabilities model.

You need to critically evaluate business capabilities that have been carried along for years but are no longer needed. There can be a great deal of organizational inertia holding them in place. If it's nothing more than that, discontinue the capabilities and repurpose the freed-up resources. Conversely, if there are business capabilities that are underutilized, it may be possible to leverage them to an even greater extent, turning them into assets.

Prepare a Future-State Business Capabilities Model

When you consider business change impacts as a source for new business capabilities, bear in mind that they are at a very low level. You may need to abstract or reframe the change impacts as business capabilities. You should mostly use the what and how dimensions of the change impact matrix. If you do use the how dimension, avoid specifying the method implied in the how. A business capabilities model should not contain processes or implementation methods.

When one of your current business capabilities needs to be enhanced, you will need to understand your company's current strengths/weaknesses with respect to that capability. The capability may be changed to such a great extent that it is easier to discontinue the capability "as is" and introduce an entirely new business capability. You can use the why dimension changes to gauge how much modification is necessary.

Goal #10: Specify Required Business Solution

"Specify Required Business Solution" means you have a complete description of how the required business capabilities will be implemented and how your value objectives will be achieved in the transformation. The business solution must include everything that is created, enhanced, or removed. This goes beyond technology and physical assets and includes processes, policies, organization structures, work content, and locations. There can be no gaps or inconsistencies, and the new parts of the solution must be fully integrated into the existing solution. If the required business solution isn't defined in its entirety, then neither the business capabilities nor the value objectives can be realized—and the transformation cannot be completed.

Business Solutions and Documentation

This book does not advocate one business solution over another or provide instructions for how to design business solutions. The treatment will focus on readiness with respect to the business solution—that is, validating whether the business solution satisfies the readiness standards, and if not, recommending steps to remediate gaps or deficiencies. However, since this readiness goal is concerned with business solutions, it is necessary to provide the reader with some idea of the nature of business solutions and their accompanying documentation.

The objective of the business solution is to solve for the change impacts induced by your business transformation. Change impacts were captured in the transformation change impact matrix produced in the readiness preparation for Goal #6: Understand the Impact of the Change. Recall that the change impact matrix organized change impacts by business change (the rows) and change impact dimension (the columns) as shown in figure 78.

Each type of change impact is addressed by a specific type of business solution. In turn, each type of business solution requires a specific type of documentation. The most likely business solution and documentation types are summarized in figure 97 (below) for each change impact.

If your company does not possess the skills and experience to develop and document a business solution, then you should engage an external business solution partner to help you. Business readiness goals #10, #15, and #16 (figure 92) depend heavily on competency in business solution development.

#	Change Impact Dimension	Change Impacts	Solution Types	Documentation Types
1	**WHAT** Content & Deliverables	Changes to work content or the deliverables for the job that must be done [ ] Add New [ ] Discontinue [ ] Modify [ ] Combine [ ] Split	External Work Products & Services	External Product and Service Catalogs, Specifications, Marketing Materials, Contracts, Service Agreements, etc.
			Internal Work Products & Services	Internal Product and Service Catalogs, Specifications, etc.
2	**HOW** Methods & Procedures	Changes to work methods, policies or procedures [ ] Add New [ ] Discontinue [ ] Modify	Processes & Workflows	Process Flow Diagrams
			Procedures	Work Instructions
			Policies	Guidelines & Service Agreements
			Knowledge & Skills	Training Materials
			Tools & Equipment	Blueprints, Specifications, Instruction Manuals, etc.
			Software & Hardware Technology	System Specifications, Instruction Manuals, etc.
3	**WHO** Relationships	Changes to work relationships including internal, reporting, customer, supplier, regulatory, etc. [ ] Add New [ ] Discontinue [ ] Modify	Organizational Structure	Organizational Charts
			Internal Staff	Staffing Plans, Job Specifications, etc.
			Trading Partners	Contractual Agreements, Contacts, etc.
			Agencies	Policies, Regulations, Procedures, Contracts, etc.

#	Change Impact Dimension	Change Impacts	Solution Types	Documentation Types
4	**WHERE** Locations	Changes to work location including workspaces, offices, customers and suppliers [ ] Add New [ ] Discontinue [ ] Modify	Buildings & Facilities	Leases & Deeds, Construction Plans, Blueprints, Specifications and Operations Manuals
			Offices & Workspaces	Office/Workspace Layouts, Specifications, etc.
5	**WHEN** Timing & Cycles	Changes to the timing (start/stop) or cycles of work [ ] Add New [ ] Discontinue [ ] Modify	Business Calendar & Cadence	Company Calendar & Business Event Guidelines
			Time and Attendance Policies	Employee Guidelines & Agreements
6	**WHY** Purpose & Motivation	Changes to work purpose, reason or motivation [ ] Add New [ ] Discontinue [ ] Modify	Company Mission & Purpose	Company & Investor Relation Materials
			Company Policies	Employee Guidelines & Agreements
			Code of Conduct	Employee Handbook
			Incentives & Compensation	Labor Agreements, Contracts, Plan Specifications, etc.

Figure 97: Business Solution Types and Documentation Types for Each Change Impact Dimension

Readiness Assessment

Readiness Assessment Standards

The readiness assessment standards are formally expressed as follows:

1. Your documented business transformation solution is complete.
2. Your documented business transformation solution is consistent.

If you know these, you have attained readiness with respect to "Specify Required Business Solution." If you don't, you will need to complete the readiness preparation described later. As with all the readiness assessments, metrics are defined to evaluate your attainment of these standards.

Readiness Assessment Metrics

These metrics examine your company's readiness and allow you to identify the gaps in your understanding.

➤ Standard 1: Your documented business transformation solution is complete.

   a. Does your business solution address all the change impacts induced by your transformation?
   b. Is your business solution aligned to the future-state business capabilities model?
   c. Does your business solution clearly identify the solution elements that must be purchased, licensed, or built, as well as those already in place?
   d. Does your business solution contain any gaps that would prevent or degrade business operations?

➤ Standard 2: Your documented business transformation solution is consistent.

   a. Have you identified the portion of the existing business solution (carrying out current-state business capabilities) that will remain after the transformation and the portion that will be discontinued?
   b. Does your new business solution coexist (in a noncontradictory manner) with the portion of the existing business solution that will remain after the transformation?

The complete readiness assessment for the goal "Identify Required Business Capabilities" is shown in figure 98 (below).

Creating an Actionable Assessment

The readiness assessment summarized in figure 98 (below) can be made actionable by converting the standards and metrics into deliverables and then combining them with the corresponding activities for producing them. Templates for readiness assessments and preparations are provided in the companion guide to this book.

Readiness Assessment	#10: Specify Required Business Solution	
Assessment Standards	1. Your documented business transformation solution is complete	2. Your documented business transformation solution is consistent
Assessment Metrics	a. Does your business solution address all the change impacts induced in your transformation?	a. Have you identified the portion of the existing business solution that will remain after the transformation and the portion which will be discontinued?
	b. Is your business solution aligned to the future state business capabilities model?	b. Does your new business solution coexist (in a non-contradictory manner) with the portion of the existing business solution that will remain after the transformation?
	c. Does your business solution clearly identify the solution elements which must be purchased, licensed, or built, as well as those already in place?	
	d. Does your business solution contain any gaps that would prevent or degrade business operations?	

Figure 98: Readiness Assessment #10: Specify Required Business Solution

Readiness Assessment Considerations

As you evaluate whether your business solution addresses each change impact induced in your transformation, make sure all dimensions of the change impact profile are considered in the solution design: what, how, who, where, when, and why. The business solution must cover more than the what and how impacts.

You should be able to identify the elements in your business solution that will support each business capability in your future-state business capabilities model. This will be easier for the newly added business capabilities and more challenging for the existing business capabilities, especially if your current business solution is insufficiently documented.

Your proposed future-state business solution must include the sources for all solution elements (purchased, licensed, built, or already existing) as this information will be used to refine estimates for the transformation investment (time and cost). If prepackaged, off-the-shelf software/hardware or other preexisting services are used, they can induce gaps in addressing change impacts—some of which could impact your business operations. You must identify the gaps and ensure they can be addressed by some other solution element (purchased, licensed, built, or already existing).

It can be tricky to evaluate whether your new business solution coexists (in a noncontradictory manner) with the portion of the existing business solution that remains after the transformation. You could have preexisting consistency issues as well. Without adequate documentation, these can be difficult to find. You can interview the people responsible for carrying out the flow of work through these solution elements to help discover preexisting inconsistencies. You can also use this same group to detect inconsistencies between new solution elements and the existing business solution remaining after the transformation.

Readiness Preparation

The readiness assessment standards for Specifying the Required Business Solution were defined as follows:

1. Your documented business transformation solution is complete.
2. Your documented business transformation solution is consistent.

If your business is unable to attain these readiness assessment standards, then you will need to undertake the following preparation actions to remediate the gaps.

Readiness Preparation Actions

The actions you can take to help you specify the business solution required for your business transformation are formally expressed as follows:

1. Validate completeness of your business transformation solution.
2. Validate consistency of your business transformation solution.

By taking these actions, you ensure your business can attain the corresponding standards. The deliverables and activities presented next will guide you in completing these actions.

Readiness Preparation Steps

Every readiness assessment standard was assigned one or more metrics to facilitate evaluation. These metrics are now used in designing the preparation steps. One preparation step is required for each assessment metric.

➢ Action 1: Validate completeness of your business transformation solution.

Readiness was determined by answering the following three questions (i.e., readiness metrics), also shown in figure 98 (above):

   a. Does your business solution address all the change impacts induced in your transformation?
   b. Is your business solution aligned to the future-state business capabilities model?
   c. Does your business solution clearly identify the solution elements that must be purchased, licensed, or built, as well as those already in place?
   d. Does your business solution contain any gaps that would prevent or degrade business operations?

Metric A: Does your business solution address all the change impacts induced in your transformation?

The preparation step is the specification of solution elements to address each change impact induced by your transformation. The business-transformation implementation leaders first review the statement of transformation impact and change impact matrix produced in goal #6: Understand Impacts of Change to ensure the proposed business solution addresses each change impact. The change impact matrix is then tagged with the corresponding element of the business solution that addresses it. Finally, the business-transformation implementation leaders ensure all dimensions of the change impact matrix are addressed—what, how, who, where, when, and why—not just what and how.

The change impact matrix can be augmented to facilitate tagging the change impacts with the business-solution elements addressing them. Solution type, solution element, and solution element ID fields are added as shown in figure 99 (below).

- Solution type: This column represents the potential type of solution associated with each change impact dimension.
- Solution element: This is the name of the solution from your business-solution documentation.
- Solution element ID: This is a unique identifier associated with the business-solution element addressing the change impact.

Once the solution type, element, and element ID are added to the change impact matrix, it is easy to check whether every business change impact has been addressed by your future-state business solution.

#	Business Changes	What				How				...
		Content & Deliverables	Solution Type	Solution Element	Solution Element ID	Methods & Procedures	Solution Type	Solution Element	Solution Element ID	...
1	Product Scope	[ ] Add New [ ] Discontinue [ ] Modify [ ] Combine [ ] Split Product Scope Induced Products or Services	[ ] External Work Products & Services [ ] Internal Work Products & Services	<Name of Solution Element>	<Unique Identifier for Solution Element>	[ ] Add New [ ] Discontinue [ ] Modify Product Scope Induced Sourcing, Production, Selling, Marketing, Fulfillment, Financial or Business Support <Method, Policy, or Procedure>	[ ] Processes & Workflows [ ] Procedures [ ] Policies [ ] Knowledge & Skills [ ] Tools & Equipment [ ] Software & Hardware Technology	<Name of Solution Element>	<Unique Identifier for Solution Element>	...
2	Service Scope	[ ] Add New [ ] Discontinue [ ] Modify [ ] Combine [ ] Split Service Scope Induced Products or Services	[ ] External Work Products & Services [ ] Internal Work Products & Services	<Name of Solution Element>	<Unique Identifier for Solution Element>	[ ] Add New [ ] Discontinue [ ] Modify Service Scope Induced Sourcing, Production, Selling, Marketing, Fulfillment, Financial or Business Support <Method, Policy, or Procedure>	[ ] Processes & Workflows [ ] Procedures [ ] Policies [ ] Knowledge & Skills [ ] Tools & Equipment [ ] Software & Hardware Technology	<Name of Solution Element>	<Unique Identifier for Solution Element>	...
.	.	.				.	.	.	.	...

Figure 99: Business Solution Augmented Change Impact Matrix

Metric B: Is your business solution aligned to the future-state business capabilities model?

The preparation step is to map each future-state business capability to the elements of the business solution that addresses it. The business-transformation implementation leaders first review the future-state business capability model to ensure the proposed business solution addresses each new and enhanced capability. The future-state business capability model is then tagged with the corresponding element of the business solution that addresses it. Finally, the business-transformation implementation leaders ensure the discontinued business capabilities are still tagged with their corresponding business-solution elements. If a solution element is only used to address a discontinued business capability, the solution element can be discontinued as well.

The future-state business capability model can be augmented to facilitate tagging the level 3 business capabilities with the business-solution elements addressing them. The solution element and solution element ID fields are added to a tree version of the future-state business capability model. This is shown for an excerpt of the Let Us Eat Cakes Business Capability model in figure 100 (below). Once the solution element and element ID are added to the future-state business capability model, it is easy to check whether every business capability has been addressed by your future-state business solution.

Level 1	Level 2	Level 3	Solution Element	Solution Element ID
Strategic Management	Business Strategy			
	New Business Development			
	Business Initiative Management			
⋮				
Sales & Operations	Order & Billing Management	Customer Order Processing	\<Name of Solution Element\>	\<Unique Identifier for Solution Element\>
		Manage Order Placement Methods	\<Name of Solution Element\>	\<Unique Identifier for Solution Element\>
		Manage Order Payment Methods	\<Name of Solution Element\>	\<Unique Identifier for Solution Element\>
		Manage Billing & Payment	\<Name of Solution Element\>	\<Unique Identifier for Solution Element\>
	Production Scheduling	Schedule Make to Stock Production	\<Name of Solution Element\>	\<Unique Identifier for Solution Element\>
		⋮		
	⋮			
⋮				

Figure 100: Let Us Eat Cakes (Excerpt) Business Solution Augmented Future-State Business Capability Model

Metric C: Does your business solution clearly identify the solution elements that must be purchased, licensed, or built, as well as those already in place?

The preparation step is to identify the source for each element of the business solution: purchase, license, built, or already exists. The business-transformation implementation leaders first review all the business-solution elements to determine how each element will be implemented during the transformation. Each business-solution element is then tagged with the intended implementation source/method: purchase, license, build, or already exists.

The future-state business-solution document can be augmented to facilitate tagging each solution element with the source/method. The solution type and solution source fields are added as shown in figure 101 (below). Once the solution type and source are added to the future-state business-solution document, it can be used in planning implementation and delivery.

Business Solution Element	Solution Element ID	Solution Type	Solution Source
\<Name of Solution Element\>	\<Unique Identifier for Solution Element\>	[ ] External Work Products & Services [ ] Internal Work Products & Services [ ] Processes & Workflows [ ] Procedures [ ] Policies [ ] Knowledge & Skills [ ] Tools & Equipment [ ] Software & Hardware Technology [ ] Organizational Structure [ ] Internal Staff [ ] Trading Partners [ ] Agencies [ ] Buildings & Facilities [ ] Offices & Workspaces [ ] Business Calendar & Cadence [ ] Time and Attendance Policies [ ] Company Mission & Purpose [ ] Company Policies [ ] Code of Conduct [ ] Incentives & Compensation	[ ] Purchase [ ] License [ ] Build [ ] Exists
. . .	. . .	. . .	. . .

Figure 101: Source/Method Augmented Future-State Business Solution Document

Metric D: Does your business solution contain any gaps that would prevent or degrade business operations?

The preparation step is to ensure there are no solution gaps for any of the future-state business capabilities. The business-transformation implementation leaders first review the future-state business capability model to identify gaps or discontinuities among the solution elements addressing each business capability. Gaps and discontinuities are then addressed through additional business-solution elements or by redesigning the proposed business-solution elements.

➢ Action 2: Validate consistency of your business transformation solution.

Readiness was determined by answering the following two questions (i.e., readiness metrics), also shown in figure 98 (above):

a. Have you identified the portions of the existing business solution (carrying out current-state business capabilities) that will remain after the transformation and be discontinued?
b. Does your new business solution coexist (in a noncontradictory manner) with the portion of the existing business solution that will remain after the transformation?

Metric A: Have you identified the portions of the existing business solution (carrying out current-state business capabilities) that will remain after the transformation and be discontinued?

The preparation step is to determine which portions of the existing business solution will remain in place and which will be decommissioned after the transformation. The business-transformation implementation leaders first review the future-state business capability model to identify existing capabilities that will be discontinued after your business transformation. The discontinued business capabilities are then tagged for removal, and the corresponding elements of the business solution are identified for potential removal. If a solution element is only used to address a discontinued business capability, the solution element can be discontinued as well.

Metric B: Does your new business solution coexist (in a noncontradictory manner) with the portion of the existing business solution that will remain after the transformation?

The preparation step ensures there are no inconsistencies among the elements of the new business solution and the portion of the existing business solution remaining after the transformation. The business-transformation implementation leaders first review the future-state business capability model to identify inconsistencies among the solution elements addressing each business capability. Inconsistencies are then addressed through redesign of the proposed business-solution elements.

The complete readiness preparation for the goal "Specify Required Business Solution" is shown in figure 102 (below).

Readiness Preparation	#10: Specify Required Business Solution	
Preparation Actions	1. Validate completeness of your business transformation solution	2. Validate consistency of your business transformation solution
Preparation Steps	a. Specify solution elements to address each change impact induced in your transformation	a. Determine which portions of the existing business solution will remain in place and which will be decommissioned after the transformation
	b. Map each future state business capability to the elements of the business solution that addresses it	b. Ensure there are no inconsistencies among the elements of the new business solution and the portion of the existing business solution that will remain after the transformation
	c. Identify the source for each element of the business solution - purchase, license, built, already exists	
	d. Ensure there are no solution gaps for any of the future state business capabilities	

Figure 102: Readiness Preparation #11: Specify Required Business Solution

Creating an Actionable Preparation

The readiness preparation summarized in figure 102 (above) can be made actionable by converting the actions and steps into deliverables and then combining them with the corresponding activities for producing them. Templates for readiness assessments and preparations are provided in the companion guide to this book.

Readiness Preparation Considerations

Consider the following as you work through the action and preparation steps for "Specify Required Business Solution."

Validate Completeness of Your Business Transformation Solution

You must identify the complete business solution required to address all change impacts—not just the technologies used to implement the how impacts. Also, note that some solution choices can create unintended change impacts to other dimensions of the change impact profile. For example, when prepackaged software is part of the solution, the prepackaged solution may assume other solution elements are already in place. If they are not in place, they will need to be included in your business solution as well.

The future-state business capability model contains the existing business capabilities that remain after the transformation—plus the enhanced and newly added capabilities. If you do not have documentation for the solution elements supporting the existing business capabilities, you can create it at this time. While it requires additional work, it can be used during future transformations or continuous improvement efforts.

It's worthwhile to create design guidelines to help navigate the wide range of solution options. Complexity introduced during the design objective is carried through to the execution objective and beyond. It should be noted that even solution elements that are purchased or licensed will still require the build-out of policies, data, workflow, user access management, and other administrative services. These must also be included as part of the business solution.

As you evaluate solution gaps, note that each business capability implies a flow of activities where some steps are carried out by people and some through technology. Furthermore, some of the steps may be carried out by entities outside of your company. You will need to check the flow of all activity workflows to identify and resolve workflow gaps or discontinuities.

Validate Consistency of Your Business Transformation Solution

When you consider eliminating existing business-solution elements that are no longer required, note that these solution elements may be used to support more than just discontinued business capabilities. If that is the case, you will either need to partially decommission the existing business solution, if possible, or support the retained business capability with a different business-solution element.

The new business-solution elements may cause some of the existing business-solution elements to become redundant. You must ensure that the redundancies do not introduce inconsistent behavior. You can also check existing policies for conflict with the new policies.

Goal #11: Specify Value Realization

Value objectives, documented as part of the readiness preparation for Goal #2: Define the Reason for the Transformation, quantified the purpose of a transformation into tangible and intangible benefits. Value realization relates the value objectives to the required business capabilities and the corresponding parts of the business solution. Without value realization, it is difficult to tell whether the transformation's purpose can be achieved through the business solution. Also, if the solution is created and delivered incrementally, it will be difficult to know whether the value objectives can be realized incrementally as well.

Readiness Assessment

Readiness Assessment Standards

The readiness assessment standards are formally expressed as follows:

1. Your transformation value objectives can be fully achieved through your future-state business capabilities.
2. Your transformation value objectives can be fully realized through your business solution.

If you know these, you have attained readiness with respect to "Specify Value Realization." If you don't, you will need to complete the readiness preparation described later. As with all the readiness assessments, metrics are defined to evaluate your attainment of these standards.

Readiness Assessment Metrics

These metrics examine your company's readiness and allow you to identify the gaps in your understanding.

➢ Standard 1: Your transformation value objectives can be fully achieved through your future-state business capabilities.

    a. Are your value objectives mapped to one or more future-state business capabilities?

    b. If these future-state business capabilities are achieved, will your value objectives be fully achieved?

➢ Standard 2: Your transformation value objectives can be fully realized through your business solution.

    a. Are your value objectives mapped to one or more business-solution elements?

    b. If these business-solution elements are implemented, will your value objectives be fully realized?

The complete readiness assessment for the goal "Specify Value Realization" is shown in figure 103 (below).

Readiness Assessment	#11: Specify Value Realization	
Assessment Standards	**1. Your transformation value objectives can be fully achieved through your future state business capabilities**	**2. Your transformation value objectives can be fully realized through your business solution**
Assessment Metrics	a. Are your value objectives mapped to one or more future state business capabilities?	a. Are your value objectives mapped to one or more business solution elements?
	b. If these future state business capabilities are achieved will your value objectives be fully achieved?	b. If these business solution elements are implemented will your value objectives be fully realized?

Figure 103: Readiness Assessment #11: Specify Value Realization

Creating an Actionable Assessment

The readiness assessment summarized in figure 103 (above) can be made actionable by converting the standards and metrics into deliverables and then combining them with the corresponding activities for

producing them. Templates for readiness assessments and preparations are provided in the companion guide to this book.

Readiness Assessment Considerations

Mapping your value objectives to future-state business capabilities are the necessary conditions to ensure your value objectives can be met. You must be able to identify a direct achievement connection between your future-state business capabilities and your value objectives. The sufficient conditions are to verify that once your business capabilities are achieved in full, your value objectives will be achieved as well. You must be able to demonstrate that no additional business capabilities, outside of those specified in your future state, are required to achieve your value objectives.

Similarly, mapping your value objectives to your business-solution elements are the necessary conditions to ensure your value objectives can be met. You must be able to identify a direct achievement connection between your business solution and your value objectives. Likewise, the sufficient conditions are to verify that once your business solution is realized in full, your value objectives will be realized as well. You must be able to demonstrate that no additional solution elements, outside of those specified in your business solution, are required to realize your value objectives.

Readiness Preparation

The readiness assessment standards for specifying value realization were defined as follows:

1. Your transformation value objectives can be fully achieved through your future-state business capabilities.
2. Your transformation value objectives can be fully realized through your business solution.

If your business is unable to attain these readiness assessment standards, you will need to undertake the following preparation actions to remediate the gaps.

Readiness Preparation Actions

The actions you can take to help you relate your value objectives to the required business capabilities and their corresponding parts of the business solution are formally expressed as follows:

1. Map your transformation value objectives to the future-state business capabilities required to fully achieve them.

2. Map your transformation value objectives to the business-solution elements required to fully realize them.

By taking these actions, you ensure your business can attain the corresponding standards. The deliverables and activities presented next will guide you in completing these actions.

Readiness Preparation Steps

Every readiness assessment standard was assigned one or more metrics to facilitate evaluation. These metrics are now used in designing the preparation steps. One preparation step is required for each assessment metric.

➤ Action 1: Map your transformation value objectives to the future-state business capabilities required to fully achieve them.

Readiness was determined by answering the following two questions (i.e., readiness metrics), also shown in figure 103 (above):

a. Are your value objectives mapped to one or more future-state business capabilities?
b. If these future-state business capabilities are achieved, will your value objectives be fully achieved?

Metric A: Are your value objectives mapped to one or more future-state business capabilities?

The preparation step maps all value objectives to the future-state business capabilities required to fully achieve them. The business-transformation implementation leaders first review the statement of value produced in Goal #2: Define the Reason for the Transformation and the future-state capabilities model produced in Goal #9: Identify Required Business Capabilities. The future-state business capability model is then tagged with the corresponding value objective it addresses. Finally, the business-transformation implementation leaders ensure all value objectives have been assigned to one or more business capability.

The future-state business capability model can be augmented, as was done for Goal #10: Specify Required Business Solution, to facilitate tagging the level 3 business capabilities with the value objectives they address. Value objective and quantified improvement fields are added to a tree version of the future-state business capability model. This is shown for an excerpt of the Let Us Eat Cakes Business Capability Model in figure 104 (below). Once the value objective and quantified improvement information have been added to the future-state business capability model, it is easy to check whether all value objectives have been addressed by your business capabilities.

Level 1	Level 2	Level 3	Value Objective	Quantified Improvement
Strategic Management	Business Strategy			
	New Business Development			
	Business Initiative Management			
. . .				
Sales & Operations	Order & Billing Management	Customer Order Processing	<Business Value to be Improved>	<Expected Amount of Improvement>
		Manage Order Placement Methods	<Business Value to be Improved>	<Expected Amount of Improvement>
		Manage Order Payment Methods	<Business Value to be Improved>	<Expected Amount of Improvement>
		Manage Billing & Payment	<Business Value to be Improved>	<Expected Amount of Improvement>
	Production Scheduling	Schedule Make to Stock Production	<Business Value to be Improved>	<Expected Amount of Improvement>
		. . .		
	. . .			
. . .				

Figure 104: Let Us Eat Cakes (Excerpt) Value Objectives Augmented Future-State Business Capability Model

Metric B: If these future-state business capabilities are achieved, will your value objectives be fully achieved?

The preparation step ensures that when your future-state business capabilities have been achieved, your value objectives will also be fully achieved. The business-transformation implementation leaders first review the future-state business capability model augmented with your transformation value objectives to identify all the business capabilities associated with each value objective. They then determine whether each value objective is fully achieved whenever the associated business capabilities are achieved. Finally, if there is a capability that is missing, it must be added to the future-state business capabilities model. Otherwise, your value objectives will not be fully achieved.

➢ Action 2: Map your transformation value objectives to the business-solution elements required to fully realize them.

Readiness was determined by answering the following two questions (i.e., readiness metrics), also shown in figure 103 (above):

a. Are your value objectives mapped to one or more business-solution elements?
b. If these business-solution elements are implemented, will your value objectives be fully realized?

Metric A: Are your value objectives mapped to one or more business-solution elements?

The preparation step is to map all value objectives to the business-solution elements required to fully realize them. The business-transformation implementation leaders first review the statement of value produced in Goal #2: Define the Reason for the Transformation and the business solution produced in Goal #10: Specify Required Business Solution. The business-solution document is then tagged with the corresponding value objective it addresses. Finally, the business-transformation implementation leaders ensure all value objectives have been assigned to one or more business-solution element.

The business-solution document can be augmented, as was done for Goal #10: Specify Required Business Solution, to facilitate tagging each solution element with the value objectives they address. Value objective and quantified improvement fields are added as shown in figure 105 (below). Once the value objective and quantified improvement information have been added to the business-solution document, it is easy to check whether all value objectives have been addressed by your business solution.

Business Solution Element	Solution Element ID	Value Objective	Quantified Improvement
<Name of Solution Element>	<Unique Identifier for Solution Element>	<Business Value to be Improved>	<Expected Amount of Improvement>
<Name of Solution Element>	<Unique Identifier for Solution Element>	<Business Value to be Improved>	<Expected Amount of Improvement>
<Name of Solution Element>	<Unique Identifier for Solution Element>	<Business Value to be Improved>	<Expected Amount of Improvement>
. . .	. . .	. . .	. . .

Figure 105: Value Objectives Augmented Future-State Business Solution Document

Metric B: If these business-solution elements are implemented, will your value objectives be fully realized?

The preparation step ensures that when your business-solution elements have been achieved, your value objectives will also be fully realized. The business-transformation implementation leaders first review the business-solution document augmented with your transformation value objectives to identify all the business-solution elements associated with each value objective. They then determine whether each value objective is fully realized whenever the associated business-solution elements are realized. Finally, if there is a solution element that is missing, it must be added to the business solution. Otherwise, your value objectives will not be fully realized.

The complete readiness preparation for the goal "Specify Value Realization" is shown in figure 106 (below).

Readiness Preparation	#11: Specify Value Realization	
Preparation Actions	1. Map your transformation value objectives to the future state business capabilities required to fully achieve them	2. Map your transformation value objectives to the business solution elements required to fully realize them
Preparation Steps	a. Map all value objectives to your future state business capabilities required to fully achieve them	a. Map all value objectives to your business solution elements
	b. Ensure that when these future state business capabilities have been achieved, your value objectives will also be fully achieved	b. Ensure that when these business solution elements have been achieved, your value objectives will also be fully realized

Figure 106: Readiness Preparation #11: Specify Value Realization

Creating an Actionable Preparation

The readiness preparation summarized in figure 106 (above) can be made actionable by converting the actions and steps into deliverables and then combining them with the corresponding activities for producing them. Templates for readiness assessments and preparations are provided in the companion guide to this book.

Readiness Preparation Considerations

Map your transformation value objectives to the future-state business capabilities required to fully achieve them. Your future-state business capabilities must be expressed in a way that illustrates the linkage back to your value objectives. The augmentation shown in figure 104 (above) will help, but you may need to add notation to your value objectives to identify all business capabilities supporting them (this is the inverse direction). These linkages will help you carry out Goal #19: Specify Path to Value.

Map your transformation value objectives to the business-solution elements required to fully realize them.

Your business solution must be expressed in a way that illustrates the linkage back to your value objectives. You don't want to rely only on the mapping through business capabilities to your business-solution elements. It's not always possible to achieve perfect alignment and you may not be able to express every business capability you need. The augmentation shown in figure 105 (above) will help, but you may need to add notation to your value objectives to identify all business-solution elements supporting them (this is the inverse direction). As in the case with the business capabilities, these linkages will help you carry out Goal #19: Specify Path to Value.

Goal #12: Specify the Delivery Sequence

The transformation delivery is the aggregate of the value objectives, future-state business capabilities, and business-solution elements associated with the transformation. It is everything that must be delivered to achieve the purpose and scope of the transformation. The transformation delivery is illustrated in figure 107 (below).

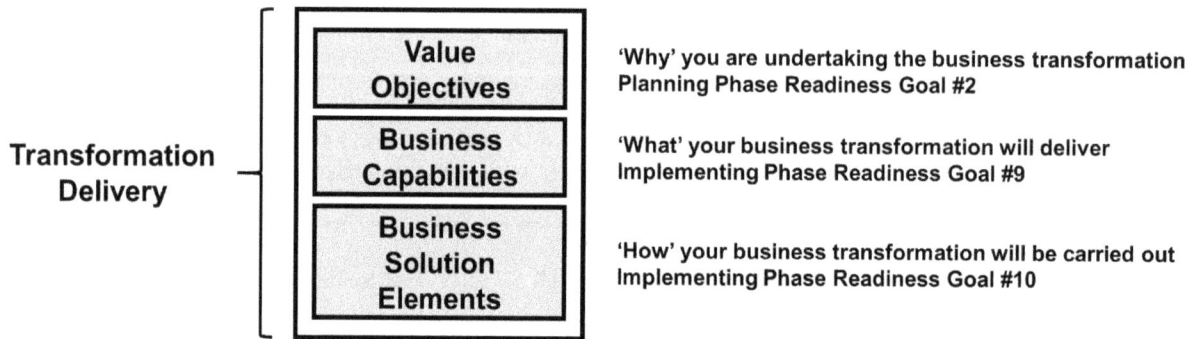

Transformation Delivery	**Value Objectives**	'Why' you are undertaking the business transformation Planning Phase Readiness Goal #2
	Business Capabilities	'What' your business transformation will deliver Implementing Phase Readiness Goal #9
	Business Solution Elements	'How' your business transformation will be carried out Implementing Phase Readiness Goal #10

Figure 107: Business Transformation Delivery

If the business transformation purpose and scope cannot be achieved in a single delivery (quite likely for larger transformations), then a business-transformation delivery sequence is required. The transformation delivery sequence is illustrated in figure 108 (below).

Sequential Ordering

The delivery sequence is the plan for incrementally fulfilling the purpose and scope. It specifies the order of the deliveries and implies a strict predecessor/successor relationship. If a delivery depends on the value objectives, business capabilities, or business-solution elements of other deliveries, then the dependent delivery must be positioned in the sequence after all the deliveries on which it depends.

Consistency

Each delivery in the sequence must be consistent. This means that the value objectives in the delivery are achieved by the business capabilities and business-solution elements in that delivery, and the business capabilities in the delivery are realized by the business-solution elements in that delivery.

Relationship to Implementation Work Plan

A business-transformation delivery sequence is different from the implementation work plan used to specify the tasks, resources, and timeline. The delivery sequence is at a much higher level than the work plan. Each delivery will have its own implementation work plan.

Transformation Delivery Sequence

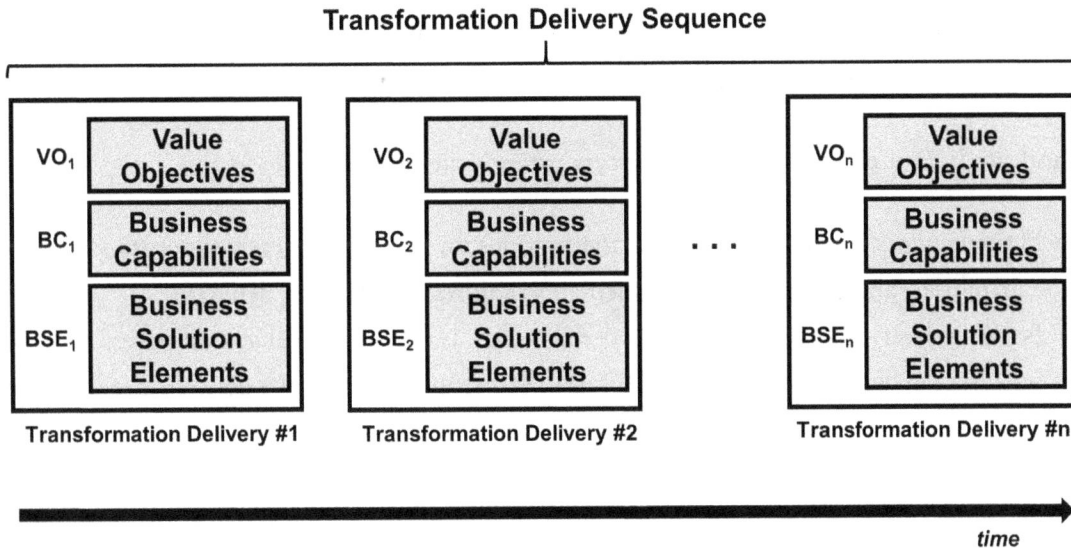

Figure 108: Business-Transformation Delivery Sequence

Readiness Assessment

Readiness Assessment Standards

The readiness assessment standards are formally expressed as follows:

1. You have planned the implementation of your transformation scope as a delivery sequence.
2. Your delivery sequence respects prerequisite deliveries.

If you know these, you have attained readiness with respect to "Specify the Delivery Sequence." If you don't, you will need to complete the readiness preparation described later. As with all the readiness assessments, metrics are defined to evaluate your attainment of these standards.

Readiness Assessment Metrics

These metrics examine your company's readiness and allow you to identify the gaps in your understanding.

➤ Standard 1: You have planned the implementation of your transformation scope as a delivery sequence.

    a. Can your entire transformation scope be implemented as a sequence of deliveries—each of which is an aggregation of value objectives, future-state business capabilities, and business-solution elements?

    b. Are the value objectives, future-state business capabilities, and business-solution elements consistent for each delivery?

➤ Standard 2: Your delivery sequence respects prerequisite deliveries.

    a. Have you satisfied all starting-point assumptions for the value objectives, future-state business capabilities, and business-solution elements required for the first delivery?

    b. Is the delivery sequence strictly ordered—that is, have the value objectives, future-state business capabilities, and business-solution elements required by a delivery been satisfied by a predecessor delivery?

The complete readiness assessment for the goal "Specify the Delivery Sequence" is shown in figure 109 (below).

Readiness Assessment	#12: Specify the Delivery Sequence	
Assessment Standards	1. You have planned the implementation of your transformation scope as a delivery sequence	2. Your delivery sequence respects pre-requisite deliveries
Assessment Metrics	a. Can your entire transformation scope be implemented as a sequence of deliveries - each of which is an aggregation of value objectives, future state business capabilities and business solution elements?	a. Have you satisfied all starting point assumptions for the value objectives, future state business capabilities and business solution elements required for the first delivery?
	b. Are the value objectives, future state business capabilities and business solution elements consistent for each delivery?	b. Is the delivery sequence strictly ordered - i.e. have the value objectives, future state business capabilities and business solution elements required by a delivery been satisfied by a predecessor delivery?

Figure 109: Readiness Assessment #12: Specify the Delivery Sequence

Creating an Actionable Assessment

The readiness assessment summarized in figure 109 (above) can be made actionable by converting the standards and metrics into deliverables and then combining them with the corresponding activities for producing them. Templates for readiness assessments and preparations are provided in the companion guide to this book.

Readiness Assessment Considerations

All transformation value objectives, future-state business capabilities, and business-solution elements should be accounted for in the deliveries. However, it's possible to use a delivery to implement scope outside of the transformation. You just need to consider whether the additional scope adds risk to the transformation.

You can have more business-solution elements in a delivery than are required to achieve the business capabilities in that delivery, but at least some future-state business capabilities must be achieved. Similarly, you can have more future-state business capabilities in a delivery than are required to achieve the value objectives, but at least one value objective must be achieved.

As you verify strict ordering of the delivery sequence, ensure there are no dependency cycles in the sequence. Subsequent deliveries can have dependencies on predecessor deliveries—but not vice versa.

Readiness Preparation

The readiness assessment standards for Specifying the Delivery Sequence were defined as follows:

1. You have planned the implementation of your transformation scope as a delivery sequence.
2. Your delivery sequence respects prerequisite deliveries.

If your business is unable to attain these readiness assessment standards, you will need to undertake the following preparation actions to remediate the gaps.

Readiness Preparation Actions

The actions you can take to help you define the transformation deliveries and delivery sequence are formally expressed as follows:

1. Create a delivery-sequence plan for implementing your transformation scope.
2. Arrange your delivery sequence to respect prerequisites.

By taking these actions, you ensure your business can attain the corresponding standards. The deliverables and activities presented next will guide you in completing these actions.

Readiness Preparation Steps

Every readiness assessment standard was assigned one or more metrics to facilitate evaluation. These metrics are now used in designing the preparation steps. One preparation step is required for each assessment metric.

➤ Action 1: Create a delivery-sequence plan for implementing your transformation scope.

Readiness was determined by answering the following two questions (i.e., readiness metrics), also shown in figure 109 (above):

a. Can your entire transformation scope be implemented as a sequence of deliveries—each of which is an aggregation of value objectives, future-state business capabilities, and business-solution elements?

b. Are the value objectives, future-state business capabilities, and business-solution elements consistent for each delivery?

Metric A: Can your entire transformation scope be implemented as a sequence of deliveries— each of which is an aggregation of value objectives, future-state business capabilities, and business-solution elements?

The preparation step partitions your transformation scope into a sequence of deliveries containing value objectives, future-state business capabilities, and business-solution elements. The business-transformation implementation leaders first review the future-state business capability model (augmented with your transformation value objectives) and the future-state business-solution document (also augmented with your transformation value objectives). These were produced in the preparation steps for Goal #11: Specify Value Realization. They then look for ways to group the value objectives, future-state business capabilities, and business-solution elements into deliveries. There may be multiple ways to form the deliveries. Here are a few guidelines for grouping:

1. Deliveries should be based on complete value objectives whenever possible.
2. Deliveries should be based on complete business capabilities whenever possible.
3. Deliveries should be based on complete business-solution elements whenever possible.

While it may not be possible to achieve all three guidelines, if you adhere to them in the order given, you will maximize the value of the deliveries. This may require multiple iterations to arrive at the optimal sequence.

Metric B: Are the value objectives, future-state business capabilities, and business-solution elements consistent for each delivery?

The preparation step ensures for each delivery, the value objectives are consistent with the future-state business capabilities and the business-solution elements. The business-transformation implementation leaders first review all the deliveries defined above. They then ensure for each delivery, the value objectives in the delivery are achieved by the business capabilities and business-solution elements in that delivery and the business capabilities in the delivery are realized by the business-solution elements in that delivery. This is the definition of consistency defined at the beginning of this section. If a delivery is not consistent, the business-transformation implementation leaders must rework the delivery composition until all deliveries are consistent.

➢ Action 2: Arrange your delivery sequence to respect prerequisites.

Readiness was determined by answering the following two questions (i.e., readiness metrics), also shown in figure 109 (above):

a. Have you satisfied all starting-point assumptions for the value objectives, future-state business capabilities, and business-solution elements required for the first delivery?
b. Is the delivery sequence strictly ordered—that is, have the value objectives, future-state business capabilities, and business-solution elements required by a delivery been satisfied by a predecessor delivery?

Metric A: Have you satisfied all starting-point assumptions for the value objectives, future-state business capabilities, and business-solution elements required for the first delivery?

The preparation step identifies the first delivery in your sequence and ensures all required preconditions for the delivery can be satisfied prior to implementation. The business-transformation implementation leaders first review all the deliveries defined for the transformation. They then identify the candidate set of deliveries that do not depend on any other deliveries. From this candidate set, a delivery is selected as the first in the sequence. The business-transformation implementation leaders then identify preconditions for the first delivery, including assumptions for achieving the value objectives, future-state business capabilities, or business-solution elements. Finally, the business-transformation implementation leaders ensure all preconditions can be fully addressed prior to implementing the first delivery. If not, then either another delivery must be selected from the candidate set or the preconditions must first be implemented.

Metric B: Is the delivery sequence strictly ordered—that is, have the value objectives, future-state business capabilities, and business-solution elements required by a delivery been satisfied by a predecessor delivery?

The preparation step orders the remaining deliveries into a sequence such that the value objectives, future-state business capabilities, and solution elements required to begin each delivery will be completed in a predecessor delivery. The business-transformation implementation leaders first review all the deliveries defined for the transformation.

They then identify the prerequisites to achieving the value objectives, future-state business capabilities, and business-solution elements in each delivery. Starting with the first delivery, the business-transformation implementation leaders order the remaining deliveries in a sequence that ensures all the prerequisites for a delivery can be fully achieved in a delivery predecessor. If not, then they continue resequencing the deliveries until this can be satisfied.

The complete readiness preparation for the goal "Specify the Delivery Sequence" is shown in figure 110 (below).

Readiness Preparation	#12: Specify the Delivery Sequence	
Preparation Actions	1. Create a delivery sequence plan for implementing your transformation scope	2. Arrange your delivery sequence to respect pre-requisites
Preparation Steps	a. Partition your transformation scope into a sequence of deliveries containing value objectives, future state business capabilities and business solution elements	a. Identify the first delivery in your sequence and ensure all required preconditions for the delivery can be satisfied prior
	b. Ensure for each delivery, the value objectives are consistent with the future state business capabilities, which are in turn consistent with the business solution elements	b. Order the remaining deliveries into a sequence such that the value objectives, future state business capabilities and solution elements required to begin the delivery have been completed in a predecessor delivery

Figure 110: Readiness Preparation #12: Specify the Delivery Sequence

Creating an Actionable Preparation

The readiness preparation summarized in figure 110 (above) can be made actionable by converting the actions and steps into deliverables and then combining them with the corresponding activities for producing them. Templates for readiness assessments and preparations are provided in the companion guide to this book.

Readiness Preparation Considerations

Create a delivery-sequence plan for implementing your transformation scope.

When partitioning your transformation scope into a sequence of deliveries, you can partition based on value objective boundaries, future-state business capability boundaries, or business-solution element boundaries. The entire transformation scope must be distributed across the set of deliveries. While it is possible your transformation contains only one delivery, most will require multiple deliveries. The key is to ensure that each delivery produces some value to your business.

When considering the consistency of your deliveries, you may not be able to realize the entire future-state business capabilities through the business-solution elements in that delivery. However, you must ensure at least some of the business-solution elements support the realization of some of the future-state business capabilities within each delivery. Similarly, you must ensure that at least some of the future-state business capabilities support the realization of some of the value objectives in each delivery.

Arrange your delivery sequence to respect prerequisites.

The best candidate for the first delivery in your delivery sequence is the one that does not depend on any of the other deliveries—and often is depended on by one or more of the other deliveries. You may also choose the delivery that realizes the greatest value.

As you are considering the sequence for the remaining deliveries, if you discover some set of deliveries are mutually dependent on each other, you will need to redefine the delivery boundaries.

Goal #13: Secure Required Resources

Project management techniques help in estimating the team members and other resources required to complete the transformation delivery within the time frame and budget. It is also critical for the team members to have the skills and experience required to complete the work. The transformation must also have sufficient leadership (high enough in the company) to motivate the transformation and effectively carry out the delivery. The readiness goal "Secure Required Resources" ensures the transformation has the right type of resources, in sufficient quantity, and at the time they are required.

Readiness Assessment

Readiness Assessment Standards

The readiness assessment standards are formally expressed as follows:

1. You have specified the resources required for executing the delivery sequence.
2. The resources required for each delivery are available when needed.

If you know these, you have attained readiness with respect to "Secure Required Resources." If you don't, you will need to complete the readiness preparation described later. As with all the readiness assessments, metrics are defined to evaluate your attainment of these standards.

Readiness Assessment Metrics

These metrics examine your company's readiness and allow you to identify the gaps in your understanding.

➤ Standard 1: You have specified the resources required for executing the delivery sequence.

   a. Have you identified the program leaders and executers (internal and external) required for each delivery?
   b. Have you identified the equipment, facilities, and other resources required for each delivery?

➤ Standard 2: The resources required for each delivery are available when needed.

   a. Will the people resources for each delivery be available at sufficient levels when required?
   b. Will the equipment, facilities, and other resources for each delivery be available at sufficient levels when required?

The complete readiness assessment for the goal "Secure Required Resources" is shown in figure 111 (below).

Readiness Assessment	#13: Secure Required Resources	
Assessment Standards	**1. You have specified the resources required for executing the delivery sequence**	**2. The resources required for each delivery are available when needed**
Assessment Metrics	a. Have you identified the program leaders and executers (internal and external) required for each delivery?	a. Will the people resources for each delivery be available at sufficient levels when required?
	b. Have you identified the equipment, facilities and other resources required for each delivery?	b. Will the equipment, facilities and other resources for each delivery be available at sufficient levels when required?

Figure 111: Readiness Assessment #13: Secure Required Resources

Creating an Actionable Assessment

The readiness assessment summarized in figure 111 (above) can be made actionable by converting the standards and metrics into deliverables and then combining them with the corresponding activities for producing them. Templates for readiness assessments and preparations are provided in the companion guide to this book.

Readiness Assessment Considerations

As you are identifying resources for each delivery, remember to include, if necessary, representatives from your customers, vendors, and other external agencies. Also, some equipment and facilities will only be needed on a temporary basis. These include team work rooms, development and testing equipment, projectors, and whiteboards.

Readiness Preparation

The readiness assessment standards for Securing the Required Resources were defined as follows:

1. You have specified the resources required for executing the delivery sequence.
2. The resources required for each delivery are available when needed.

If your business is unable to attain these readiness assessment standards, you will need to undertake the following preparation actions to remediate the gaps.

Readiness Preparation Actions

The actions you can take to help ensure you have the resources necessary for your business transformation are formally expressed as:

1. Identify the resources required for your delivery sequence.
2. Secure the resources required for your delivery sequence when needed.

By taking these actions, you ensure your business can attain the corresponding standards. The deliverables and activities presented next will guide you in completing these actions.

Readiness Preparation Steps

Every readiness assessment standard was assigned one or more metrics to facilitate evaluation. These metrics are now used in designing the preparation steps. One preparation step is required for each assessment metric.

➢ Action 1: Identify the resources required for your delivery sequence.

Readiness was determined by answering the following two questions (i.e., readiness metrics), also shown in figure 111 (above):

a. Have you identified the program leaders and executers (internal and external) required for each delivery?
b. Have you identified the equipment, facilities, and other resources required for each delivery?

Metric A: Have you identified the program leaders and executers (internal and external) required for each delivery?

The preparation step specifies the people resources required (program leaders, program executers, external-solution specialists) for each delivery in the sequence. The business-transformation implementation leaders first review the delivery sequence prepared in Goal #12: Specify the Delivery Sequence. For each delivery in the sequence, they determine the people resources needed in each delivery, including program leaders, program executers, and external-solution specialists. The skills and experience for each type of people resource must also be specified to ensure a good fit for the tasks in the delivery. Finally, the business-transformation implementation leaders tag each delivery with the people resource types and quantities required.

Metric B: Have you identified the equipment, facilities, and other resources required for each delivery?

The preparation step specifies the equipment, facilities, and other resources required for each delivery in the sequence. The business-transformation implementation leaders first review the delivery sequence. For each delivery in the sequence, they determine the equipment, facilities, and other resources needed in each delivery: meeting rooms, workspaces, computers, printers, projectors, software, and anything else the program implementation needs to carry out the deliveries. Finally, the business-transformation implementation leaders tag each delivery with the equipment and other resources required.

➤ Action 2: Secure the resources required for your delivery sequence when needed.

Readiness was determined by answering the following two questions (i.e., readiness metrics), also shown in figure 111 (above):

a. Will the people resources for each delivery be available at sufficient levels when required?
b. Will the equipment, facilities, and other resources for each delivery be available at sufficient levels when required?

Metric A: Will the people resources for each delivery be available at sufficient levels when required?

The preparation step ensures the people resources required for each delivery will be available at the time they are needed. The business-transformation implementation leaders first review the delivery sequence. For each delivery in the sequence, they note the timing requirements for the people resources needed in the delivery. They then determine whether the resources can be made available at the time the delivery is implemented. If not, temporary resources must be acquired—or the timing of the delivery must be adjusted to accommodate resource availability.

Metric B: Will the equipment, facilities, and other resources for each delivery be available at sufficient levels when required?

The preparation step ensures the equipment, facilities, and other resources required for each delivery will be available at the time they are needed. The business-transformation implementation leaders first review the delivery sequence. For each delivery in the sequence, they note the timing requirements for the equipment, facilities, and other resources needed in the delivery. They then determine whether the resources can be made available at the time the delivery is implemented. If not, additional resources must be acquired—or the timing of the delivery must be adjusted to accommodate resource availability.

The complete readiness preparation for the goal "Secure Required Resources" is shown in figure 112 (below).

Readiness Preparation	#13: Secure Required Resources	
Preparation Actions	1. Identify the resources required for your delivery sequence	2. Secure the resources required for your delivery sequence when needed
Preparation Steps	a. Specify the people resources required (program leaders, program executers, external solution specialists) for each delivery in the sequence	a. Ensure the people resources required for each delivery can be made available at the time they are needed
	b. Specify the equipment, facilities and other resources required for each delivery in the sequence	b. Ensure the equipment, facilities and other resources required for each delivery can be made available at the time they are needed

Figure 112: Readiness Preparation #13: Secure Required Resources

Creating an Actionable Preparation

The readiness preparation summarized in figure 112 (above) can be made actionable by converting the actions and steps into deliverables and then combining them with the corresponding activities for producing them. Templates for readiness assessments and preparations are provided in the companion guide to this book.

Readiness Preparation Considerations

Identify the Resources Required for Your Delivery Sequence

The statement of transformation investment developed under Goal #7: Identify Required Investment can be used to identify and prepare the resource requirements. You should also have a better understanding of the type of resources required from your future-state business-solution documentation prepared in Goal #10: Specify Required Business Solution.

Secure the Resources Required for Your Delivery Sequence When Needed

At this point in the transformation, you should understand the relative time frames for each delivery in the delivery sequence. This helps in assessing resource availability.

You will need to understand the level of effort required from all nonprogram team members (including executives and impacted users) since they may not be dedicated exclusively to the implementation.

Execution Readiness

Execution is the fulfillment of all the transformation changes included in the design. The research showed that eleven of the thirty-six reasons for failure were related to execution. They range from failure to implement sound project management practices to insufficient attention to change management. Execution is generally the longest, most resource intensive, and most expensive part of the transformation. It is when the transformation comes into existence, creating both excitement and anxiety. Readiness of execution is expressed through the attainment of the six readiness goals as shown in figure 92. Each of these readiness goals has specific readiness assessments and readiness preparations—formally developed in the remainder of this section.

Goal #14: Instill Program Management Rigor

Program and project management concepts have been around for decades. Best practices, templates, and techniques are available through many sources. The Project Management Institute has published a Body of Knowledge on this subject and offers study guides and professional certifications.

It's hard to imagine that program management still needs to be called out explicitly as a challenge, but given that a third of the reasons for business transformation failure were due to weak project management, it is included. For successful execution, business transformations require—at a minimum—a methodology for implementing the business-solution elements, a disciplined program governance structure and governance processes, and methods for monitoring, evaluating, and reporting on implementation progress.

Readiness Assessment

Readiness Assessment Standards

The readiness assessment standards are formally expressed as follows:

1. You are using a solution-delivery methodology and tools.
2. You have established program governance structures and processes.
3. You are using processes for monitoring, evaluating, and reporting progress.

If you know these, you have attained readiness with respect to "Instill Program Management Rigor." If you don't, you will need to complete the readiness preparation described later. As with all the readiness assessments, metrics are defined to evaluate your attainment of these standards.

Readiness Assessment Metrics

These metrics examine your company's readiness and allow you to identify the gaps in your understanding.

➢ Standard 1: You are using solution-delivery methodology and tools.

    a. Have you identified an appropriate delivery methodology and tool set for your business solution?

    b. Have you instituted the methodology and tool set within your business?

➢ Standard 2: You have established program governance structures and processes.

    a. Have you defined the roles and responsibilities for decision-making and escalation?

    b. Have you instituted scope, risk, and issues management processes?

➢ Standard 3: You are using processes for monitoring, evaluating, and reporting progress.

    a. Have you instituted a method for collecting and tracking implementation progress?

    b. Have you instituted a method for evaluating and reporting implementation progress?

The complete readiness assessment for the goal "Instill Program Management Rigor" is shown in figure 113 (below).

Readiness Assessment	#14: Instill Program Management Rigor		
Assessment Standards	**1. You are using solution delivery methodology and tools**	**2. You have established program governance structures and processes**	**3. You are using processes for monitoring, evaluating and reporting progress**
Assessment Metrics	a. Have you identified an appropriate delivery methodology and toolset for your business solution?	a. Have you defined the roles and responsibilities for decision making and escalation?	a. Have you instituted a method for collecting and tracking implementation progress?
	b. Have you instituted the methodology and toolset within your business?	b. Have you instituted scope, risk and issues management processes?	b. Have you instituted a method for evaluating and reporting implementation progress?

Figure 113: Readiness Assessment #14: Instill Program Management Rigor

Creating an Actionable Assessment

The readiness assessment summarized in figure 113 (above) can be made actionable by converting the standards and metrics into deliverables and then combining them with the corresponding activities for producing them. Templates for readiness assessments and preparations are provided in the companion guide to this book.

Readiness Assessment Considerations

The nature of your business solution will drive the best choice of delivery methodology/tool set. You will need to ensure the methodology/tool set can accommodate the range of change impacts realized through your business solution. Program implementation leadership should be experienced in the use of the delivery methodology and tool set. Regarding the program-governance structure and processes, they should be included as artifacts of the program management office and must be documented and shared with the program-implementation team.

Finally, you must establish and carry out a disciplined cadence for collecting and tracking implementation progress. Implementation progress must be honestly evaluated and communicated to executives as well as the program-implementation team.

Readiness Preparation

The readiness assessment standards for Instilling Program Management were defined as follows:

1. You are using a solution-delivery methodology and tools.
2. You have established program governance structures and processes.
3. You are using processes for monitoring, evaluating, and reporting progress.

If your business is unable to attain these readiness assessment standards, you will need to undertake the following preparation actions to remediate the gaps.

Readiness Preparation Actions

The actions you can take to ensure you are using disciplined program management are formally expressed as follows:

1. Select and put in place an appropriate solution-delivery methodology.
2. Define and implement program-governance structure and processes.
3. Define and implement methods for monitoring, evaluating, and reporting on program progress.

By taking these actions, you ensure your business can attain the corresponding standards. The deliverables and activities presented next will guide you in completing these actions.

Readiness Preparation Steps

Every readiness assessment standard was assigned one or more metrics to facilitate evaluation. These metrics are now used in designing the preparation steps. One preparation step is required for each assessment metric.

➢ Action 1: Select and put in place an appropriate solution-delivery methodology.

Readiness was determined by answering the following two questions (i.e., readiness metrics), also shown in figure 113 (above):

a. Have you identified the most appropriate delivery methodology and tool set for your business solution?
b. Have you instituted the methodology and tool set within your business?

Metric A: Have you identified the most appropriate delivery methodology and tool set for your business solution?

The preparation step is to select the best delivery methodology and tool set for your business solution. Experienced solution-integration partners typically define their own solution-delivery methodology and tool set and recommend using what they have developed. If you are not using an experienced integration partner (not advisable), the business-transformation implementation leaders will need to select a delivery methodology from those that are commercially available. They must then review the range of change impacts addressed by the future-state business solution (prepared in Goal #10: Specify Required Business Solution) to determine whether the recommended delivery methodology/ tool set can handle the change impacts and solution elements.

Metric B: Have you instituted the methodology and tool set within your business?

The preparation step ensures you develop competency within your business on the use of the methodology and tool set. The business-transformation implementation leaders must obtain or prepare training materials on the use of the methodology and tool set. They must then ensure the tool set is available to the program-implementation team. Finally, the business-transformation implementation leaders must train the program-implementation team on the use of the methodology and tools.

➤ Action 2: Define and implement program governance structure and processes.

Readiness was determined by answering the following two questions (i.e., readiness metrics), also shown in figure 113 (above):

a. Have you defined the roles and responsibilities for decision-making and escalation?
b. Have you instituted scope, risk, and issues-management processes?

Metric A: Have you defined the roles and responsibilities for decision-making and escalation?

The preparation step defines and implements a program-governance structure with roles and responsibilities for implementation decisions and escalation. The Program Management Institute offers program governance structure samples and guidelines for roles and responsibilities. The business-transformation implementation leaders select a governance structure that will work for your solution delivery. They then ensure the program-implementation team understands the structure/ roles/responsibilities. Finally, the business-transformation implementation leaders ensure program governance is adhered to throughout the program implementation.

Metric B: Have you instituted scope, risk, and issues-management processes?

The preparation step ensures processes for managing scope changes, program risks, and issues are defined and implemented. Sample processes for scope change, program risk, and issues management are widely available. The business-transformation implementation leaders select processes that will work within your business. They document the processes and include them as artifacts of the program-management office. Finally, the business-transformation implementation leaders train the program-implementation team on usage.

➤ Action 3: Define and implement methods for monitoring, evaluating, and reporting on program progress.

Readiness was determined by answering the following two questions (i.e., readiness metrics), also shown in figure 111 (above):

a. Have you instituted a method for collecting and tracking implementation progress?
b. Have you instituted a method for evaluating and reporting implementation progress?

Metric A: Have you instituted a method for collecting and tracking implementation progress?

The preparation step is to design and implement methods for collecting and tracking implementation progress. Again, there are commercially available applications suitable for large-scale implementations. The business-transformation implementation leaders select an application that will work within your business. They then document the methods for recording, collecting, and tracking progress and include them as artifacts in the office of program management. Finally, the business-transformation implementation leaders train the program-implementation team on usage of the implementation progress tracking methods.

Metric B: Have you instituted a method for evaluating and reporting implementation progress?

The preparation step is to design and implement methods for evaluating and reporting implementation progress. The business-transformation implementation leaders will establish a cadence for review, evaluation, and corrective actions with respect to implementation progress. They then retain the reports in a program-management artifact repository and make them available to the executives as well as the program-implementation team. The complete readiness preparation for the goal "Instill Program Management Rigor" is shown in figure 114 (below).

Readiness Preparation	#14: Instill Program Management Rigor		
Preparation Actions	1. Select and put in place an appropriate solution delivery methodology	2. Define and implement program governance structure and processes	3. Define and implement methods for monitoring, evaluating and reporting on program progress
Preparation Steps	a. Select the best delivery methodology and toolset for your business solution	a. Define and implement a program governance structure with roles and responsibilities for decisions and escalation	a. Design and implement a method for collecting and tracking implementation progress
	b. Develop competency within your business on the use of the methodology and toolset	b. Define and implement processes for managing scope changes, program risks and issues	b. Design and implement a method for evaluating and reporting implementation progress

Figure 114: Readiness Preparation #14: Instill Program Management Rigor

Creating an Actionable Preparation

The readiness preparation summarized in figure 114 (above) can be made actionable by converting the actions and steps into deliverables and then combining them with the corresponding activities for producing them. Templates for readiness assessments and preparations are provided in the companion guide to this book.

Readiness Preparation Considerations

Select and Put in Place an Appropriate Solution-Delivery Methodology

If you are using a business solution-delivery methodology recommended by a technology solution-delivery partner, ensure the delivery methodology and tool set is robust enough to handle the entire business solution and not just the technical portions of the solution. It is preferable to use one solution-delivery methodology and tool set since using more than one creates confusion and sometimes conflicting direction to the implementation team.

The solution-delivery methodology and tools will most likely be new for the program-implementation team. However, program leadership should be proficient in using the methodology/tools. You can engage a solution-integration partner to help administer the methodology/tool set until your business develops proficiency. The solution-delivery methodology and tool set can be reused on future program-implementation efforts, and it is generally worth building internal competency.

Define and implement program governance structure and processes.

Ensure there is clear accountability and responsibility for decisions and be disciplined in use-of-program governance. If a decision cannot be resolved at a lower level of the governance structure, it must be escalated to the next highest level and so on. There are significant consequences for undisciplined program decision-making, including financial and legal impacts.

Ensure program decisions, scope changes, program risks, and issues are documented and retained in a repository, which is accessible to the program-implementation team. These will be referred to during implementation and can save a lot of time wasted in backtracking.

Define and implement methods for monitoring, evaluating, and reporting on program progress.

If your company already has methods in place for monitoring, evaluating, and reporting on program progress, use what you have rather than creating or purchasing something new. At the very least, you will need to track program task completion, program costs, and schedule. More sophisticated applications support resource utilization and earned-value analysis. Whether you purchase a tool set or develop one, it's better to start simply at first rather than creating something so complex it becomes burdensome to use.

As you evaluate and report on implementation progress, insist on discipline and honesty. Utilize corrective actions to recover from slips on spend or milestone completion, but don't discourage honesty. Problems only become worse over time.

Goal #15: Standardize Solution

Complexity and customization increase the total life cycle cost of a solution and can negatively impact a solution's agility, flexibility, and scalability. Complex or customized solutions are not inherently bad or to be avoided at all cost, but they should be used appropriately. Complexity and customization become problems when it is unclear why they are proposed or there is no identifiable value over standard solutions. A solution-delivery methodology should at least include an assessment of complexity/customization to ensure it is considered in the execution of the transformation.

Standard Solutions versus Custom Solutions

Standard solutions contain a higher percentage of predesigned/prebuilt content than custom solutions. The predesigned/prebuilt content represents industry best practices that have been generalized to accommodate a wide range of businesses. The predesigned/prebuilt content can in some cases be an advantage or a disadvantage.

Custom solutions offer much less predesigned/prebuilt content; the solutions are tailored specifically to each need. As might be suspected, this can be an advantage in some cases and a disadvantage in others.

There are pros and cons to both standard and custom solutions, and some companies exclusively prefer one type over the other. The guidance in this section is to standardize whenever possible and at least require justification when custom solutions are proposed. The following attributes for the two types of solutions will help you in assessing the pros and cons for your business transformation.

Solution Fit

- Custom solutions are designed specifically for the unique requirements of your business.
- Standard solutions are prewired to handle major requirements but may not address all requirements.

Solution Advantage

- Custom solutions offer proprietary advantages over competitors.
- Standard solutions are based on commonly accepted best practices.

Life Cycle Cost

- Custom solutions cost more to develop but may cost less to integrate with the rest of your business-solution elements and cost less to maintain/enhance.
- Standard solutions cost less to develop but are costlier to modify outside of the standard offering.

Delivery Time Frame

- Custom solutions require more time to develop but may take less time to integrate with the rest of your business-solution elements and less time to maintain/enhance.
- Standard solutions require less time to develop but may take more time to modify outside of the standard offering.

Solution Adoption

- Custom solutions are more readily adopted as they are tailored specifically to business need but are also frequently tailored to avoid beneficial change impacts.

- Standard solutions are less readily adopted as the offering is generalized for a wide range of businesses/industries.

Support

- Custom solutions are dependent on the person or company that developed the solution to enhance and maintain them.
- Standard solutions have a much larger community of support to enhance and maintain them.

Simple Solutions versus Complex Solutions

Complexity with respect to business solutions will be taken to mean the range of business variation the solution can accommodate. If one solution is more complex than another, it means it can address a greater variety of business situations. A solution becomes overly complex when the business variation it addresses is seldom or never experienced, or more likely, no effort has been taken to reduce the business variation to begin with. Business variation is not necessarily bad, but it does require a more complex business solution. The guidance in this section is to reduce variation whenever possible and at least require justification when complex business solutions are proposed to address variation.

Readiness Assessment

Readiness Assessment Standards

The readiness assessment standards are formally expressed as follows:

1. Business solutions are evaluated for complexity and customization.
2. Complex or customized solutions have business justification.

If you know these, you have attained readiness with respect to "Standardize Solution." If you don't, you will need to complete the readiness preparation described later. As with all the readiness assessments, metrics are defined to evaluate your attainment of these standards.

Readiness Assessment Metrics

These metrics examine your company's readiness and allow you to identify the gaps in your understanding.

> Standard 1: Business solutions are evaluated for complexity and customization.

    a. Do you have a method for submitting requests for additional complexity and customization?

    b. Do requests for customization and complexity include the cost/impact as well as the business value?

> Standard 2: Complex or customized solutions have business justification

    a. Are requests for additional complexity and customization reviewed within the program governance structure?

    b. Is business value justification required whenever a more complex or custom solution is chosen over a simpler or standard solution?

The complete readiness assessment for the goal "Standardize Solution" is shown in figure 115 (below).

Readiness Assessment	#15: Standardize Solution	
Assessment Standards	1. Business solutions are evaluated for complexity and customization	2. Complex or customized solutions have business justification
Assessment Metrics	a. Do you have a method for submitting requests for additional complexity and customization?	a. Are requests for additional complexity and customization reviewed within the program governance structure?
	b. Do requests for customization and complexity include the cost/impact as well as the business value?	b. Is business value justification required whenever a more complex or custom solution is chosen over a simpler or standard solution?

Figure 115: Readiness Assessment #15: Standardize Solution

Creating an Actionable Assessment

The readiness assessment summarized in figure 115 (above) can be made actionable by converting the standards and metrics into deliverables and then combining them with the corresponding activities for producing them. Templates for readiness assessments and preparations are provided in the companion guide to this book.

Readiness Assessment Considerations

Requests for added complexity and customization generally result in changes to program scope. Therefore, the method for submitting requests for additional complexity and customization can be part of the program management office's scope change management process. The decision-maker responsible for evaluating the requests should be clearly identified and have full authority to approve/deny the request.

Readiness Preparation

The readiness assessment standards for standardizing your solution were defined as follows:

1. Business solutions are evaluated for complexity and customization.
2. Complex or customized solutions have business justification.

If your business is unable to attain these readiness assessment standards, you will need to undertake the following preparation actions to remediate the gaps.

Readiness Preparation Actions

The actions you can take to ensure your business solutions are as standardized as possible are formally expressed as follows:

1. Instill a program-level process for evaluating complexity and customization in business solutions.
2. Require business-value justification for all complex and customized solutions.

By taking these actions, you ensure your business can attain the corresponding standards. The deliverables and activities presented next will guide you in completing these actions.

Readiness Preparation Steps

Every readiness assessment standard was assigned one or more metrics to facilitate evaluation. These metrics are now used in designing the preparation steps. One preparation step is required for each assessment metric.

➤ Action 1: Instill a program level process for evaluating complexity and customization in business solutions.

Readiness was determined by answering the following two questions (i.e., readiness metrics), also shown in figure 115 (above):

a. Do you have a method for submitting requests for additional complexity and customization?
b. Do requests for customization and complexity include the cost/impact as well as the business value?

Metric A: Do you have a method for submitting requests for additional complexity and customization?

The preparation step is to define and put in place a program-level process for submitting requests for complexity and customization. The business-transformation implementation leaders first create a complexity/customization request submittal/approval procedure. They then create a form for collecting information on the nature of the request. Finally, the business-transformation implementation leaders provide a mechanism to collect and retain requests for review and archive.

Metric B: Do requests for customization and complexity include the cost/impact as well as the business value?

The preparation step ensures requests for complexity/customization are required to include estimates of value and cost/impact. The business-transformation implementation leaders add fields to capture a description of the business value and cost to develop/implement the complexity/customization. There should also be space to capture any change impacts/side effects of taking on a more complex/customized solution.

➤ Action 2: Require business value justification for all complex and customized solutions.

Readiness was determined by answering the following two questions (i.e., readiness metrics), also shown in figure 115 (above):

a. Are requests for additional complexity and customization reviewed within the program-governance structure?
b. Is business-value justification required whenever a more complex or custom solution is chosen over a simpler or standard solution?

Metric A: Are requests for additional complexity and customization reviewed within the program-governance structure?

The preparation step defines and puts in place a program-governance process to review requests for additional complexity and customization. The business-transformation implementation leaders first define the governance process and decision-making authority for reviewing and approving/denying requests for additional complexity and customization. They then conduct complexity/customization request reviews in accordance with a published cadence. Finally, the business-transformation implementation leaders ensure the outcome of the review is published and made available to the program-implementation team and executive stakeholders.

Metric B: Is business-value justification required whenever a more complex or custom solution is chosen over a simpler or standard solution?

The preparation step ensures more complex or customized solutions are only chosen over simpler or standard solutions when their value exceeds their cost/impact. The business-transformation implementation leaders first prepare and distribute a decision process and criteria for reviewing and approving/denying requests for additional complexity and customization. They then must ensure the guidelines are strictly followed.

The complete readiness preparation for the goal "Standardize Solution" is shown in figure 116 (below).

Creating an Actionable Preparation

The readiness preparation summarized in figure 116 (below) can be made actionable by converting the actions and steps into deliverables and then combining them with the corresponding activities for producing them. Templates for readiness assessments and preparations are provided in the companion guide to this book.

Readiness Preparation	#15: Standardize Solution	
Preparation Actions	1. Instill a program level process for evaluating complexity and customization in business solutions	2. Require business value justification for all complex and customized solutions
Preparation Steps	a. Define and put in place a program level process for submitting requests for additional complexity and customization	a. Define and put in place a program governance process to review requests for additional complexity and customization
	b. Require requests for complexity/customization to include estimates of value and cost/impact	b. Ensure more complex or customized solutions are only chosen over simpler or standard solutions when their value exceeds their cost/impact

Figure 116: Readiness Preparation #15: Standardize Solution

Readiness Preparation Considerations

Instill a Program-Level Process for Evaluating Complexity and Customization in Business Solutions

Requests for complexity and customization should be retained, as the same request can be raised many times during the implementation, especially when they are made on behalf of users resisting the business changes.

Complexity can often be created in one business function to simplify the work in other functional areas. The net must be an overall simplification—or an improvement in quality/capability. Complexity should not be used to move work around the organization if there is no business benefit.

Require business-value justification for all complex and customized solutions.

This must be followed consistently and in a disciplined manner—the cost and impact can be huge. Frequently the request for additional complexity and customization is intended to offset the change impact in the transformation. This can be a legitimate use, provided it does not impact the value objectives or future-state business capabilities.

The disposition of the complexity/customization request should be clearly communicated as there is generally concern associated with both approval and denial decisions. Once a request is approved, you most likely will need to revise the program schedule and budget as there will be an accompanying increase in scope.

Goal #16: Integrate Solution

Your business solution should be described in total after achieving Goal #10: Specify Required Business Solution, but the integration may not be fully specified. A solution that is integrated will be complete and flow contiguously throughout the components. It will not have missing or disjointed steps. The solution-delivery methodology you choose should include an assessment of integrated flow throughout your business solution.

Integrated versus Unintegrated Solutions

You can determine whether your business solution is integrated by considering two important properties of the work that flows through the solution: connectedness and cohesiveness. These properties are illustrated in figure 117 (below).

Connected versus Disconnected Workflow

A connected workflow has no gaps between adjacent solution elements. Whatever is intended to flow between the solution elements—process work steps, data, and electronic signals—will flow completely and without interruption. Conversely, a disconnected workflow has gaps between adjacent elements where the flow stops abruptly in an upstream element and then continues later in the downstream element. Disconnected workflow is often incomplete as well as interrupted. In figure 117, quadrants 1 and 2 show disconnected workflow, and quadrants 3 and 4 show connected workflow.

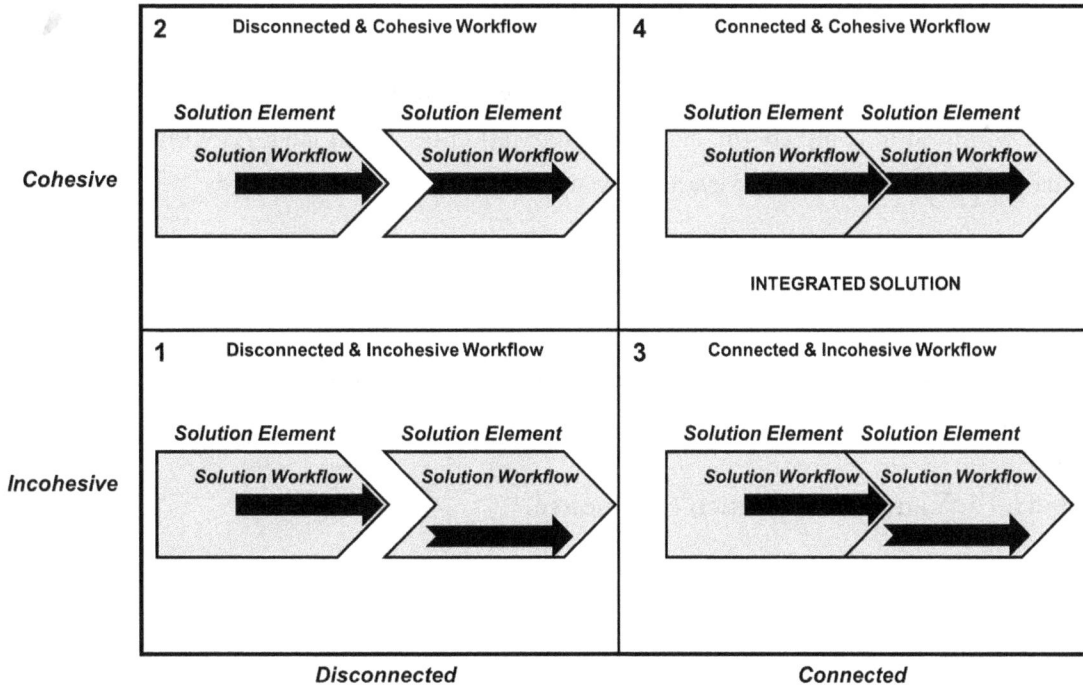

Figure 117: Solution Integration—Workflow Properties

Cohesive versus Incohesive Workflow

A cohesive workflow is functionally aligned between adjacent solution elements. Whatever is intended to flow between the solution elements will flow harmoniously and with the context carried across solution element boundaries. Conversely, an incoherent workflow does not preserve the context of the work as it passes across the boundaries. For example, an incoherent workflow may not preserve dimensional units on data or preserve work ownership as it moves from one solution element to another. In figure 117, quadrants 1 and 3 show incoherent workflow and quadrants 2 and 4 show coherent workflow.

An integrated solution is one where the workflows are both connected and coherent across solution elements. This is represented by quadrant 4 in figure 117 (above):

Readiness Assessment

Readiness Assessment Standards

The readiness assessment standards are formally expressed as follows:

1. Your business solution flows across solution elements.

2. Your business solution flow is functionally cohesive.

If you know these, then you have attained readiness with respect to "Integrate Solution." If you don't, you will need to complete the readiness preparation described later. As with all the readiness assessments, metrics are defined to evaluate your attainment of these standards.

Readiness Assessment Metrics

These metrics examine your company's readiness and allow you to identify the gaps in your understanding.

➤ Standard 1: Your business solution is connected.

    a. Are workflows uninterrupted across solution elements?

    b. If you are using a delivery sequence, do you have a way to temporarily bridge gaps until all deliveries are completed?

➤ Standard 2: Your business solution is cohesive.

    a. Are workflows functionally aligned across solution elements?

    b. If you are using a delivery sequence, do you have a way to temporarily bridge the solution flow until all deliveries are completed?

The complete readiness assessment for the goal "Integrate Solution" is shown in figure 118 (below).

Readiness Assessment	#16: Integrate Solution	
Assessment Standards	**1. Your business solution is connected**	**2. Your business solution is cohesive**
Assessment Metrics	a. Are workflows uninterrupted across solution elements?	a. Are workflows functionally aligned across solution elements?
	b. If you are using a delivery sequence, do you have a way to temporarily bridge gaps until all deliveries are completed?	b. If you are using a delivery sequence, do you have a way to temporarily bridge the solution flow until all deliveries are completed?

Figure 118: Readiness Assessment #16: Integrate Solution

Creating an Actionable Assessment

The readiness assessment summarized in figure 118 (above) can be made actionable by converting the standards and metrics into deliverables and then combining them with the corresponding activities for producing them. Templates for readiness assessments and preparations are provided in the companion guide to this book.

Readiness Assessment Considerations

As you evaluate whether your solution elements are connected, you'll need to understand whether workflow (data and processes) are manually handled multiple times when crossing solution element boundaries. It is best if the flow happens without any human intervention, but that is not always possible.

As you consider whether your solution elements are cohesive, you should ensure data or workflow crossing solution elements can be utilized as is by the downstream solution element—without human intervention to transform the data or workflow once it is passed to the downstream solution element.

Readiness Preparation

The readiness assessment standards for Integrating your Solution were defined as follows:

1. Your business solution is connected.
2. Your business solution is functionally cohesive.

If your business is unable to attain these readiness assessment standards, you will need to undertake the following preparation actions to remediate the gaps.

Readiness Preparation Actions

The actions you can take to help you ensure your solution is integrated are formally expressed as follows:

1. Connect your business solution across all solution elements.
2. Create cohesive flow across your business solution.

By taking these actions, you ensure your business can attain the corresponding standards. The deliverables and activities presented next will guide you in completing these actions.

Readiness Preparation Steps

Every readiness assessment standard was assigned one or more metrics to facilitate evaluation. These metrics are now used in designing the preparation steps. One preparation step is required for each assessment metric.

➢ Action 1: Connect your business solution across all solution elements.

Readiness was determined by answering the following two questions (i.e., readiness metrics), also shown in figure 118 (above):

a. Are workflows uninterrupted across solution elements?
b. If you are using a delivery sequence, do you have a way to temporarily bridge gaps until all deliveries are completed?

Metric A: Are workflows uninterrupted across solution elements?

The preparation step ensures there are physical or functional connections where the business solution crosses solution element boundaries. The business-transformation implementation leaders first review all elements in the business solution. They then identify where there are flows of work (activities, data, and policies) crossing business-solution elements. Finally, the business-transformation implementation leaders must ensure there are physical or functional connections when the flow of work crosses the boundaries between solution elements. There can be no missing or disjointed flows.

Metric B: If you are using a delivery sequence, do you have a way to temporarily bridge gaps until all deliveries are completed?

The preparation step ensures there are temporary functional bridges when the business solution is implemented via a delivery sequence. The business-transformation implementation leaders first review all elements in the business solution. They then identify where there are gaps in the flows of work (activities, data, and policies) crossing business-solution elements. The business-transformation implementation leaders then review the delivery sequence to identify the delivery in which the gaps will be resolved (i.e., gaps in the flow of work crossing business-solution elements are implemented in a subsequent delivery). Finally, the business-transformation implementation leaders ensure temporary functional bridges (e.g., through human intervention) are created to address the gaps until completion of the delivery in which the gaps are permanently resolved.

➢ Action 2: Create cohesive flow across your business solution.

Readiness was determined by answering the following two questions (i.e., readiness metrics), also shown in figure 118 (above):

a. Are workflows functionally aligned across solution elements?
b. If you are using a delivery sequence, do you have a way to temporarily bridge the solution flow until all deliveries are completed?

Metric A: Are workflows functionally aligned across solution elements

The preparation step ensures functionally aligned and contiguous flow of work across your business-solution elements. The business-transformation implementation leaders first review all elements in the business solution. They then identify where there are flows of work (activities, data, and policies) crossing business-solution elements. Finally, the business-transformation implementation leaders must ensure workflows are functionally aligned when the flow of work crosses the boundaries between solution elements.

Metric B: If you are using a delivery sequence, do you have a way to temporarily bridge the solution flow until all deliveries are completed?

The preparation step ensures there are temporary functionally aligned solution flows when the business solution is implemented across a delivery sequence. The business-transformation implementation leaders first review all elements in the business solution. They then identify where there is functional misalignment in the flows of work (activities, data, and policies) crossing business-solution elements. The business-transformation implementation leaders then review the delivery sequence to identify the delivery in which the functional misalignment will be resolved (i.e., the functional misalignment is addressed). Finally, the business-transformation implementation leaders ensure temporary functional alignment (e.g., through human intervention) is created to address the functional misalignment until completion of the delivery in which it is permanently resolved.

The complete readiness preparation for the goal "Integrate Solution" is shown in figure 119 (below).

Readiness Preparation	#16: Integrate Solution	
Preparation Actions	**1. Connect your business solution across all solution elements**	**2. Create cohesive flow across your business solution**
Preparation Steps	a. Create physical or functional connections where the business solution crosses solution element boundaries	a. Create functionally aligned and contiguous flow of work across your business solution elements
	b. Create temporary functional connection bridges when the business solution is implemented across a delivery sequence	b. Create temporary functionally aligned solution flow when the business solution is implemented across a delivery sequence

Figure 119: Readiness Preparation #16: Integrate Solution

Creating an Actionable Preparation

The readiness preparation summarized in figure 119 (above) can be made actionable by converting the actions and steps into deliverables and then combining them with the corresponding activities for producing them. Templates for readiness assessments and preparations are provided in the companion guide to this book.

Readiness Preparation Considerations

Connect Your Business Solution across All Solution Elements

As you work to ensure your business-solution elements are connected, you will need to also ensure that no preexisting connections within and among solution elements have become disconnected by the introduction of new business-solution elements.

When implementing the solution through multiple deliveries, you may need temporary human intervention to move data and workflow processes across the boundaries of solution elements (or even within solution elements). You'll have to evaluate whether the temporary human intervention is acceptable, and you must ensure some delivery in the sequence eliminates the human intervention.

Create functionally cohesive flow across your business solution.

As you work to ensure your business-solution elements are functionally aligned, you will need to also ensure that no preexisting functional alignment within and among solution elements has been become misaligned by the introduction of the new business-solution elements.

Again, if you are using a delivery sequence, it may be acceptable to temporarily use human intervention to transform data and workflow processes once they cross downstream solution element boundaries. You'll have to evaluate whether the temporary human intervention is acceptable, and as in the case with connected solutions, some delivery in the sequence must eliminate the human intervention.

Goal #17: Manage Business-Solution Change

It's hard to imagine a business transformation without at least some effort devoted to change management. Change management typically means helping people overcome their fear and resistance to change. There are many methodologies and approaches available, including useful practices and insights into the nature of organizational change itself. If the business-solution change is ineffectively managed, you run the risk of incomplete implementation, which can often be worse than a delayed implementation. While managing human change resistance is a significant part of change management, there are other change impacts induced from your business solution. This readiness goal ensures you consider all of them and are prepared to address them.

Readiness Assessment

Readiness Assessment Standards

The readiness assessment standards are formally expressed as follows:

1. You understand the impact of your business solution on your business.
2. Your business is ready to adopt your business solution.

If you know these, you have attained readiness with respect to "Manage Business-Solution Change." If you don't, you will need to complete the readiness preparation described later. As with all the readiness assessments, metrics are defined to evaluate your attainment of these standards.

Readiness Assessment Metrics

These metrics examine your company's readiness and allow you to identify the gaps in your understanding.

➤ Standard 1: You understand the impact of your business solution on your business.

   a. Have you identified the impacts of your business solution on your business?
   b. Have you expressed the impacts of your business solution in a statement of business solution impact?

➤ Standard 2: Your business is ready to adopt your business solution.

   a. Is your business ready to adopt the business solution impacts?
   b. If not, do you know what is required to adopt your business solution impacts?

The complete readiness assessment for the goal "Manage Business Solution" is shown in figure 120 (below).

Readiness Assessment	#17: Manage Business Solution Change	
Assessment Standards	1. You understand the impact of your business solution on your business	2. Your business is ready to adopt your business solution
Assessment Metrics	a. Have you identified the impacts of your business solution on your business?	a. Is your business ready to adopt the business solution impacts?
	b. Have you expressed the impacts of your business solution in a Statement of Business Solution Impact?	b. If not, do you know what is required to adopt your business solution impacts?

Figure 120: Readiness Assessment #17: Manage Business-Solution Change

Creating an Actionable Assessment

The readiness assessment summarized in figure 120 (above) can be made actionable by converting the standards and metrics into deliverables and then combining them with the corresponding activities for producing them. Templates for readiness assessments and preparations are provided in the companion guide to this book.

Readiness Assessment Considerations

The business impacts from your transformation were identified during the planning phase, but this was before the business solution was defined. The business solution will introduce additional change impacts on your business. You must also capture the change impacts induced by your business solution. They will be specific to how you have chosen to achieve your business capabilities and value objectives.

Similarly, the change impact readiness assessment conducted during the planning phase helps you evaluate your company's readiness to absorb the business change impacts. However, this is not an indication that your business will be ready to adopt the impacts of your business solution. You will need to conduct the business solution adoption assessment to determine your level of readiness to adopt the impacts from your business solution.

Finally, the change impact readiness gap closure prepared during the planning phase helps you close the gaps in readiness to begin your business transformation, but it will not tell you how to close the gaps in readiness to adopt your business solution. You will need to conduct the business solution adoption gap closure to close the gaps in business solution adoption readiness.

Readiness Preparation

The readiness assessment standards for managing business-solution change were defined as follows:

1. You understand the impact of your business solution on your business.
2. Your business is ready to adopt your business solution.

If your business is unable to attain these readiness assessment standards, you will need to undertake the following preparation actions to remediate the gaps.

Readiness Preparation Actions

The actions you can take to help evaluate and address the change impacts induced by your business solution are formally expressed as follows:

1. Prepare statement of business solution impact.
2. Assess readiness to adopt business solution.

By taking these actions, you ensure your business can attain the corresponding standards. The deliverables and activities presented next will guide you in completing these actions.

Readiness Preparation Steps

Every readiness assessment standard was assigned one or more metrics to facilitate evaluation. These metrics are now used in designing the preparation steps. One preparation step is required for each assessment metric.

➢ Action 1: Prepare statement of business solution impact.

Readiness was determined by answering the following two questions (i.e., readiness metrics), also shown in figure 120 (above):

a. Have you identified the impacts of your business solution on your business?
b. Have you expressed the impacts of your business solution in a statement of business solution impact?

Metric A: Have you identified the impacts of your business solution on your business?

The preparation step creates a business solution impact matrix. The business-transformation implementation leaders first use the business solution augmented change impact matrix created in Goal #10: Specify Required Business Solution (shown in figure 99: Business Solution Augmented Change Impact Matrix) to prepare the business solution impact matrix template. An example of this template is shown in figure 121, figure 122, and figure 123 (below). The matrix was distributed across three figures to show all six change impact dimensions. The "Solution Change Impact" column was added to capture whether there will be an impact to your business from the solution element. Solution change impacts are aligned with each type of solution element (see figure 97: Business Solution Types and Documentation Types for Each Change Impact Dimension). For example, the solution type "External Work Products and Services" could result in a change impact associated with this solution, and similarly for all other solution types.

The business-transformation implementation leaders will then review each business-solution element associated with each business change to determine whether it will result in an impact to the business. Any business-solution change impact is noted in the matrix.

#	Business Changes	What					How				
		Content & Deliverables	Solution Type	Solution Element	Solution Element ID	Solution Change Impact	Methods & Procedures	Solution Type	Solution Element	Solution Element ID	Solution Change Impact
1	Product Scope	[ ] Add New [ ] Discontinue [ ] Modify [ ] Combine [ ] Split Product Scope Induced Products or Services	[ ] External Work Products & Services [ ] Internal Work Products & Services	\<Name of Solution Element>	\<Unique Identifier for Solution Element>	[ ] External Work Products Impact [ ] External Work Services Impact [ ] Internal Work Products Impact [ ] Internal Work Services Impact	[ ] Add New [ ] Discontinue [ ] Modify Product Scope Induced Sourcing, Production, Selling, Marketing, Fulfillment, Financial or Business Support \<Method, Policy, or Procedure>	[ ] Processes & Workflows [ ] Procedures [ ] Policies [ ] Knowledge & Skills [ ] Tools & Equipment [ ] Software & Hardware Technology	\<Name of Solution Element>	\<Unique Identifier for Solution Element>	[ ] Processes & Workflows Impact [ ] Procedures Impact [ ] Policies Impact [ ] Knowledge & Skills Impact [ ] Tools & Equipment Impact [ ] Software & Hardware Technology Impact
. . .	. . .	. . .		.	.	.	. . .	.	.	.	.

Figure 121: Business-Solution Change Impact Matrix—Part 1

#	Business Changes	Who					Where				
		Relationships	Solution Type	Solution Element	Solution Element ID	Solution Change Impact	Locations	Solution Type	Solution Element	Solution Element ID	Solution Change Impact
1	Product Scope	[ ] Add New [ ] Discontinue [ ] Modify Product Scope Induced Relationship \<Internal, Reporting, Customer, Supplier, Regulatory Agency>	[ ] Organizational Structure [ ] Internal Staffing [ ] Trading Partner [ ] Agencies	\<Name of Solution Element>	\<Unique Identifier for Solution Element>	[ ] Organizational Structure Impact [ ] Internal Staffing Impact [ ] Trading Partner Impact [ ] Agencies Impact	[ ] Add New [ ] Discontinue [ ] Modify Product Scope Induced Location \<Workspaces, Offices, Customers, Suppliers>	[ ] Buildings & Facilities [ ] Offices & Workspaces	\<Name of Solution Element>	\<Unique Identifier for Solution Element>	[ ] Buildings & Facilities Impact [ ] Offices & Workspaces Impact
. . .	. . .	. . .		.			.	.	.	.	.

Figure 122: Business-Solution Change Impact Matrix—Part 2

#	Business Changes	When					Why				
		Timing & Cycles	Solution Type	Solution Element	Solution Element ID	Solution Change Impact	Purpose & Motivation	Solution Type	Solution Element	Solution Element ID	Solution Change Impact
1	Product Scope	[ ] Add New [ ] Discontinue [ ] Modify Product Scope Induced Timing or Cycles {Not Common}	[ ] Business Calendar & Cadence [ ] Time and Attendance Policies	\<Name of Solution Element>	\<Unique Identifier for Solution Element>	[ ] Business Calendar & Cadence Impact [ ] Time and Attendance Policies Impact	[ ] Add New [ ] Discontinue [ ] Modify Product Scope Induced Purpose or Motivation {Not Common}	[ ] Company Mission & Purpose [ ] Company Policies [ ] Code of Conduct [ ] Incentives & Compensation	\<Name of Solution Element>	\<Unique Identifier for Solution Element>	[ ] Company Mission & Purpose Impact [ ] Company Policies Impact [ ] Code of Conduct Impact [ ] Incentives & Compensation Impact
. . .	. . .	.					. . .	.	.	.	.

Figure 123: Business-Solution Change Impact Matrix—Part 3

Metric B: Have you expressed the impacts of your business solution in a statement of business solution impact?

The preparation step is to prepare a statement of business solution impact. The business-transformation implementation leaders use the business solution impact matrix produced above to create a statement of business solution impact. This should be of the form: "To complete the delivery of the business solution, we will address and adopt the following business change impacts <insert your business solution impacts>."

➢ Action 2: Assess readiness to adopt business solution.

Readiness was determined by answering the following two questions (i.e., readiness metrics), also shown in figure 120 (above):

a. Is your business ready to adopt the business solution impacts?
b. If not, do you know what is required to adopt your business solution impacts?

Metric A: Is your business ready to adopt the business solution impacts?

The preparation step creates and conducts a business solution adoption readiness assessment. The business-transformation implementation leaders first use the business-solution change impact matrix (produced above) to create the business solution adoption readiness assessment. An example of this template is shown in figure 124 (below). The "Solution Change Impact Adoption Gaps" column was added to capture any gaps your business has in adopting the impacts of your business solution. The template captures both willingness and ability gaps.

The business-transformation implementation leaders will then review each business solution impact associated with each business change to determine whether it will create a willingness or ability gap in adopting the business solution impact. Any adoption gap is noted in the assessment.

#	Business Changes	What							...
		Content & Deliverables	Solution Type	Solution Element	Solution Element ID	Solution Change Impact	Solution Change Impact Adoption Gaps	...
1	Product Scope	[ ] Add New [ ] Discontinue [ ] Modify [ ] Combine [ ] Split Product Scope Induced Products or Services	[ ] External Work Products & Services [ ] Internal Work Products & Services	<Name of Solution Element>	<Unique Identifier for Solution Element>	[ ] External Work Product Impact [ ] External Work Service Impact [ ] Internal Work Product Impact [ ] Internal Work Service Impact	**Willingness Gaps** [ ] Reluctance [ ] Uncertainty **Ability Gaps** [ ] Competency [ ] License/Permission [ ] Resource	...
.	.	.	.	.	.	.	.	...
.	.	.	.	.	.	.	.	

Figure 124: Business Solution Adoption Readiness Assessment

Metric B: If not, do you know what is required to adopt your business solution impacts?

The preparation step creates the business solution adoption gap closure. The business-transformation implementation leaders first use the business solution adoption readiness assessment (produced above), to create the business solution adoption gap closure template. An example of this template is shown in figure 125 (below). The "Solution Change Impact Adoption Gap Closure" column was added to capture how you will close gaps in the adoption of your business solution impacts. The template captures gap closure methods for both willingness and ability gaps.

The business-transformation implementation leaders will then review each business solution impact associated with each business change to determine how adoption gaps will be closed. The closure for any adoption gap is noted in the matrix.

#	Business Changes	Content & Deliverables	Solution Type	Solution Element	Solution Element ID	Solution Change Impact	Solution Change Impact Adoption Gaps	Solution Change Impact Adoption Gap Closure	...
						What			...
1	Product Scope	[ ] Add New [ ] Discontinue [ ] Modify [ ] Combine [ ] Split Product Scope Induced Products or Services	[ ] External Work Products & Services [ ] Internal Work Products & Services	<Name of Solution Element>	<Unique Identifier for Solution Element>	[ ] External Work Product Impact [ ] External Work Service Impact [ ] Internal Work Product Impact [ ] Internal Work Service Impact	**Willingness Gaps** [ ] Reluctance [ ] Uncertainty **Ability Gaps** [ ] Competency [ ] License/Permission [ ] Resource	**Willingness Gap Closure** [ ] Incentives [ ] Disincentives **Ability Gap Closure** [ ] Training [ ] Acquire [ ] Add	...
.	.	.	.	.	.	.	.	.	...

Figure 125: Business Solution Adoption Gap Closure

The complete readiness preparation for the goal "Manage Business-Solution Change" is shown in figure 126 (below).

Readiness Preparation	#17: Manage Business Solution Change	
Preparation Actions	1. Prepare Statement of Business Solution Impact	2. Assess Readiness to Adopt Business Solution
Preparation Steps	a. Create a Business Solution Impact Matrix	a. Prepare and conduct a Business Solution Adoption Readiness Assessment
	b. Prepare a Statement of Business Solution Impact	b. Create a Business Solution Adoption Gap Closure

Figure 126: Readiness Preparation #17: Manage Business-Solution Change

Creating an Actionable Preparation

The readiness preparation summarized in figure 126 (above) can be made actionable by converting the actions and steps into deliverables and then combining them with the corresponding activities for producing them. Templates for readiness assessments and preparations are provided in the companion guide to this book.

Readiness Preparation Considerations

Prepare Statement of Business Solution Impact

It is critical to identify all the user impacts introduced by your business solution as they are used in identifying both adoption gaps as well as the means to close those gaps. While it is not uncommon to have impacts from almost all elements of your business solution, they fortunately do not have the same degree of impact. This will be reflected in whether you will have a gap in adoption and if so, the level of effort required to close the gap.

Assess Readiness to Adopt Business Solution

You will need to assess change resistance within your business culture as well as among the individuals impacted by the solution. Some of the adoption gaps may become a hurdle to realizing the value of your business transformation. These will be considered in the readiness preparation for Goal #19: Specify Path to Value.

As you prepare your plan to close business solution adoption gaps, you will need to effectively manage/reduce resistance to change. Gap closure methods include incentives, disincentives, training, and if necessary, new resources. Unfortunately, not everyone is willing and able to adopt the new business solution.

Business-solution change management has primarily dealt with people readiness. There are other aspects of the business solution (technology, hardware and software, data, equipment, and supplies), which also must be made "ready." The business-solution change impact, business solution adoption assessment, and business solution adoption gap closure can be extended to address the nonhuman solution elements as well.

Goal #18: Communicate with Stakeholders

Stakeholder communication played an essential role in establishing "purpose" in the planning phase of the transformation. In the implementing phase of the transformation, the stakeholder group expands to anyone impacted by the transformation—including users, customers, suppliers, and external agencies. Stakeholder communication has three objectives: keeping your business motivated during the lengthy implementation, ensuring stakeholders are aware of the implementation progress, and letting stakeholders know how the transformation will impact them.

Poor communication was cited as a major source of failure in the research studies. Communication is challenged when the content or frequency are inappropriate, if your audience has not been fully identified, or when there is no mechanism for stakeholders to provide feedback. Feedback during implementation is critical to gauging change resistance and business solution adoption. Overcoming these challenges is the central theme of communication readiness.

Readiness Assessment

Readiness Assessment Standards

The readiness assessment standards are formally expressed as follows:

1. You have defined an implementation phase stakeholder communication plan.
2. You are effectively executing on your implementation phase stakeholder communication plan.

If you know these, then you have attained readiness with respect to "Communicate with Stakeholders." If you don't, you will need to complete the readiness preparation described later. As with all the readiness assessments, metrics are defined to evaluate your attainment of these standards.

Readiness Assessment Metrics

These metrics examine your company's readiness and allow you to identify the gaps in your understanding.

➤ Standard 1: You have defined an implementation phase stakeholder communication plan.

   a. Have you identified the types of communication content required for your business transformation?
   b. Have you identified the different stakeholder groups to receive the communications?
   c. Have you defined a communication cadence aligned with the implementation phase milestones?

> Standard 2: You are effectively executing on your implementation phase stakeholder communication plan.

  a. Is the proper content prepared and delivered to the stakeholder groups in accordance with the communication cadence?
  b. Is there a mechanism in place to receive and address feedback on the delivered communications?

The complete readiness assessment for the goal "Communicate with Stakeholders" is shown in figure 127 (below).

Readiness Assessment	#18: Communicate with Stakeholders	
Assessment Standards	1. You have defined an Implementation Phase stakeholder communication plan	2. You are effectively executing on your Implementation Phase stakeholder communication plan
Assessment Metrics	a. Have you identified the types of communication content required for your business transformation?	a. Is the proper content prepared and delivered to the stakeholder groups in accordance with the communication cadence?
	b. Have you identified the different stakeholder groups to receive the communications?	b. Is there a mechanism in place to receive and address feedback on the delivered communications?
	c. Have you defined a communication cadence aligned with the Implementation Phase milestones?	

Figure 127: Readiness Assessment #18: Communicate with Stakeholders

Creating an Actionable Assessment

The readiness assessment summarized in figure 127 (above) can be made actionable by converting the standards and metrics into deliverables and then combining them with the corresponding activities for producing them. Templates for readiness assessments and preparations are provided in the companion guide to this book.

Readiness Assessment Considerations

Communication during the implementation phase is very important. Employees and other stakeholders will naturally be curious about progress and want to know how the transformation will impact them personally. It's important to have a blend of communication types: motivational, progress, and impact.

Content should be tailored to the audience. There may be sensitive information reserved for executive stakeholders. At a minimum, you should have internal and external stakeholder groups. The communication cadence should be at least as frequent as the implementation phase milestones and preferably more frequent.

It's important to have a forum for feedback from impacted users and other stakeholder groups, which accomplishes two things. First, it lets people know they have a channel to raise concerns and ask questions. Second, it provides valuable information you can use to tailor future communications.

Readiness Preparation

The readiness assessment standards for communicating with stakeholders were defined as follows:

1. You have defined an implementation phase stakeholder communication plan.
2. You are effectively executing on your implementation phase stakeholder communication plan.

If your business is unable to attain these readiness assessment standards, you will need to undertake the following preparation actions to remediate the gaps.

Readiness Preparation Actions

The actions you can take to help establish strong communications during your implementation are formally expressed as follows:

1. Prepare an implementation phase stakeholder communication plan.
2. Execute on your implementation phase stakeholder communication plan.

By taking these actions, you ensure your business can attain the corresponding standards. The deliverables and activities presented next will guide you in completing these actions.

Readiness Preparation Steps

Every readiness assessment standard was assigned one or more metrics to facilitate evaluation. These metrics are now used in designing the preparation steps. One preparation step is required for each assessment metric.

> ➢ Action 1: Prepare an implementation phase stakeholder communication plan.

Readiness was determined by answering the following three questions (i.e., readiness metrics), also shown in figure 127 (above):

    a. Have you identified the types of communication content required for your business transformation?

    b. Have you identified the different stakeholder groups to receive the communications?

    c. Have you defined a communication cadence aligned with the implementation phase milestones?

Metric A: Have you identified the types of communication content required for your business transformation?

The preparation step identifies the types of communication content required for your business transformation. The business-transformation implementation leaders determine the types of communication content required for your business transformation. There are three basic types of communication content: motivational, progress, and impact. The content for each type of communication will depend on the business transformation. Motivational content can be drawn from Goal 9: Identify Required Business Capabilities and Goal 10: Specify Required Business Solution. Progress content can be drawn from Goal 12: Specify the Delivery Sequence. Impact content can be drawn from Goal 17: Manage Business Change.

Metric B: Have you identified the different stakeholder groups to receive the communications?

The preparation step identifies the different stakeholder groups to receive the communications. The business-transformation implementation leaders first identify the different stakeholder groups—for example, executives, delivery team, impacted users, customers, suppliers, regulatory agencies, and other external agencies. They then determine which stakeholder groups will receive each of the content types: motivational, progress, and impact. The business-transformation implementation leaders then determine whether any of the content needs to be tailored to the specific groups and how the content will be adjusted.

Metric C: Have you defined a communication cadence aligned with the implementation phase milestones?

The preparation step defines a communication cadence aligned with the implementation phase milestones. The communication cadence defines the frequency and order of the various communications delivered to the stakeholder groups. The delivery sequence can be used to build the communication cadence as it will contain milestones and dates. The business-transformation implementation leaders align the communication cadence to support the activities and milestones in the delivery sequence.

➢ Action 2: Execute on your implementation phase stakeholder communication plan.

Readiness was determined by answering the following two questions (i.e., readiness metrics), also shown in figure 127 (above):

a. Is the proper content prepared and delivered to the stakeholder groups in accordance with the communication cadence?

b. Is there a mechanism in place to receive and address feedback on the delivered communications?

Metric A: Is the proper content prepared and delivered to the stakeholder groups in accordance with the communication cadence?

The preparation step prepares content appropriate for each stakeholder group and delivers the content in accordance with the defined communication cadence. The business-transformation implementation leaders first prepare the content for each communication—with respect to the defined cadence. They then adjust content as required for each stakeholder group and obtain any required approvals. Finally, the business-transformation implementation leaders deliver the communications with instructions on how to provide both positive and critical feedback.

Metric B: Is there a mechanism in place to receive and address feedback on the delivered communications?

The preparation step ensures there is a mechanism to receive and address feedback on the delivered communications. The business-transformation implementation leaders set up a mechanism to receive feedback from all stakeholder groups on the implementation communications. They then setup a mechanism to respond to feedback from all stakeholder groups on the implementation communications. The business-transformation implementation leaders review communications feedback and prepare responses to the stakeholder groups as appropriate. Finally, they deliver the feedback to the stakeholder groups.

The complete readiness preparation for the goal "Communicate with Stakeholders" is shown in figure 128 (below).

Creating an Actionable Preparation

The readiness preparation summarized in figure 128 (below) can be made actionable by converting the actions and steps into deliverables and then combining them with the corresponding activities for

producing them. Templates for readiness assessments and preparations are provided in the companion guide to this book.

Readiness Preparation	#18: Communicate with Stakeholders	
Preparation Actions	1. Prepare an Implementation Phase stakeholder communication plan	2. Execute on your Implementation Phase stakeholder communication plan
Preparation Steps	a. Identify the types of communication content required for your business transformation	a. Prepare content appropriate for each stakeholder group and deliver in accordance with the communication cadence
	b. Identify the different stakeholder groups to receive the communications	b. Create a mechanism to receive and address feedback on the delivered communications
	c. Define a communication cadence aligned with the Implementation Phase milestones	

Figure 128: Readiness Preparation #18: Communicate with Stakeholders

Readiness Preparation Considerations

Prepare an Implementation Phase Stakeholder Communication Plan

While some of your progress and impacts may be of a sensitive nature, it is important to paint an accurate picture. Impacted users prefer the truth to filtered communications that are only positive.

You may wish to include issues that were encountered and addressed, or in process of being addressed. You may also wish to include testimonials from impacted users, which help establish credibility with colleagues and peer groups.

There is a balance between accuracy and unintentional/unnecessary alarm. You can be honest without explaining all details to each stakeholder group. This is critical with customers and other external entities. Competitors can exploit the challenges in your transformation to get your customers to switch to them.

As an alternative to an implementation milestone cadence, you may also wish to establish a regular communication cadence on a weekly or monthly basis—independent of the delivery sequence. It can complement the cadence based on the delivery sequence, or if it's frequent enough, it can replace the delivery sequence-based cadence. You may also incorporate transformation implementation communications into a preestablished communication cadence for your business.

Execute on your implementation phase stakeholder communication plan.

You should designate an owner for preparing and delivering communications. It's important to ensure consistent messaging and timing. There may be occasions where content approval is required for each stakeholder group. This needs to be factored into the communication process.

It's critical to let stakeholder groups know they have a channel to raise concerns and ask questions. It's also important to respond to all questions and feedback. This is part of the solution adoption process. You will get valuable information from the questions/feedback, which you can use to tailor future communications as well as adjust the implementation, if necessary.

Goal #19: Specify Path to Value

In Goal #11: Specify Value Realization, the transformation value objectives were mapped to the required business capabilities—and their corresponding parts of the business solution. In this goal, the path to value explains how the value is achieved and validated. First, any hurdles to achieve the business capabilities and value objectives are identified. Second, mitigation strategies are designed to overcome these hurdles.

Value Hurdles and Hurdle Mitigations

Value hurdles are impediments to achieving your value objectives. They originate within your business solution and take the form of implementation or adoption hurdles. Hurdles have the potential to prevent the realization of your value objectives.

Hurdle mitigations are activities to eliminate or reduce the impact of value hurdles. Some hurdle mitigations address implementation hurdles, and some address adoption hurdles.

The hurdles and corresponding mitigations form the path to value. This is shown schematically in figure 129 (below). Without an explicit path to value, there is no way to understand what is preventing a value objective from being realized—or what can be done to address it.

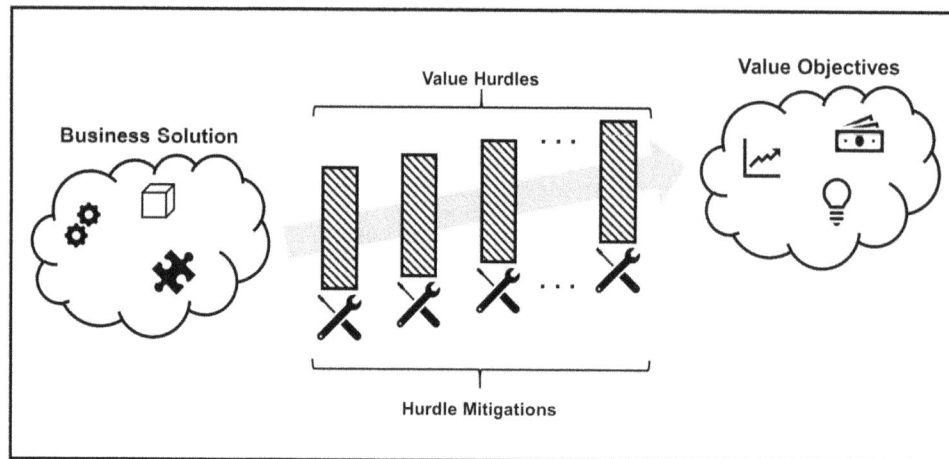

Figure 129: Path to Value—From Business Solution to Value Objectives

Readiness Assessment

Readiness Assessment Standards

The readiness assessment standards are formally expressed as follows:

1. You have identified all hurdles that could prevent the realization of a value objective.
2. You have identified mitigations to address all value objective hurdles.

If you know these, you have attained readiness with respect to "Specify Path to Value." If you don't, you will need to complete the readiness preparation described later. As with all the readiness assessments, metrics are defined to evaluate your attainment of these standards.

Readiness Assessment Metrics

These metrics examine your company's readiness and allow you to identify the gaps in your understanding.

➢ Standard 1: You have identified all hurdles that could prevent the realization of a value objective.

  a. Have you identified everything in your business solution that must be fully implemented to realize your value objectives?
  b. Have you identified everything in your business solution that must be fully adopted to realize your value objectives?

> Standard 2: Your business is ready to adopt your business solution.

   a. Have you identified a way to eliminate or reduce the impact of all business solution-implementation hurdles?

   b. Have you identified a way to eliminate or reduce the impact of all business solution-adoption hurdles?

The complete readiness assessment for the goal "Specify Path to Value" is shown in figure 130 (below).

Creating an Actionable Assessment

The readiness assessment summarized in figure 130 (below) can be made actionable by converting the standards and metrics into deliverables and then combining them with the corresponding activities for producing them. Templates for readiness assessments and preparations are provided in the companion guide to this book.

Readiness Assessment	#19: Specify Path to Value	
Assessment Standards	1. You have identified all hurdles that could prevent the realization of a value objective	2. You have identified mitigations to address all value objective hurdles
Assessment Metrics	a. Have you identified everything in your business solution, that must be fully implemented, to realize your value objectives?	a. Have you identified a way to eliminate or reduce the impact of all business solution implementation hurdles?
	b. Have you identified everything in your business solution, that must be fully adopted, to realize your value objectives?	b. Have you identified a way to eliminate or reduce the impact of all business solution adoption hurdles?

Figure 130: Readiness Assessment #19: Specify Path to Value

Readiness Assessment Considerations

It's possible your notation used to identify the solution elements required to achieve your value objectives is imperfect. Some value objectives may be realized directly through the solution elements, and some value objectives may be realized indirectly through business capabilities. You must ensure that you have captured both the direct and indirect solution elements. Similarly, as you consider everything in your business solution that must be adopted to realize your value objectives, you must examine both direct and indirect solution elements.

Solution delivery methodologies will normally include solution reviews and testing at key milestones to validate correct and complete implementation of the solution and mitigate the implementation hurdles.

In mitigating business solution-adoption hurdles, your action plan should address ability and willingness hurdles. Ability hurdles are mitigated through resource capacity, training, and equipment/tools. Willingness hurdles are mitigated through incentives and disincentives.

Readiness Preparation

The readiness assessment standards for specifying path to value were defined as follows:

1. You have identified all hurdles that could prevent the realization of a value objective.
2. You have identified mitigations to address all value objective hurdles.

If your business is unable to attain these readiness assessment standards, you will need to undertake the following preparation actions to remediate the gaps.

Readiness Preparation Actions

The actions you can take to help you identify value objective hurdles and implement hurdle mitigations are formally expressed as:

1. Identify all hurdles that could prevent the realization of a value objective.
2. Identify mitigations to address all value objective hurdles.

By taking these actions, you ensure your business can attain the corresponding standards. The deliverables and activities presented next will guide you in completing these actions.

Readiness Preparation Steps

Every readiness assessment standard was assigned one or more metrics to facilitate evaluation. These metrics are now used in designing the preparation steps. One preparation step is required for each assessment metric.

➢ Action 1: Identify all hurdles that could prevent the realization of a value objective.

Readiness was determined by answering the following two questions (i.e., readiness metrics), also shown in figure 130 (above):

a. Have you identified everything in your business solution that must be fully implemented to realize your value objectives?
b. Have you identified everything in your business solution that must be fully adopted to realize your value objectives?

Metric A: Have you identified everything in your business solution that must be fully implemented to realize your value objectives?

The preparation step is to identify the business solutions elements that must be fully implemented to realize your value objectives. These are the solution implementation hurdles. Fortunately, most of the identification work was covered by earlier readiness goals. There are two types of solution elements to consider—those directly associated with the value objectives and those indirectly associated with the value objectives—by way of the business capabilities. This is shown schematically in figure 131 (below).

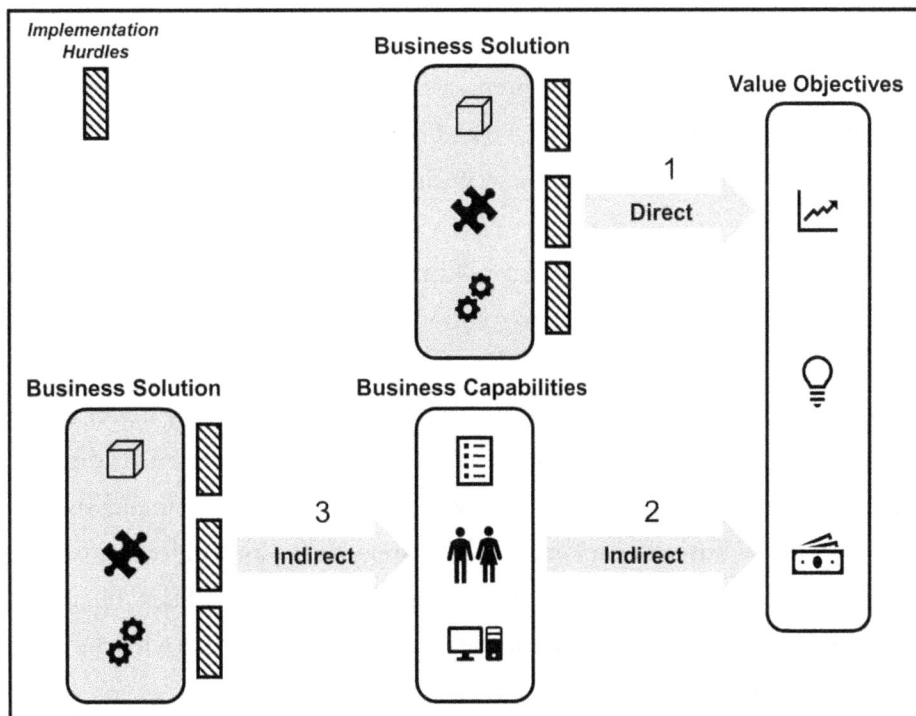

Figure 131: Business-Solution Implementation Hurdles

Direct Business-Solution Elements

From earlier in this chapter (Goal #11: Specify Value Realization), a value objective can only be achieved if all the business capabilities on which it depends are fully achieved and if all the solution elements on which it depends are fully realized. In figure 131, the implementation hurdles are shown as crosshatched boxes. The direct dependency path is labeled "1," and the indirect dependency path is labeled with "2" and "3."

Direct dependency business-solution elements were introduced in the readiness preparation for Goal #11. They were illustrated in figure 105: Value Objectives Augmented Future-State Business Solution Document. These business-solution elements directly supported the value objectives.

Indirect Business-Solution Elements

Identifying indirectly dependent business-solution elements requires two steps. The first step is to identify the business capabilities on which the value objectives depend. This part of the dependency path is labeled "2" in figure 131 (above). These business capabilities were also introduced in the readiness preparation for Goal #11 and illustrated in figure 104: Let Us Eat Cakes (Excerpt) Value Objectives Augmented Future-State Business Capability Model. The business capabilities supported the value objectives.

The second step is to identify the business-solution elements on which these business capabilities depend. This part of the dependency path is labeled "3" in figure 131 (above). These business-solution elements were introduced in the readiness preparation for Goal #10: Specify Required Business Solution and illustrated in figure 100: Let Us Eat Cakes (Excerpt) Business Solution Augmented Future-State Business Capability Model. These business-solution elements indirectly support the value objectives.

The implementation hurdles are then the set of business-solution elements that directly support the value objectives plus the set of business-solution elements that indirectly support the value objectives.

The business-transformation implementation leaders first determine the direct business-solution elements using the method described above to identify business-solution elements directly supporting the value objectives. They then identify the indirect business-solution elements using the method described above to identify business capabilities that support the value objectives and subsequently identify the business-solution elements that support those business capabilities. Finally, the business-transformation implementation leaders combine the direct solution elements with the indirect solution elements to form the set of solution implementation hurdles.

Metric B: Have you identified everything in your business solution that must be fully adopted to realize your value objectives?

The preparation step is to identify the business-solution change impact gaps that must be fully adopted to realize your value objectives. These are the solution-adoption hurdles. Most of the identification work was done earlier in this chapter. Again, there are two types of business-solution change impact gaps to consider—those directly associated with the value objectives and those indirectly associated with the value objectives by way of the business capabilities. This is shown schematically in figure 132 (below).

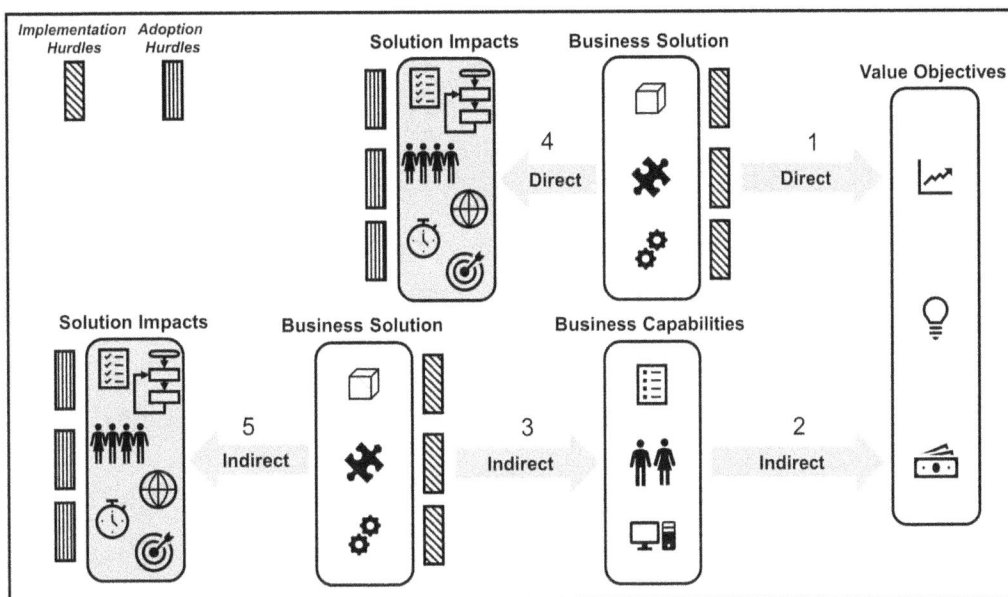

Figure 132: Business Solution-Adoption Hurdles

Direct Business-Solution Change Impacts

From earlier in this chapter (Goal #17: Manage Business-Solution Change), a business-solution element can induce solution change impacts. In figure 131, the adoption hurdles are shown as vertically striped boxes. The direct dependency path is labeled "4," and the indirect dependency path is labeled "5."

Solution change impacts were introduced in the readiness preparation for Goal #17. They were illustrated in figure 121: Business-Solution Change Impact Matrix—Part 1, figure 122: Business-Solution Change Impact Matrix—Part 2, and figure 123: Business-Solution Change Impact Matrix—Part 3. The business-solution change impact matrix was then used to identify whether a solution change impact also created an adoption gap. The adoption gaps were depicted in figure 124: Business

Solution Adoption Readiness Assessment. The direct business-solution change impacts are the adoption gaps for the direct business-solution elements.

Indirect Business-Solution Change Impacts

The indirect business-solution change impacts are shown on the path labeled "5" in figure 131. They are the adoption gaps for the indirect business-solution elements and are identified using the same method as described for direct business-solution change impacts.

The adoption hurdles are then the set of gaps associated with direct business-solution change impacts plus the set of gaps associated with indirect business-solution change impacts.

The business-transformation implementation leaders first determine the adoption gaps associated with the direct business-solution change impacts using the method described above to identify direct business-solution element gaps. They then determine the adoption gaps associated with the indirect business-solution change impacts using the method described above to identify indirect business-solution element gaps. Finally, the business-transformation implementation leaders combine the adoption gaps from the direct business-solution change impacts with the adoption gaps from the indirect business-solution change impacts to form the complete set of solution-adoption hurdles.

➤ Action 2: Identify mitigations to address all value objective hurdles.

Readiness was determined by answering the following two questions (i.e., readiness metrics), also shown in figure 130 (above):

a. Have you identified a way to eliminate or reduce the impact of all business solution-implementation hurdles?

b. Have you identified a way to eliminate or reduce the impact of all business solution-adoption hurdles?

Metric A: Have you identified a way to eliminate or reduce the impact of all business solution-implementation hurdles?

The preparation step is to enact design reviews and implementation testing for all business-solution element hurdles. These are the solution implementation hurdle mitigations. From Action 1 (above), the implementation hurdles were the set of business-solution elements that directly supported the value objectives plus the set of business-solution elements that indirectly supported the value objectives. Hurdle mitigations must be specified for the entire set of implementation hurdles shown schematically in figure 133 (below).

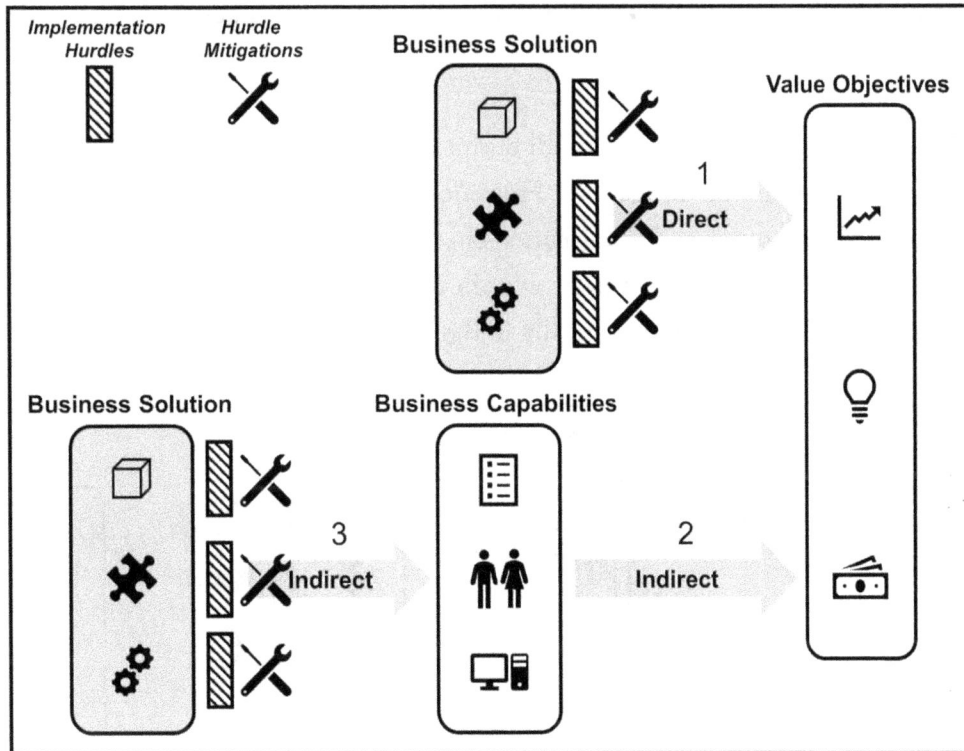

Figure 133: Business-Solution Implementation Hurdle Mitigations

Mitigating Business-Solution Implementation Hurdles

A solution implementation hurdle is mitigated by eliminating or reducing the chances of an incomplete or incorrect implementation of the corresponding business-solution element. The most direct way to mitigate implementation hurdles is by validating the solution's completeness and correctness against the specifications.

The business-transformation implementation leaders first review the list of business solution-implementation hurdles and for each hurdle, conduct the following:

- solution element design and build review
- solution element functional and technical testing

The business-transformation implementation leaders then plan to address (reimplement/remediate) any business-solution element that fails to meet the test of correctness and completeness.

Metric B: Have you identified a way to eliminate or reduce the impact of all business solution-adoption hurdles?

The preparation step is to enact closures for all business-solution change impact gap hurdles. These are the solution adoption hurdle mitigations. From Action 1 (above), the adoption hurdles were the set of gaps associated with direct business-solution change impacts plus the set of gaps associate with the indirect business-solution change impacts. Hurdle mitigations must be specified for the entire set of implementation hurdles shown schematically in figure 134 (below).

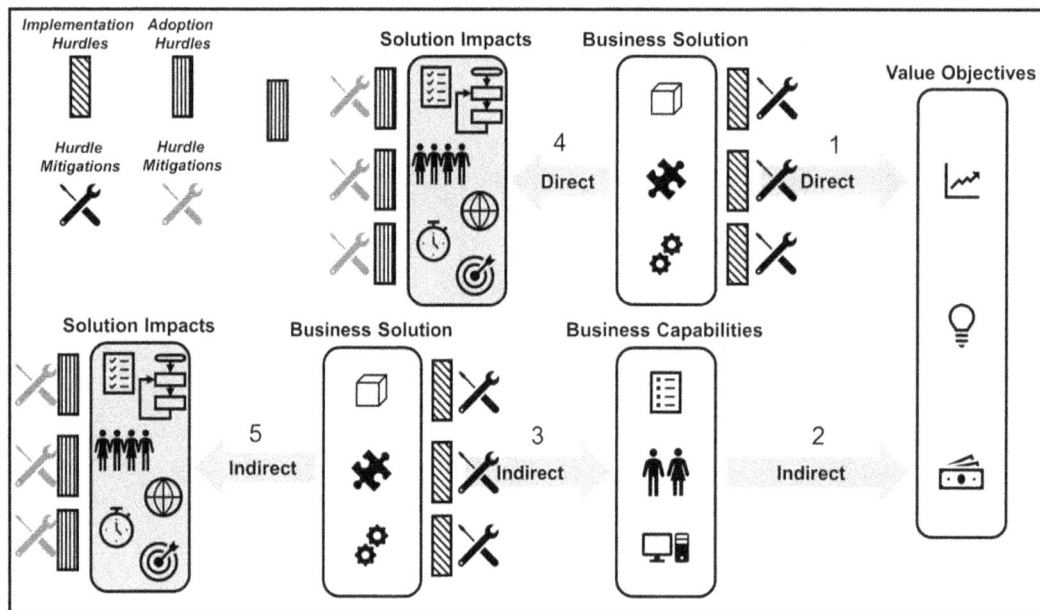

Figure 134: Business Solution Adoption Hurdle Mitigations

Mitigating Business Solution-Adoption Hurdles

A solution adoption hurdle is mitigated by eliminating or reducing the chances of incomplete or incorrect adoption of the corresponding business-solution element. In the readiness preparation for Goal #17: Manage Business-Solution Change, gap closures were identified for the solution change impacts that had adoption gaps. Gap closures were depicted in figure 125: Business Solution Adoption Gap Closure. These adoption gap closures are the business solution adoption hurdle mitigations.

Adoption gaps were closed using one of two methods depending on the type of adoption gap.

- Willingness adoption gaps were closed using incentives or disincentives.
- Ability adoption gaps were closed through training or by adding equipment, tools, or human or other resources.

The business-transformation implementation leaders review the list of business solution-adoption hurdles and for each hurdle and implement the appropriate adoption gap closure from those below:

- incentives/disincentives
- training
- equipment/tools/other resource
- additional people

The complete readiness preparation for the goal "Specify Path to Value" is shown in figure 135 (below).

Readiness Preparation	#19: Specify Path to Value	
Preparation Actions	1. Identify all hurdles that could prevent the realization of a value objective	2. Identify mitigations to address all value objective hurdles
Preparation Steps	a. Identify the business solution elements, that must be fully implemented, to realize your value objectives	a. Enact design reviews and implementation testing for all business solution element hurdles
	b. Identify the business solution change impact gaps, that must be fully adopted, to realize your value objectives	b. Enact gap closures for all business solution change impact gap hurdles

Figure 135: Readiness Preparation #19: Specify Path to Value

Creating an Actionable Preparation

The readiness preparation summarized in figure 135 (above) can be made actionable by converting the actions and steps into deliverables and then combining them with the corresponding activities for producing them. Templates for readiness assessments and preparations are provided in the companion guide to this book.

Readiness Preparation Considerations

Identify All Hurdles That Could Prevent the Realization of a Value Objective

As you work to identify the set of business-solution elements that support your value objectives, you may discover that the business-solution elements indirectly supporting your value objectives are already in the set of business-solution elements directly supporting your value objectives. That is okay—provided they are noted somewhere.

Not all business-solution change impacts have the potential to prevent the realization of a value objective. You only need to identify as hurdles those that will prevent the adoption of a business-solution element.

Identify mitigations to address all value objective hurdles.

Solution element reviews and testing are not foolproof and rarely can be exhaustively implemented. Testing can be automated, but the design of the test cannot. The cost to mitigate a business-solution element implementation or adoption hurdle should be much less than the cost to implement the business-solution element in the first place. If not, then the complexity of the solution is greater than the value it brings.

Chapter Takeaway Points

- We defined the five readiness goals for the design objective: identify required business capabilities, specify required business solution, specify value realization, specify the delivery sequence, and secure required resources.
- We defined the six readiness goals for the execution objective: instill program management rigor, standardize solution, integrate solution, manage business-solution change, communicate with stakeholder, and specify path to value.
- We defined readiness assessment standards and metrics for each of the readiness goals.
- We defined readiness preparations actions and steps for each of the readiness goals.
- We described how to make the readiness assessment and preparation actionable and identified items for consideration during a transformation.
- We described guidelines for producing a three-level business capabilities model and how to use the model to capture the post-transformation future state.
- We described how to use change impacts to identify various types of business solutions and how to document the business solution types.

- We described how to augment the change impact matrix with the business-solution elements addressing each change impact.
- We described how to augment the future-state business capability model with the business-solution elements addressing each business capability.
- We described how to document the type and source of each business-solution element.
- We described how to augment the future-state business capability model to show which capabilities are required to achieve your value objectives.
- We described how to augment the future-state business-solution document to show which business-solution elements are required to achieve your value objectives.
- We defined a business transformation delivery sequence as a sequentially ordered set of value objectives, business capabilities, and business-solution elements that must be delivered to achieve the purpose and scope of your business transformation.
- We described the minimum program management rigor required to support a business transformation that includes a solution-delivery methodology, program-governance structure and processes, and methods for monitoring, evaluating, and reporting on program progress.
- We described a method for describing and evaluating standard and custom business solutions and simple and complex business solutions.
- We described how to justify custom and complex business solutions over standard and simple solutions.
- We described a method for describing and evaluating integrated and unintegrated business solutions and connected and disconnected business solutions.
- We described how to ensure your business solutions are both integrated and connected.
- We described how to use a business-solution change impact matrix to capture the change impacts stemming from your choice of business-solution elements.
- We described how to create a business solution adoption readiness assessment to evaluate whether your business-solution change impacts result in adoption gaps.
- We described how to create a business solution adoption gap closure plan to close the adoption gaps resulting from the change impacts of your business solution.
- We described the types of communication, stakeholder groups, and communication cadence required during the implementation phase of your business transformation.
- We defined the path to value—from business solution to value objectives—including value hurdles and hurdle mitigations.
- We described how to identify the direct and indirect business-solution elements constituting implementation hurdles.
- We described how to identify the direct and indirect solution change impacts constituting adoption hurdles.
- We described how to mitigate implementation and adoption hurdles.

Chapter 6

OPTIMIZING PHASE READINESS

Success has always been easy to measure. It is the distance
between one's origins and one's final achievement.
—Michael Korda

The optimizing phase is where the value of the transformation is realized. The transformational change must be fully adopted within your business, the transformation's purpose must be fully achieved, and your business must attain an operational state of continuous improvement.

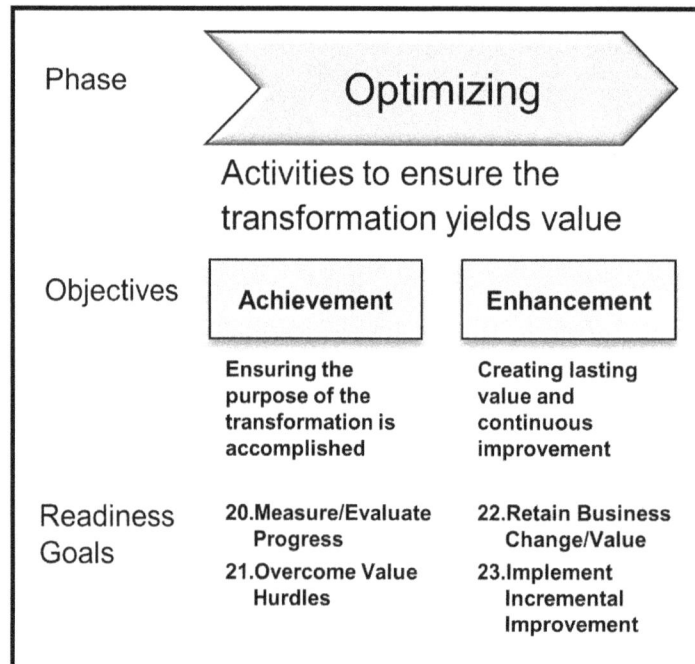

Phase	**Optimizing**	
	Activities to ensure the transformation yields value	
Objectives	**Achievement**	**Enhancement**
	Ensuring the purpose of the transformation is accomplished	Creating lasting value and continuous improvement
Readiness Goals	20.Measure/Evaluate Progress 21.Overcome Value Hurdles	22.Retain Business Change/Value 23.Implement Incremental Improvement

Figure 136: Optimizing Phase Readiness Goals

This chapter introduces readiness for the optimizing phase of a business transformation. It is organized in two sections. The first section covers readiness for the achievement objective, and the second covers readiness for the enhancement objective. As with previous chapters, each section will specify the readiness assessments and readiness preparations for the respective readiness goals. The readiness goals for the achievement and enhancement objectives are shown again in figure 136 (below).

Achievement Readiness

Achievement in the optimizing phase of a business transformation means achievement of the transformation's purpose. All changes and change impacts have been adopted and the value has been realized. Readiness of achievement is expressed through the attainment of two readiness goals as shown in figure 136 (above). Each of these readiness goals has specific readiness assessments and readiness preparations—formally expressed in the remainder of this section.

Goal #20: Measure/Evaluate Progress

Achieving the transformation means you can objectively demonstrate that the transformation's purpose, scope, and value objectives have been realized—and the required business capabilities and solutions have been implemented. Realization and implementation are measurable and at great risk if not measured and evaluated. This requires a framework of metrics, baseline, and target values and a method for tracking/publishing progress.

Metrics and Measurement

To ground the discussion on measuring and evaluating progress, it's helpful to have a few working definitions. Refer to figure 137 (below) for a pictorial overview.

Measures

Measures are unit specific values quantifying the state of an observation. The observation can be of anything in your business of relevance.

Metrics

Metrics are combinations of measures used to track and assess the status of a specific action or result. Metrics establish standards for the status and facilitate tracking to those standards.

Key Performance Indicators (KPIs)

KPIs are metrics that demonstrate progress in achieving your objectives. In this case, the objectives are adoption of your business solution, attainment of business capabilities, and realization of your value objectives. All KPIs are metrics, but not all metrics are KPIs.

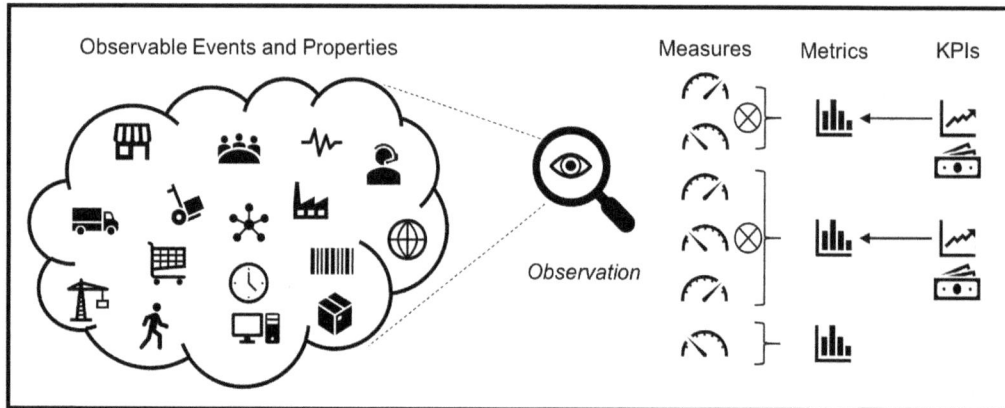

Figure 137: Measure, Metrics and KPIs

Example

Recall how Let Us Eat Cakes added an online ordering system for prepaid pickup orders. One of the value objectives of the transformation was to profitably service the on-the-go customer segment. A KPI that can be used to demonstrate progress toward that objective is on-the-go customer profitability. The metric for this KPI is the simple difference of two measures: on-the-go customer revenue and on-the-go cost of sales.

On-the-Go Customer Profitability

To ensure realization of the object to profitably service the on-the-go customer segment, Let Us Eat Cakes will need to establish a baseline and target for on-the-go customer profitability, and track and publish their progress over time. If on-the-go customer profitability does not track toward the intended target, Let Us Eat Cakes will need to take corrective action as described in Goal #21: Overcome Value Hurdles.

Readiness Assessment

Readiness Assessment Standards

The readiness assessment standards are formally expressed as follows:

1. You have a system in place to track progress in achieving the purpose and value of your business transformation.
2. You know the starting points and end goals for your progress tracking system.

If you know these, you have attained readiness with respect to "Measure/Evaluate Progress." If you don't, you will need to complete the readiness preparation described later. As with all the readiness assessments, metrics are defined to evaluate your attainment of these standards.

Readiness Assessment Metrics

These metrics examine your company's readiness and allow you to identify the gaps in your understanding.

➢ Standard 1: You have a system in place to track progress in achieving the purpose and value of your business transformation.

    a. Have you defined the metrics corresponding to adoption of the business solution, attainment of business capabilities, and realization of the value objectives?

    b. Have you defined and put in place a method for measuring, tracking, and publishing the metrics?

➢ Standard 2: You know the starting points and end goals for your progress tracking system.

    a. Have you established a metric baseline?

    b. Have you established metric targets?

The complete readiness assessment for the goal "Measure/Evaluate Progress" is shown in figure 138 (below).

Readiness Assessment	#20: Measure/Evaluate Progress	
Assessment Standards	1. You have a system in place to track progress in achieving the purpose and value of your business transformation	2. You know the starting points and end goals for your progress tracking system
Assessment Metrics	a. Have you defined the metrics corresponding to adoption of the business solution, attainment of business capabilities and realization of the value objectives?	a. Have you established a metric baseline?
	b. Have you defined and put in place a method for measuring, tracking and publishing the metrics?	b. Have you established metric targets?

Figure 138: Readiness Assessment #20: Measure/Evaluate Progress

Creating an Actionable Assessment

The readiness assessment summarized in figure 138 (above) can be made actionable by converting the standards and metrics into deliverables and then combining them with the corresponding activities for producing them. Templates for readiness assessments and preparations are provided in the companion guide to this book.

Readiness Assessment Considerations

As you evaluate the design of your KPIs, you must ensure they directly (or at least indirectly) track the progress of the business solution, attainment of business capabilities, and realization of the value objectives. The corresponding metrics must have clear and agreed-on definitions and units of measure and be comprised of quantified observable events that can be measured, tracked, and published.

Readiness Preparation

The readiness assessment standards for measuring/evaluating progress were defined as follows:

1. You have a system in place to track progress in achieving the purpose and value of your business transformation.
2. You know the starting points and end goals for your progress tracking system.

If your business is unable to attain these readiness assessment standards, you will need to undertake the following preparation actions to remediate the gaps.

Readiness Preparation Actions

The actions you can take to help ensure you can measure and evaluate the progress toward achieving the purpose of your transformation are formally expressed as follows:

1. Define and implement a system for tracking your progress in achieving the purpose and value of your business transformation
2. Establish starting points and end goals for your tracking system

By taking these actions, you ensure your business can attain the corresponding standards. The deliverables and activities presented next will guide you in completing these actions.

Readiness Preparation Steps

➢ Action 1: Define and implement a system for tracking your progress in achieving the purpose and value of your business transformation.

Readiness was determined by answering the following two questions (i.e., readiness metrics), also shown in figure 138 (above):

a. Have you defined the metrics corresponding to adoption of the business solution, attainment of business capabilities, and realization of the value objectives?
b. Have you defined and put in place a method for measuring, tracking, and publishing the metrics?

Metric A: Have you defined the metrics corresponding to adoption of the business solution, attainment of business capabilities, and realization of the value objectives?

The preparation step is to define metrics for tracking the adoption of your business solution, attainment of business capabilities, and realization of your value objectives. The business-transformation implementation leaders first review the mapping of business transformation value objectives to business capabilities from Goal #11: Specify Value Realization. They then identify metrics to track and assess the status of attaining the business capabilities and value objectives of the transformation. These become the KPIs for achieving your business capabilities and value objectives.

The business-transformation implementation leaders then review the willingness and ability gaps in achieving adoption of your business solution from Goal #17: Manage Business-Solution Change. They then identify metrics to track and assess the status of closing business solution adoption willingness and ability gaps. These become the KPIs for attaining adoption of your business solution.

Metric B: Have you defined and put in place a method for measuring, tracking, and publishing the metrics?

The preparation step is to define and develop a method for measuring, tracking, and publishing the metrics. The business-transformation implementation leaders first define the component measures for each KPI identified above, and if required, a method for combining them to produce the KPIs. Component measures must be quantifiable representations of directly observable actions. They must also have units assigned to them so they can represent a standard when combined into metrics.

The business-transformation implementation leaders then implement (develop or acquire) a mechanism for collecting the individual measures, combining them into metrics, and storing them for use in tracking, publishing, and evaluation. This will be your metric collection, tracking and publishing system. Finally, the business-transformation implementation leaders place the metric collection, tracking, and publishing system into productive use.

➤ Action 2: Establish starting points and end goals for your tracking system.

Readiness was determined by answering the following two questions (i.e., readiness metrics), also shown in figure 138 (above):

a. Have you established a metric baseline?
b. Have you established metric targets?

Metric A: Have you established a metric baseline?

The preparation step is to measure and establish baselines for each of your metrics. The business-transformation implementation leaders first designate a suitable reference point based on time, milestone, or some other condition. They then collect and publish all the metrics as a baseline for the KPIs for achieving your business capabilities and value objectives, and the KPIs for attaining adoption of your business solution.

Metric B: Have you established metric targets?

The preparation step is to establish targets for your metrics. The business-transformation implementation leaders define values for each of the KPIs such that when these values are reached, you can declare successful achievement of the purpose and value of your business transformation. These values represent the targets for your business transformation metric collection, tracking, and publishing system.

The complete readiness preparation for the goal "Measure/Evaluate Progress" is shown in figure 139 (below).

Readiness Preparation	#20: Measure/Evaluate Progress	
Preparation Actions	**1. Define and implement a system for tracking your progress in achieving the purpose and value of your business transformation**	**2. Establish starting points and end goals for your tracking system**
Preparation Steps	a. Define metrics for tracking the adoption of your business solution, attainment of business capabilities and realization of your value objectives	a. Measure and establish baselines for your metrics
	b. Define and develop a method for measuring, tracking and publishing the metrics	b. Establish targets for your metrics

Figure 139: Readiness Preparation #20: Measure/Evaluate Progress

Creating an Actionable Preparation

The readiness preparation summarized in figure 139 (above) can be made actionable by converting the actions and steps into deliverables and then combining them with the corresponding activities for producing them. Templates for readiness assessments and preparations are provided in the companion guide to this book.

Readiness Preparation Considerations

Define and implement a system for tracking your progress in achieving the purpose and value of your business transformation.

As you are defining the metrics to serve as KPIs for your transformation, you may need proxy measures if you can't directly measure what is required to produce the KPI. There are many metrics that are easy to measure, but they do not have a causal or at least correlated relationship with the key performance indicators. You need to demonstrate the relationship between what you can measure and the objectives you intend to achieve.

Also, the published metrics must be shared with those that can evaluate progress and implement corrective actions when necessary.

Establish starting points and end goals for your tracking system.

If it's possible, you should capture the baseline just prior to implementation of the business solution. However, it may be the case that the metrics are not valid until just after the implementation of the solution. Set your starting point as early as is practical to measure.

If a delivery sequence is used to carry out the implementation, the targets may be a series of target values over time. Targets can be tied to specific action plans in addressing the value hurdles identified in Goal #21: Overcome Value Hurdles.

Goal #21: Overcome Value Hurdles

Realizing the value of your transformation begins in the planning phase when you define the transformation's purpose and value. It continues through the implementing phase as you create a path from value objectives, to solution, to impacts, adoption gaps, and gap closures. This culminates in specific hurdles to value and their corresponding mitigations. In the optimizing phase, a method was given to help you measure your progress toward achieving the purpose and value. The final step is to apply the effort necessary to overcome the value hurdles. The entire process is illustrated in figure 140 (below). Each step is shown together with the respective readiness goal in which that step is introduced and addressed. If you neglect to assign and prioritize accountability for overcoming value hurdles, or are ineffective in executing the hurdle mitigations, your efforts will fail to produce measurable results.

Readiness Assessment

Readiness Assessment Standards

The readiness assessment standards are formally expressed as follows:

1. Your business is committed to adopting your business solution and achieving the purpose and value of your business transformation.
2. Your business is effectively executing on the strategies and plans to overcome your value hurdles.

If you know these, you have attained readiness with respect to "Overcome Value Hurdles." If you don't, you will need to complete the readiness preparation described later. As with all the readiness assessments, metrics are defined to evaluate your attainment of these standards.

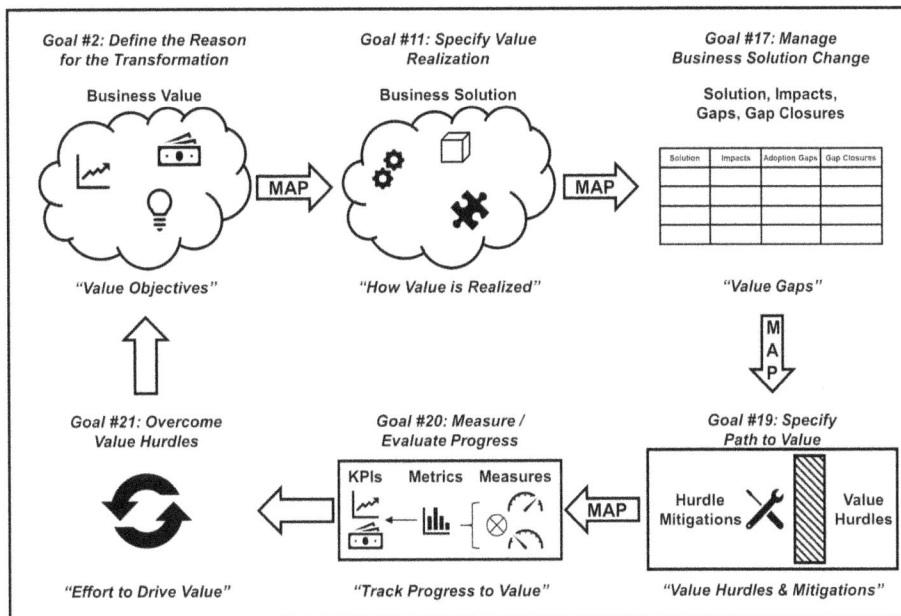

Figure 140: Realizing Business Value

Readiness Assessment Metrics

These metrics examine your company's readiness and allow you to identify the gaps in your understanding.

➢ Standard 1: Your business is committed to adopting your business solution and achieving the purpose and value of your business transformation.

   a. Have you assigned an owner, both accountable and responsible, for driving adoption of the business solution and realizing the value objectives?
   b. Have you provided the owner with sufficient resources to overcome impediments to solution adoption and value realization?

➢ Standard 2: Your business is effectively executing on the strategies and plans to overcome your value hurdles.

   a. Are you taking the required actions to overcome the hurdles to adoption and value realization?

b.   Are adoption/value relapses quickly corrected and successes quickly reinforced?

The complete readiness assessment for the goal "Overcome Value Hurdles" is shown in figure 141 (below).

Readiness Assessment	#21: Overcome Value Hurdles	
Assessment Standards	1. Your business is committed to adopting your business solution and achieving the purpose and value of your business transformation	2. Your business is effectively executing on the strategies and plans to overcome your value hurdles
Assessment Metrics	a. Have you assigned an owner, both accountable and responsible, for driving adoption of the business solution and realizing the value objectives?	a. Are you taking the required actions to overcome the hurdles to adoption and value realization?
	b. Have you provided the owner with sufficient resources to overcome impediments to solution adoption and value realization?	b. Are adoption/value relapses quickly corrected and successes quickly reinforced?

Figure 141: Readiness Assessment #21: Overcome Value Hurdles

Creating an Actionable Assessment

The readiness assessment summarized in figure 141 (above) can be made actionable by converting the standards and metrics into deliverables and then combining them with the corresponding activities for producing them. Templates for readiness assessments and preparations are provided in the companion guide to this book.

Readiness Assessment Considerations

The owner assigned to drive adoption of the business solution and realize the value objectives should be respected within your business and have the experience to lead these efforts. Resources, including money and employee time, must be prioritized and committed to overcoming the value hurdles.

There must be a plan in place and project management practices employed to execute the plan, monitor progress, and communicate status. Successes/wins should be celebrated and at least brought to light through regular communication. Finally, you should know whether the impacted users are struggling to master the new business solution, sliding backward, or making steady progress.

Readiness Preparation

The readiness assessment standards for overcoming value hurdles were defined as follows:

1. Your business is committed to adopting your business solution and achieving the purpose and value of your business transformation.
2. Your business is effectively executing on the strategies and plans to overcome your value hurdles.

If your business is unable to attain these readiness assessment standards, you will need to undertake the following preparation actions to remediate the gaps.

Readiness Preparation Actions

The actions you can take to ensure your business overcomes the hurdles to value are formally expressed as follows:

1. Commit the business to adopt the business solution and achieve the purpose and value of your business transformation.
2. Drive effective execution of the strategies and plans to overcome your value hurdles.

By taking these actions, you ensure your business can attain the corresponding standards. The deliverables and activities presented next will guide you in completing these actions.

Readiness Preparation Steps

➤ Action 1: Commit the business to adopt the business solution and achieve the purpose and value of your business transformation.

Readiness was determined by answering the following two questions (i.e., readiness metrics), also shown in figure 141 (above):

a. Have you assigned an owner, both accountable and responsible, for driving adoption of the business solution and realizing the value objectives?
b. Have you provided the owner with sufficient resources to overcome impediments to solution adoption and value realization?

Metric A: Have you assigned an owner, both accountable and responsible, for driving adoption of the business solution and realizing the value objectives?

The preparation step is to assign an executive owner with accountability and responsibility for driving adoption of the business solution and realizing the value objectives. The CEO must assign an owner who is respected and has the experience to lead the adoption and value realization efforts. The CEO should then communicate throughout the organization that this person is both accountable and responsible for leading the activities to overcome value hurdles.

Metric B: Have you provided the owner with sufficient resources to overcome impediments to solution adoption and value realization?

The preparation step provides this owner with sufficient resources and authority to overcome impediments to solution adoption and value realization. The CEO must provide the owner with enough resources and the authority to overcome impediments to solution adoption and value realization. The owner should have the authority to enact the plans but coordinate the implementation timeline through functional leaders. All functional executives must support the owner in carrying out the action plan.

➤ Action 2: Drive effective execution of the strategies and plans to overcome your value hurdles.

Readiness was determined by answering the following two questions (i.e., readiness metrics), also shown in figure 141 (above):

a. Are you taking the required actions to overcome the hurdles to adoption and value realization?
b. Are adoption/value relapses quickly corrected and successes quickly reinforced?

Metric A: Are you taking the required actions to overcome the hurdles to adoption and value realization?

The preparation step is to execute on the action plan to overcome hurdles to adoption and value realization. The owner first develops a cadence for implementation: weekly goals/objectives, task assignments, progress reviews, status reporting. The owner can use Goal #11 for value goals, Goal #17 and #19 for business solution adoption plans and value realization plans, respectively; and Goal #20 for the measurement and tracking system. Finally, the owner escalates to the executive team required plan corrections and any issues or deficiencies in the execution.

ARE YOU READY FOR YOUR BUSINESS TRANSFORMATION?

Metric B: Are adoption/value relapses quickly corrected and successes quickly reinforced?

The preparation step is to quickly correct relapses in adoption/value realization and reinforce successful adoption/value realization. The owner regularly monitors the progress of business solution adoption and realization of value objectives. Whenever successful adoption/value realization is achieved, it is reinforced through incentives and visibility throughout the business. If relapses in either solution adoption or value realization are encountered, the owner must determine the root cause, escalate this to the executive leaders, and correct them as quickly as possible.

The complete readiness preparation for the goal "Overcome Value Hurdles" is shown in figure 142 (below).

Readiness Preparation	#21: Overcome Value Hurdles	
Preparation Actions	1. Commit the business to adopt the business solution and achieve the purpose and value of your business transformation	2. Drive effective execution of the strategies and plans to overcome your value hurdles
Preparation Steps	a. Assign an executive owner with accountability and responsibility for driving adoption of the business solution and realizing the value objectives	a. Execute on the action plan to overcome hurdles to adoption and value realization
	b. Provide this owner with sufficient resources and authority to overcome impediments to solution adoption and value realization	b. Quickly correct the relapses in adoption/value realization and reinforce the successful adoption/value realization

Figure 142: Readiness Preparation #21: Overcome Value Hurdles

Creating an Actionable Preparation

The readiness preparation summarized in figure 142 (above) can be made actionable by converting the actions and steps into deliverables and then combining them with the corresponding activities for producing them. Templates for readiness assessments and preparations are provided in the companion guide to this book.

Readiness Preparation Considerations

Commit the business to adopt the business solution and achieve the purpose and value of your business transformation.

The implementation steering committee or some other committee of executives, could be the party responsible for driving solution adoption and value realization, but the committee should still have a leader to facilitate actions, address issues, and report on progress.

Drive effective execution of the strategies and plans to overcome your value hurdles.

You may elect to continue using the program management implementation methodology and perhaps even the same team to drive execution of the hurdle mitigation plan. You can hold forums with impacted users to understand what is working well, where struggles or relapses are occurring, why they are occurring and what can be done to address them. Wins should be institutionalized, and setbacks should be addressed immediately.

Enhancement Readiness

Enhancement in the optimizing phase of a business transformation implies the business has attained a new operating state—one in which the value of the transformation continues to increase over time. This is important as the disruption created by a transformation is not sustainable. However, incrementally improving an operating state is sustainable and far less disruptive. Readiness of enhancement is expressed through the attainment of two readiness goals shown earlier in figure 136. Each of these readiness goals has specific readiness assessments and readiness preparations—formally expressed in the remainder of this section.

Goal #22: Retain Your Business Change/Value

The transformation loses its impact if your business cannot retain the changes and value achieved. This will occur when your business neglects to assign and prioritize accountability for retaining adoption of the business changes and value objectives. If accountability has been assigned, then resources will need to be allocated, and change adoption and value objective metrics must also be defined, tracked, and published to help retain the transformation.

Readiness Assessment

Readiness Assessment Standards

The readiness assessment standards are formally expressed as follows:

1. Your business is committed to retaining the purpose and value of your business transformation.
2. Your business is effectively executing on the plans to retain the purpose and value of your business transformation.

If you know these, then you have attained readiness with respect to "Retain Your Business Change/ Value." If you don't, then you will need to complete the readiness preparation described later. As with all the readiness assessments, metrics are defined to evaluate your attainment of these standards.

Readiness Assessment Metrics

These metrics examine your company's readiness and allow you to identify the gaps in your understanding.

➢ Standard 1: Your business is committed to retaining the purpose and value of your business transformation.

    a. Have you assigned an owner to drive retention of your business transformation change and value?
    b. Have you provided resources to remediate relapses in business change and value should they occur?

➢ Standard 2: Your business is effectively executing on the plans to retain the purpose and value of your business transformation.

    a. Have you put in place a system to track the retention of your business transformation change and value?
    b. Are you taking action to diagnose and quickly remediate relapses in business transformation change and value?

The complete readiness assessment for the goal "Retain Your Business Change/Value" is shown figure 143 (below).

Readiness Assessment	#22: Retain Your Business Change/Value	
Assessment Standards	**1. Your business is committed to retaining the purpose and value of your business transformation**	**2. Your business is effectively executing on the plans to retain the purpose and value of your business transformation**
Assessment Metrics	a. Have you assigned an owner to drive retention of your business transformation change and value?	a. Have you put in place a system to track the retention of your business transformation change and value?
	b. Have you provided resources to remediate relapses in business change and value should they occur?	b. Are you taking action to diagnose and quickly remediate relapses in business transformation change and value?

Figure 143: Readiness Assessment #22: Retain Your Business Change/Value

Creating an Actionable Assessment

The readiness assessment summarized in figure 143 (above) can be made actionable by converting the standards and metrics into deliverables and then combining them with the corresponding activities for producing them. Templates for readiness assessments and preparations are provided in the companion guide to this book.

Readiness Assessment Considerations

As in the case of Goal #21: Overcome Value Hurdles, the owner assigned to drive retention of your business transformation should be respected within your business and have the experience to lead these efforts. Resources must be prioritized and committed to the retention as well.

Finally, you should be able to measure whether your business is having difficulty retaining the changes and value objectives from the transformation.

Readiness Preparation

The readiness assessment standards for retaining your business change/value were defined as follows:

1. Your business is committed to retaining the purpose and value of your business transformation.
2. Your business is effectively executing on the plans to retain the purpose and value of your business transformation.

If your business is unable to attain these readiness assessment standards, you will need to undertake the following preparation actions to remediate the gaps.

Readiness Preparation Actions

The actions you can take to help you retain the changes and value of your transformation are formally expressed as follows:

1. Commit the business to retain the purpose and value of your business transformation.
2. Drive effective execution of the plans to retain the purpose and value of your business transformation.

By taking these actions, you ensure your business can attain the corresponding standards. The deliverables and activities presented next will guide you in completing these actions.

Readiness Preparation Steps

➢ Action 1: Commit the business to retain the purpose and value of your business transformation.

Readiness was determined by answering the following two questions (i.e., readiness metrics), also shown in figure 143 (above):

a. Have you assigned an owner to drive retention of your business transformation change and value?
b. Have you provided resources to remediate relapses in business change and value should they occur?

Metric A: Have you assigned an owner to drive retention of your business transformation change and value?

The preparation step is to assign an executive owner to drive retention of your business transformation change and value. The CEO must assign an owner who is respected and has the experience to lead the retention efforts (disciplined, strong diagnostic skills). The CEO should then communicate throughout the organization that this person is both accountable and responsible for leading the activities to retain the business transformation change and value.

Metric B: Have you provided resources to remediate relapses in business change and value should they occur?

The preparation step provides this owner with sufficient resources and authority to remediate relapses in business change and value should they occur. The CEO must provide the owner with enough resources and the authority to carry out the plans to retain the business transformation change and value. All functional executives must support the owner in carrying out the action plan.

> Action 2: Drive effective execution of the plans to retain the purpose and value of your business transformation.

Readiness was determined by answering the following two questions (i.e., readiness metrics), also shown in figure 143 (above):

a. Have you put in place a system to track the retention of your business transformation change and value?
b. Are you taking action to diagnose and quickly remediate relapses in business transformation change and value?

Metric A: Have you put in place a system to track the retention of your business transformation change and value?

The preparation step is to define and put in place a method for measuring, tracking, and publishing the metrics to track retention of your business transformation change and value. The owner can leverage the KPIs, measures, and mechanism for tracking, publishing, and evaluation developed in Goal #20: Measure/Evaluate Progress. Finally, the owner will place the metric collection, tracking, and publishing system into productive use.

Metric B: Are you taking action to diagnose and quickly remediate relapses in business transformation change and value?

The preparation step is to execute actions to diagnose and quickly remediate relapses in business transformation change and value. The owner regularly monitors the metrics to determine if there are relapses in business transformation change and value. If relapses occur, the owner needs to analyze them to determine root cause and then escalate to executive leaders for remediation as quickly as possible.

The complete readiness preparation for the goal "Retain Your Business Change/Value" is shown in figure 144 (below).

Readiness Preparation	#22: Retain Your Business Change/Value	
Preparation Actions	1. Commit the business to retain the purpose and value of your business transformation	2. Drive effective execution of the plans to retain the purpose and value of your business transformation
Preparation Steps	a. Assign an executive owner to drive retention of your business transformation change and value	a. Define and develop a method for measuring, tracking and publishing the metrics to track the retention of your business transformation change and value
	b. Provide this owner with sufficient resources and authority to remediate relapses in business change and value should they occur	b. Execute actions to diagnose and quickly remediate relapses in business transformation change and value

Figure 144: Readiness Preparation #22: Retain Your Business Change/Value

Creating an Actionable Preparation

The readiness preparation summarized in figure 144 (above) can be made actionable by converting the actions and steps into deliverables and then combining them with the corresponding activities for producing them. Templates for readiness assessments and preparations are provided in the companion guide to this book.

Readiness Preparation Considerations

Commit the business to retain the purpose and value of your business transformation.

The implementation steering committee or some other committee of executives could be the party responsible for driving the retention of your business transformation, but the committee should still have a leader to facilitate tracking the KPIs, diagnosing relapses, implementing remediation plans, and reporting on progress.

Drive effective execution of the plans to retain the purpose and value of your business transformation.

Some relapses in your transformation may be due to other changes occurring within your business and not directly related to the business transformation. If that is the case, remediation may require revising, or even discontinuing, the other business changes.

Goal #23: Implement Incremental Improvement

The final readiness goal addresses your company's ability to incrementally improve the operating performance beyond your original business transformation. Incremental improvement is less disruptive than a business transformation. It is therefore in your company's best interest to pursue this course. Incremental improvement, like the other goals in the optimizing phase, is jeopardized if your business either neglects to assign and prioritize accountability or neglects to commit resources and efforts toward continuous improvement.

Readiness Assessment

Readiness Assessment Standards

The readiness assessment standards are formally expressed as follows:

1. Your business is committed to continuously improving on your business transformation.
2. Your business is effectively implementing a continuous improvement strategy.

If you know these, you have attained readiness with respect to "Implement Incremental Improvement." If you don't, you will need to complete the readiness preparation described later. As with all the readiness assessments, metrics are defined to evaluate your attainment of these standards.

Readiness Assessment Metrics

These metrics examine your company's readiness and allow you to identify the gaps in your understanding.

➢ Standard 1: Your business is committed to continuously improving on your business transformation.

    a. Have you assigned an owner to drive incremental improvement efforts?

b. Have you provided resources to implement continuous improvement efforts?

➤ Standard 2: Your business is effectively implementing a continuous improvement strategy.

a. Have you created an incremental improvement plan?

b. Are you effectively executing on your incremental improvement plan?

The complete readiness assessment for the goal "Implement Incremental Improvement" is shown figure 145 (below).

Readiness Assessment	#23: Implement Incremental Improvement	
Assessment Standards	1. Your business is committed to continuously improving on your business transformation	2. Your business is effectively implementing a continuous improvement strategy
Assessment Metrics	a. Have you assigned an owner to drive incremental improvement efforts?	a. Have you created an incremental improvement plan?
	b. Have you provided resources to implement continuous improvement efforts?	b. Are you effectively executing on your incremental improvement plan?

Figure 145: Readiness Assessment #23: Implement Incremental Improvement

Creating an Actionable Assessment

The readiness assessment summarized in figure 145 (above) can be made actionable by converting the standards and metrics into deliverables and then combining them with the corresponding activities for producing them. Templates for readiness assessments and preparations are provided in the companion guide to this book.

Readiness Assessment Considerations

As in the case with Goal 21 and Goal 22, the owner should be respected within the organization and have the experience to lead continuous improvement efforts. Resources must be prioritized and committed toward these efforts. Finally, the incremental improvement plan must be consistent with the spirit of the business transformation's purpose and value, and not undo the business capabilities and values achieved through the transformation.

Readiness Preparation

The readiness assessment standards for implementing incremental improvement were defined as follows:

1. Your business is committed to continuously improving on your business transformation.
2. Your business is effectively implementing a continuous improvement strategy.

If your business is unable to attain these readiness assessment standards, you will need to undertake the following preparation actions to remediate the gaps.

Readiness Preparation Actions

The actions you can take to help you instill incremental improvement beyond the business transformation are formally expressed as follows:

1. Commit the business to continuously improve on the value and purpose of your business transformation.
2. Prepare and implement a continuous improvement strategy.

By taking these actions, you ensure your business can attain the corresponding standards. The deliverables and activities presented next will guide you in completing these actions.

Readiness Preparation Steps

➤ Action 1: Commit the business to continuously improve on the value and purpose of your business transformation.

Readiness was determined by answering the following two questions (i.e., readiness metrics), also shown in figure 145 (above):

a. Have you assigned an owner to drive incremental improvement efforts?
b. Have you provided resources to implement continuous improvement efforts?

Metric A: Have you assigned an owner to drive incremental improvement efforts?

The preparation step is to assign an executive owner to drive incremental improvement on your business transformation. The CEO must assign an owner who is respected and has the experience to lead the incremental improvement efforts (disciplined, strong, continuous improvement background). The CEO should then communicate throughout the organization that this person is both accountable and responsible for leading the activities to incrementally improve on the business transformation's purpose and value.

Metric B: Have you provided resources to implement continuous improvement efforts?

The preparation step provides this owner with sufficient resources and authority to carry out continuous improvement efforts. The CEO must provide the owner with enough resources and the authority to carry out the incremental improvement plans. All functional executives must support the owner in carrying out the action plan.

➢ Action 2: Commit the business to continuously improve on the value and purpose of your business transformation.

Readiness was determined by answering the following two questions (i.e., readiness metrics), also shown in figure 145 (above):

a. Have you created an incremental improvement plan?
b. Are you effectively executing on your incremental improvement plan?

Metric A: Have you created an incremental improvement plan?

The preparation step is to define and develop a plan for incrementally improving on your business transformation's purpose and value. The owner will create an incremental improvement road map with goals/objectives and then validate and prioritize these with the executive team. Planning can draw from improvements to business capabilities, improvements to value objectives and business-solution elements, or improvements to adoption of the business solution. Finally, the owner will utilize program management techniques to plan and resource the improvements.

Metric B: Are you effectively executing on your incremental improvement plan?

The preparation step is to execute the action plan to incrementally improve your business transformation. The owner will utilize the program management discipline to execute, evaluate progress, address issues, and report on status.

The complete readiness preparation for the goal "Implement Incremental Improvement" is shown in figure 146 (below).

Readiness Preparation	#23: Implement Incremental Improvement	
Preparation Actions	**1. Commit the business to continuously improve on the value and purpose of your business transformation**	**2. Prepare and implement a continuous improvement strategy**
Preparation Steps	a. Assign an executive owner to drive incremental improvement on your business transformation	a. Define and develop a plan for incrementally improving on your business transformation purpose and value
	b. Provide this owner with sufficient resources and authority to carry out continuous improvement efforts	b. Execute on the action plan to incrementally improve your business transformation

Figure 146: Readiness Preparation #23: Implement Incremental Improvement

Creating an Actionable Preparation

The readiness preparation summarized in figure 146 (above) can be made actionable by converting the actions and steps into deliverables and then combining them with the corresponding activities for producing them. Templates for readiness assessments and preparations are provided in the companion guide to this book.

Readiness Preparation Considerations

Commit the business to continuously improve on the value and purpose of your business transformation.

The owner assigned to drive incremental improvement could be the same person responsible for retaining business change/value. At the very least, if the efforts to incrementally improve on the business transformation overlap with efforts to retain the original business transformation changes, the two efforts will need to be coordinated.

Prepare and implement a continuous improvement strategy.

The continuous improvement plan can be incorporated into your annual capital improvement planning process. Improvement plan goals and objectives can include items that were descoped from the original business transformation. You must also ensure that incremental improvement efforts are consistent with the purpose and value of the original business transformation. If the business environment changed during or since the implementation of the transformation, improvement plans should be validated against these changes.

Chapter Takeaway Points

- We defined the two readiness goals for the achievement objective: measure/evaluate progress and overcome value hurdles.

- We defined the two readiness goals for the enhancement objective: retain business change/value and implement incremental improvement.

- We defined readiness assessment standards and metrics for each of the readiness goals.

- We defined readiness preparations actions and steps for each of the readiness goals.

- We described how to make the readiness assessment and preparation actionable and identified items for consideration during a transformation.

- We described how to setup a system of KPIs, metrics, and measurements to track and evaluate progress toward achieving the transformation's purpose and value.

- We illustrated the entire value realization process from defining the transformation's purpose/value addressed in goal #2: define the reason for the transformation through overcoming hurdles to value in goal #21: overcome value hurdles.

- Techniques were provided for ensuring you retain the value of your business transformation and can improve beyond the original purpose and value.

Chapter 7

PUTTING READINESS TO USE

Isn't it a pleasure to study and practice what you have learned?
—Confucius

This chapter considers how to put business transformation readiness techniques into practice. It begins with an application of readiness to the challenges facing the Let Us Eat Cakes bakery and closes by addressing how to approach transformation readiness within your own company.

Let Us Eat Cakes Revisited

Let Us Eat Cakes was a fictitious pickup/dine-in bakery with five locations serving local neighborhoods. To drive growth, they began an effort to service on-the-go customers using an online ordering/ payment system. The objective was to provide commuters with quick and convenient order placement and pickup. However, issues emerged after a few months into their modernization effort—none of which were anticipated—but all of which were the natural consequences of adding an online presence.

Readiness Issues at Let Us Eat Cakes

Let Us Eat Cakes began their investment to modernize before they understood all the implications of the modernization. As the modernization effort proceeded, the experienced employees started to ask relevant questions around the design of the solution.

1. How would they handle the additional volume of on-the-go customers without overflowing the sales and dining areas?
2. How would customers who paid for their purchases online pick up their orders and be on their way quickly? Where would they park?

3. Do the online commuter customers want/need assistance in designing specialty cakes?

4. How would customer credit card data be handled securely?

5. Who would support the new website?

6. Would a second shift be required to process online orders placed after normal business hours?

7. Where and how would online orders be staged for pickup?

8. Will the restaurant supply vendor change their delivery schedule to avoid the commuter customer rush?

Furthermore, Let Us Eat Cakes didn't know whether they had identified all their challenges. They needed to assess their level of readiness before taking on its transformation.

As reality began to sink in, the leadership questioned whether they should continue their modernization effort—even though they had already spent one-third of their budget to develop the website. On the one hand, they knew they needed to support the on-the-go customer segment to meet growth objectives, and canceling the modernization effort was not an attractive option. On the other hand, the challenges still needed to be addressed, and there could be others.

Moving forward caused a lot of anxiety. Consequently, Let Us Eat Cakes suffered from the plague of transformation paralysis. They needed to better prepare their business to undertake the modernization effort.

Readiness Solutions at Let Us Eat Cakes

Let Us Eat Cakes' issues are materializing during the implementing phase of its transformation. However, the root cause stems from insufficient work in the planning phase, most of which can be attributed to three readiness goals:

- Goal #2: Define the Reason for the Transformation
- Goal #5: Identify What Needs to Change
- Goal #6: Understand the Impact of the Change

The first readiness goal is aligned with the purpose objective, and the second and third readiness goals are aligned with the scope objective. This is illustrated within the context of the change cycle in figure 147 (below).

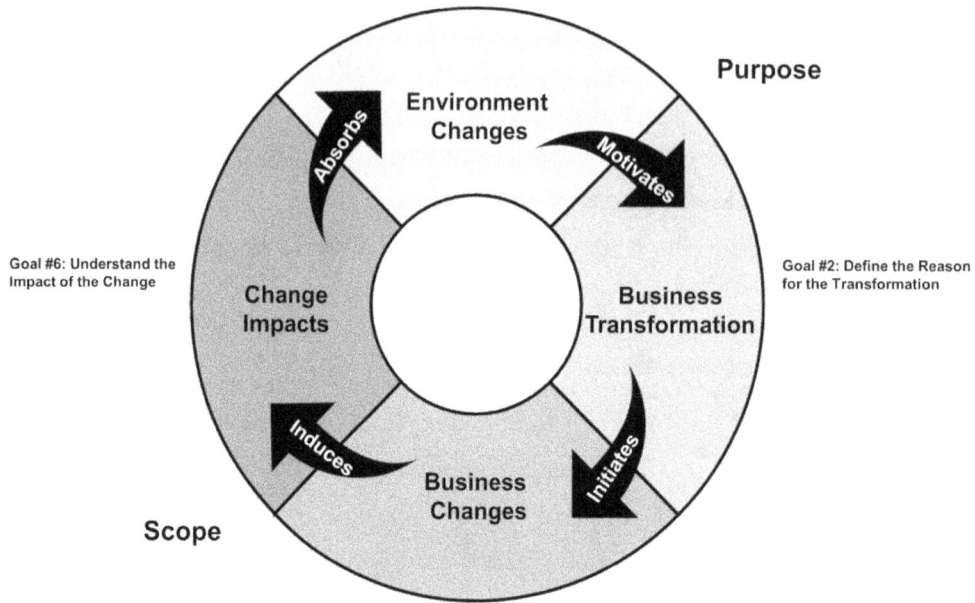

Figure 147: Let Us Eat Cakes Change Cycle

Purpose Readiness

The readiness assessment for Goal #2: Define the Reason for the Transformation is shown again in figure 148 (below).

Readiness Assessment	#2: Identify the Reason for the Transformation		
Assessment Standards	**1. You understand the reason for your transformation**	**2. Your reason is aligned with your company's mission**	**3. Your reason produces a compelling next state with lasting value**
Assessment Metrics	a. Do you know what is motivating your company to transform its business?	a. Does your reason follow logically from the current state of your business?	a. Does the reason create a compelling next state?
	b. Have you created a formal Statement of Purpose for the transformation?	b. Is it reasonable to get to the next state from the current state?	b. Does the next state create lasting value for your company?
	c. Is the Statement of Purpose clear and without ambiguity?	c. Is the next state on the path of your mission?	c. Does the Statement of Purpose express the Value to the company?

Figure 148: Let Us Eat Cakes Goal #2 Readiness Assessment

While Let Us Eat Cakes has an informal understanding of the purpose of its transformation, it is not enough to allow them to identify the impacts induced by their business changes. If the senior leaders at Let Us Eat Cakes had conducted the readiness assessment for Goal #2, they would understand their readiness gaps and proceed with the preparation shown in figure 149 (below).

Readiness Preparation	#2: Identify the Reason for the Transformation		
Preparation Actions	1. Produce a Transformation Statement of Purpose	2. Align your Statement of Purpose within the context of your Company's Purpose	3. Produce a formal Statement of Value for your Transformation
Preparation Steps	a. Business Transformation Statement of Motivation	a. Statement of Purpose Validation	a. Transformation Vision Statement
	b. Business Transformation Statement of Purpose	b. Statement of Purpose Feasibility	b. Transformation Value Proposition
	c. Business Transformation Confirmation of Clarity	c. Statement of Purpose Congruence	c. Statement of Purpose/Value

Figure 149: Let Us Eat Cakes Goal #2 Readiness Preparation

The motivation for carrying out their modernization effort (preparation step 1a in figure 149) is illustrated in figure 150 (below).

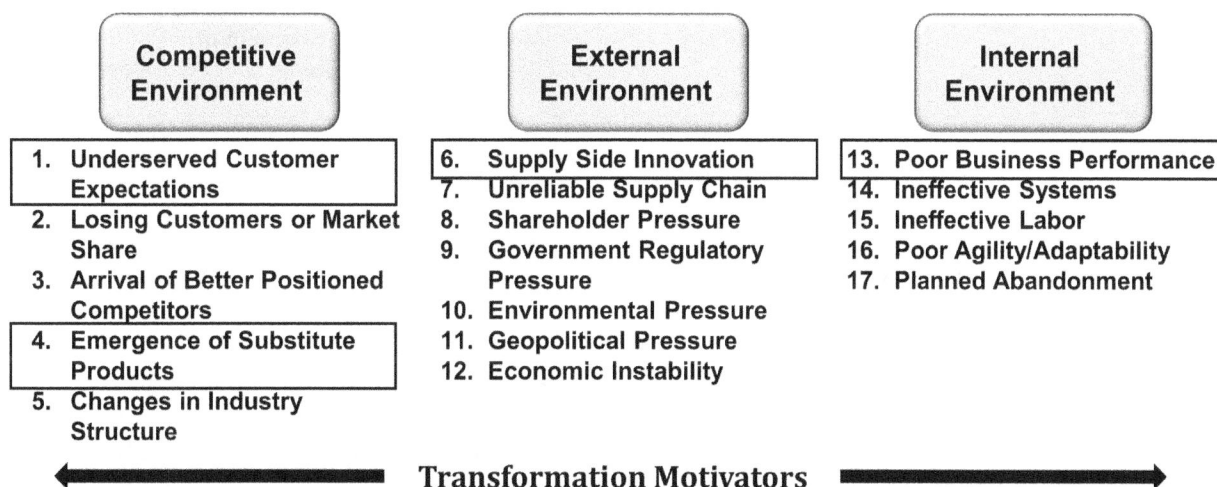

Competitive Environment

1. Underserved Customer Expectations
2. Losing Customers or Market Share
3. Arrival of Better Positioned Competitors
4. Emergence of Substitute Products
5. Changes in Industry Structure

External Environment

6. Supply Side Innovation
7. Unreliable Supply Chain
8. Shareholder Pressure
9. Government Regulatory Pressure
10. Environmental Pressure
11. Geopolitical Pressure
12. Economic Instability

Internal Environment

13. Poor Business Performance
14. Ineffective Systems
15. Ineffective Labor
16. Poor Agility/Adaptability
17. Planned Abandonment

◄ **Transformation Motivators** ►

Figure 150: Let Us Eat Cakes' Business Transformation Motivators

Let Us Eat Cakes' modernization motivators include the following:

1. Underserved Customer Expectations. On-the-go customers wanted to be in and out quickly.

4. Emergence of Substitute Products. Customers have other options for baked goods.

6. Supply-Side Innovation. Availability of mobile-enabled order placement capability.

13. Poor Business Performance. Additional growth was needed from the on-the-go segment.

Once Let Us Eat Cakes understands the motivation for their modernization, they can use the remainder of the Goal #2 readiness preparation to fully articulate the purpose and value. Most importantly, they will be well positioned to define the scope of business changes and change impacts.

Scope Readiness

Goal #5: Identify What Needs to Change

The readiness assessment for Goal #5: Identify What Needs to Change, is shown again in figure 151 (below). It's clear, even from a quick read through of the standards and metrics, that Let Us Eat Cakes did not thoroughly capture the scope of their modernization. A key output of the readiness preparation for Goal #5 (shown again in figure 152 below) is the statement of business change. This relates the motivators of a transformation to the business changes initiated. The potential business changes initiated are shown again in figure 153 (below).

Readiness Assessment	#5: Identify What Needs to Change		
Assessment Standards	1. You know what needs to change in your business to achieve the transformation	2. You have a Statement of Transformation Scope	3. Your stakeholders are aligned around the Statement of Transformation Scope
Assessment Metrics	a. Have you identified EVERYTHING in your business that needs to change to achieve your transformation?	Have you prepared a formal statement of transformation scope?	a. Have you reviewed the statement of transformation scope with all stakeholders for validation and commitment?
	b. Have you assigned a priority and sequence to the set of changes?		b. Do you have validation and commitment?

Figure 151: Let Us Eat Cakes Goal #5 Readiness Assessment

Readiness Preparation	#5: Identify What Needs to Change		
Preparation Actions	1. Prepare Inventory of Business Changes	2. Prepare Statement of Transformation Scope	3. Secure Stakeholder Commitment to the Statement of Transformation Scope
Preparation Steps	a. Statement of Business Change	Statement of Transformation Scope	a. Stakeholder Statement of Transformation Scope Communication
	b. Business Change Priority & Sequence Plan		b. Stakeholder Statement of Transformation Scope Acknowledgement

Figure 152: Let Us Eat Cakes Goal #5 Readiness Preparation

As these are still potential business changes, Let Us Eat Cakes must still identify the changes it will initiate during their modernization. The business changes they initiated include the following:

2. service scope (online ordering and payment)

3. industry/market served (on-the-go customers)

4. customer experience (quick and convenient pay-in-advance experience)

5. technology platform (mobile-enabled website for placing orders)

9. sales/distribution channel (online purchasing and quick pickup)

Let Us Eat Cakes is now able to create a statement of business change and a formal statement of transformation scope. These statements can then be reviewed with their key stakeholders to ensure commitment to the modernization effort and allow Let Us Eat Cakes to identify the impacts induced by the business changes.

	Transformation Motivators (Reasons for your Transformation)	1. Product Scope	2. Service Scope	3. Industry/Market Served	4. Customer Experience	5. Technology Platform	6. Cost Structure	7. Ownership Structure	8. Internal Organization	9. Sales/Distribution Channel	10. Core Capabilities Definition	11. Outsourcing & Insourcing	12. Risk Profile	13. Regulatory Profile	14. Geographic Structure	15. Corporate Culture/Values
Competitive Environment	1. Underserved Customer Expectations	●	●	●	●	●				●	●					
	2. Losing Customers or Market Share															
	3. Arrival of Better Positioned Competitors															
	4. Emergence of Substitute Products	●	●	●	●						●					
	5. Changes in Industry Structure															
External Environment	6. Supply Side Innovation	●	●		●	●	●				●					
	7. Unreliable Supply Chain															
	8. Shareholder Pressure															
	9. Government Regulatory Pressure															
	10. Environmental Pressure															
	11. Geopolitical Pressure															
	12. Economic Instability															
Internal Environment	13. Poor Business Performance	●	●	●	●	●	●	●	●	●	●	●				
	14. Ineffective Systems															
	15. Ineffective Labor															
	16. Poor Agility/Adaptability															
	17. Planned Abandonment															

Figure 153: Let Us Eat Cakes Potential Business Changes Initiated

Goal #6: Understand the Impact of the Change

The readiness assessment for Goal #6: Understand the Impact of the Change is shown again in figure 154 (below). This goal addresses Let Us Eat Cakes' readiness issues by first identifying all the impacts from their modernization effort and then evaluating whether they are ready to begin addressing those impacts. Two key outputs of the readiness preparation for Goal #6 (shown in figure 155 below), are the business change impact profile and change impact matrix. The change impact profile relates business changes to the potential impacts (what, how, who, where, when, and why) they will induce.

Readiness Assessment	#6: Understand the Impact of the Change	
Assessment Standards	1. You understand the impact of the Change Scope on your business	2. Your business is ready to undertake the Change Scope
Assessment Metrics	a. Have you identified the business impacts of all the changes required for the transformation?	a. Do you know which of the changes will be difficult for your business to enact or adopt? Is your business ready to begin implementing the changes?
	b. Have you expressed the magnitude of the impact to your business - in a Statement of Transformation Impact?	b. If not, what is required to occur or be in place to commence with change implementation and adoption? Can your business address all open change implementation/adoption readiness gaps prior to investment?

Figure 154: Let Us Eat Cakes Goal #6 Readiness Assessment

Readiness Preparation	#6: Understand the Impact of the Change	
Preparation Actions	1. Prepare Statement of Transformation Impact	2. Assess Readiness to Begin Transformation
Preparation Steps	a. Change Impact Profile and Transformation Change Impact Matrix	a. Transformation Change Readiness Assessment
	b. Statement of Transformation Impact	b. Transformation Change Readiness Gap Closure

Figure 155: Let Us Eat Cakes Goal #6 Readiness Preparation

Each of the readiness issues experienced during Let Us Eat Cakes' modernization are the result of impacts to the what, how, who, where, when, and why dimensions. For example, consider this question asked by one of their experienced employees: "How will we handle the additional volume of on-the-go customers without overflowing the sales and dining areas?"

This question implies impacts to the how, who, and where dimensions were indeed induced by their modernization.

1. How. A method is now needed to address more customer volume than in the past.
2. Who. There is a new customer segment (on-the-go customers) with whom a relationship must be established.
3. Where. The additional volume must be addressed in some other area of the bakery than the sales and dining areas used for their other customer segments.

The change impact dimensions for the remaining readiness issues is shown in figure 157 (below).

#	Business Changes	Quantified Change Impact Profile						Total
		What	How	Who	Where	When	Why	
1	Product Scope							
2	Service Scope	10	10	5	5	0	5	35
3	Industry/Market Served	5	5	10	5	5	10	40
4	Customer Experience	10	10	10	0	0	10	40
5	Technology Platform	10	10	5	0	0	5	30
6	Cost Structure							
7	Ownership Structure							
8	Internal Organization							
9	Sales/Distribution Channel	10	10	10	10	5	10	55
10	Core Capabilities Definition							
11	Outsourcing & Insourcing							
12	Risk Profile							
13	Regulatory Profile							
14	Geographic Structure							
15	Corporate Culture/Values							
	Total Change Impact	45	45	40	20	10	40	200

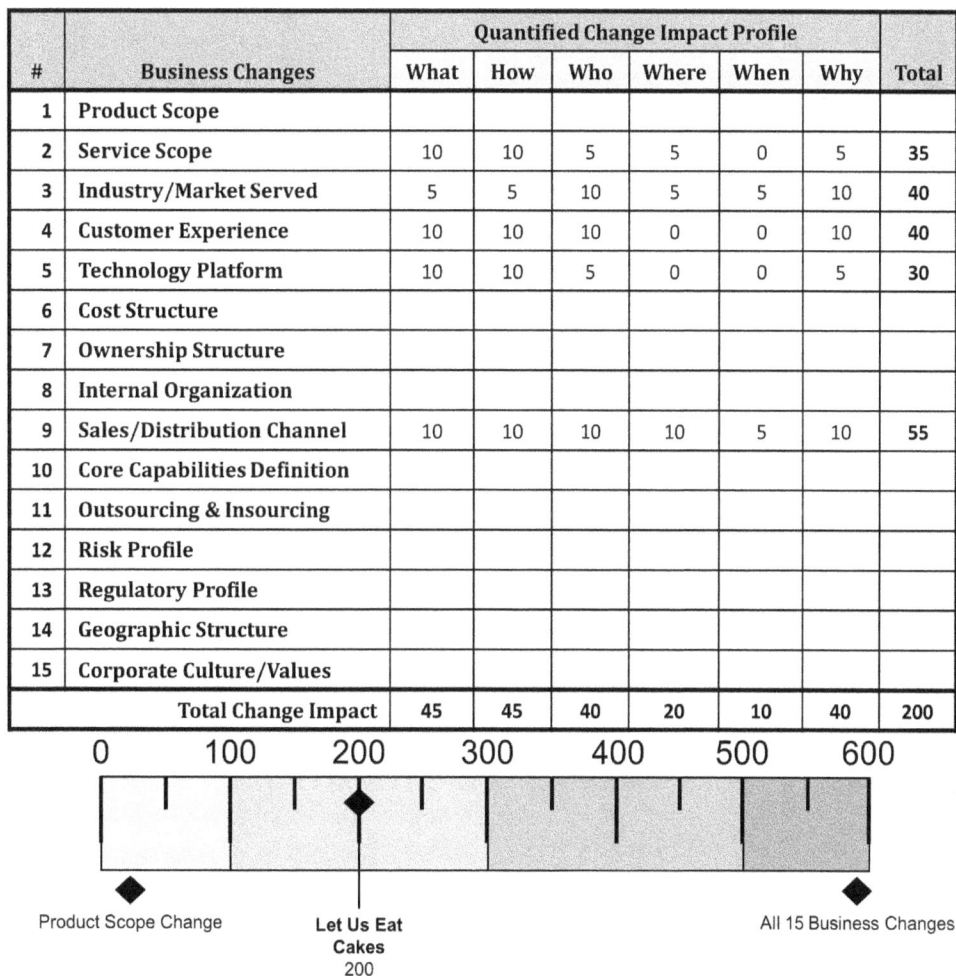

Figure 156: Let Us Eat Cakes Change Impact Profile

#	Readiness Issues	Change Impacts Induced					
		What	How	Who	Where	When	Why
1	How would they handle the additional volume of "on the go" customers without overflowing the sales and dining areas?		✓	✓	✓		
2	How would customers who paid online pick up their orders and be on their way quickly? Where would they park?		✓	✓	✓		
3	Do the online commuter customers want/need assistance in designing specialty cakes?	✓		✓			
4	How would prepay customer credit card data be handled securely?	✓	✓	✓			
5	Who would support the new website?	✓					
6	Would a second shift be required to handle online orders placed after normal business hours?	✓		✓		✓	
7	Where and how would online orders be staged for pick-up?	✓	✓	✓	✓		
8	Will the restaurant supply vendor change their delivery schedule to avoid the commuter customer rush?			✓		✓	

Figure 157: Let Us Eat Cakes Readiness Issues and Induced Change Impacts

Figure 157 shows how each readiness issue results from impacts induced by the changes in their modernization effort. The transformation change impact matrix would have helped them identify the change impacts before they turned into readiness issues (see figure 158). The complete matrix would contain a row for each of the business changes initiated during their modernization (service scope, industry/market served, customer experience, technology platform, and sales/distribution channel).

#	Business Changes	**What** Content & Deliverables Changes to work content or the deliverables for the job that must be done	**How** Methods & Procedures Changes to work methods, policies or procedures	**Who** Relationships Changes to work relationships including internal, reporting, customer, supplier, regulatory, etc.	**Where** Locations Changes to work location including workspaces, offices, customers and suppliers	**When** Timing & Cycles Changes to the timing (start/stop) or cycles of work	**Why** Purpose & Motivation Changes to work purpose, reason or motivation
2	Service Scope	[ ] Add New [ ] Discontinue [ ] Modify [ ] Combine [ ] Split Service Scope Induced Products or Services	[ ] Add New [ ] Discontinue [ ] Modify Service Scope Induced Sourcing, Production, Selling, Marketing, Fulfillment, Financial or Business Support <Method, Policy, or Procedure>	[ ] Add New [ ] Discontinue [ ] Modify Service Scope Induced Relationship <Internal, Reporting, Customer, Supplier, Regulatory Agency>	[ ] Add New [ ] Discontinue [ ] Modify Service Scope Induced Location <Workspaces, Offices, Customers, Suppliers>	[ ] Add New [ ] Discontinue [ ] Modify Service Scope Induced Timing or Cycles {Not Common}	[ ] Add New [ ] Discontinue [ ] Modify Service Scope Induced Purpose or Motivation
3	Industry/Market Served	[ ] Add New [ ] Discontinue [ ] Modify [ ] Combine [ ] Split Industry or Market Served Induced Products or Services	[ ] Add New [ ] Discontinue [ ] Modify Industry/Market Served Induced Sourcing, Production, Selling, Marketing, Fulfillment, Financial or Business Support <Method, Policy, or Procedure>	[ ] Add New [ ] Discontinue [ ] Modify Industry or Market Served Induced Relationship <Internal, Reporting, Customer, Supplier, Regulatory Agency>	[ ] Add New [ ] Discontinue [ ] Modify Industry or Market Served Induced Location <Workspaces, Offices, Customers, Suppliers>	[ ] Add New [ ] Discontinue [ ] Modify Industry or Market Served Induced Timing or Cycles {Not Common}	[ ] Add New [ ] Discontinue [ ] Modify Industry or Market Served Induced Purpose or Motivation
.	.	.	.	.	.	.	.

Figure 158: Let Us Eat Cakes Transformation Change Impact Matrix Template

Now suppose Let Us Eat Cakes had completed a transformation change impact matrix for their modernization. This is shown in figure 159 (below) for the service scope and industry/market served business changes. The "[✓] Add New" and "[✓] Modify" change impacts induced by these changes will uncover most of their readiness issues.

The change impacts induced by service scope address the following:

4. How would customer credit card data be handled securely?
5. Would a second shift be required to handle online orders placed after normal business hours?
6. Where and how would online orders be staged for pickup?

The change impacts induced by industry/market served address the following:

1. How would they handle the additional volume of on-the-go customers without overflowing the sales and dining areas?
2. How would customers who paid online pick up their orders and be on their way quickly? Where would they park?
3. Do the online commuter customers want/need assistance in designing specialty cakes?
4. Will the restaurant supply vendor change their delivery schedule to avoid the commuter customer rush?

The change impacts induced by technology platform address the following:

5. Who would support the new website?

#	Business Changes	What Content & Deliverables Changes to work content or the deliverables for the job that must be done	How Methods & Procedures Changes to work methods, policies or procedures	Who Relationships Changes to work relationships including internal, reporting, customer, supplier, regulatory, etc.	Where Locations Changes to work location including workspaces, offices, customers and suppliers	When Timing & Cycles Changes to the timing (start/stop) or cycles of work	Why Purpose & Motivation Changes to work purpose, reason or motivation
2	Service Scope	[✓] **Add New** • Online order placement • Online credit card pre-payment • Online pickup date/time specification [✓] **Modify** • Instore order pickup	[✓] **Add New** • Online credit card processing for online orders [✓] **Modify** • Order processing for online orders • Order fulfillment for pickup orders	[✓] **Add New** • Online order customers • Online order processing & fulfillment employees	[✓] **Add New** • Home/Mobile locations for order placement [✓] **Modify** • Order fulfillment for pickup orders	[✓] **Add New** • New shift to process and fulfill online orders placed in the evening	[✓] **Modify** • Business growth to come through online order service
3	Industry/Market Served	[✓] **Add New** • Custom order design for commuter customers • Quick pickup for prepaid commuter customer orders	[✓] **Modify** • Order pickup process for "on the go" commuter customers • Order fulfillment for pickup orders	[✓] **Add New** • Commuter "on the go" customer segment • Employees to support "on the go" order pickup	[✓] **Add New** • Order pickup space for "on the go" customers • Parking space for "on the go" customers	[✓] **Modify** • Early order pickup for commuter customers • Restaurant supply vendor delivery time change	[✓] **Modify** • Business growth to come through "on the go" commuter customer segment

Figure 159: Let Us Eat Cakes Change Impact Matrix—Service Scope and Industry/Market Segment

While no technique can anticipate the entire spectrum of change across a business transformation, taking the time to complete a change impact matrix will greatly reduce readiness issues uncovered during the transformation.

Design Readiness

To round out the discussion on readiness for Let Us Eat Cakes' modernization effort, it's worthwhile mentioning a few words on Goal #9: Identify Required Business Capabilities. The readiness issues materialized as gaps in their solution. This is not surprising as Let Us Eat Cakes spent most of their effort on the implementation of the online solution and very little on understanding the business capabilities required to support online ordering and the commuter customer segment.

Business capability models emphasize general competencies and avoid prematurely committing to specific solutions. In the case of Let Us Eat Cakes, the business capabilities model elicits new opportunities and addresses some of their readiness issues. The top level had seven business capabilities, and the second level had thirty-four business capabilities as shown in figure 160 (below).

The first step in utilizing the business capabilities model is to identify the business capabilities affected by the change impacts. For example, the change impacts shown in the matrix in figure 158 can be mapped onto the second/third level business model for sales and operations as shown in figure 161 (below).

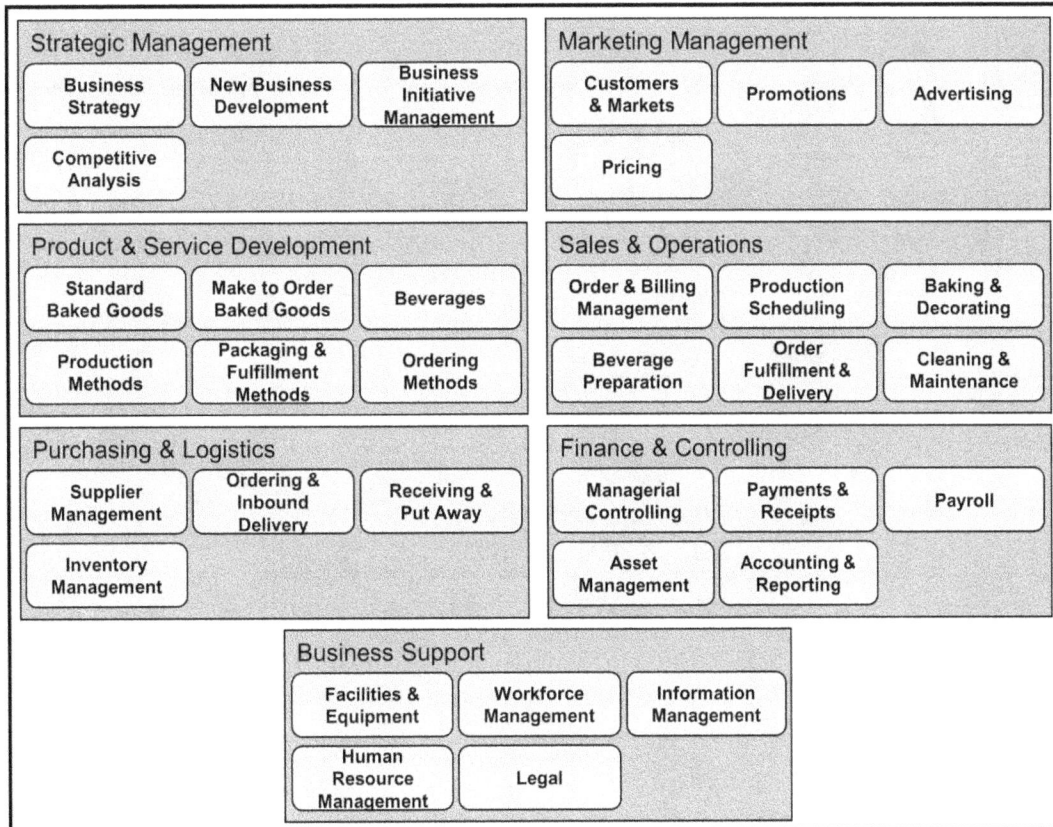

Figure 160: Let Us Eat Cakes Business Capabilities Model

The specific change impacts are now associated with generalized business capabilities: Service Scope: "What—Content and Deliverables" has the following change impacts:

[✓] Add New
- Online order placement
- Online credit card prepayment
- Online pickup date/time specification

The business capabilities affected by these impacts are denoted with a "*" in figure 161:

- Online order placement. Order and billing management—manage order placement methods.
- Online credit card prepayment. Order and billing management—manage order payment methods.
- Online pickup date/time specification. Order fulfillment and delivery—serving and pickup

Aligning the change impacts to the business capabilities allows Let Us Eat Cakes to generalize their solution to a broader purpose.

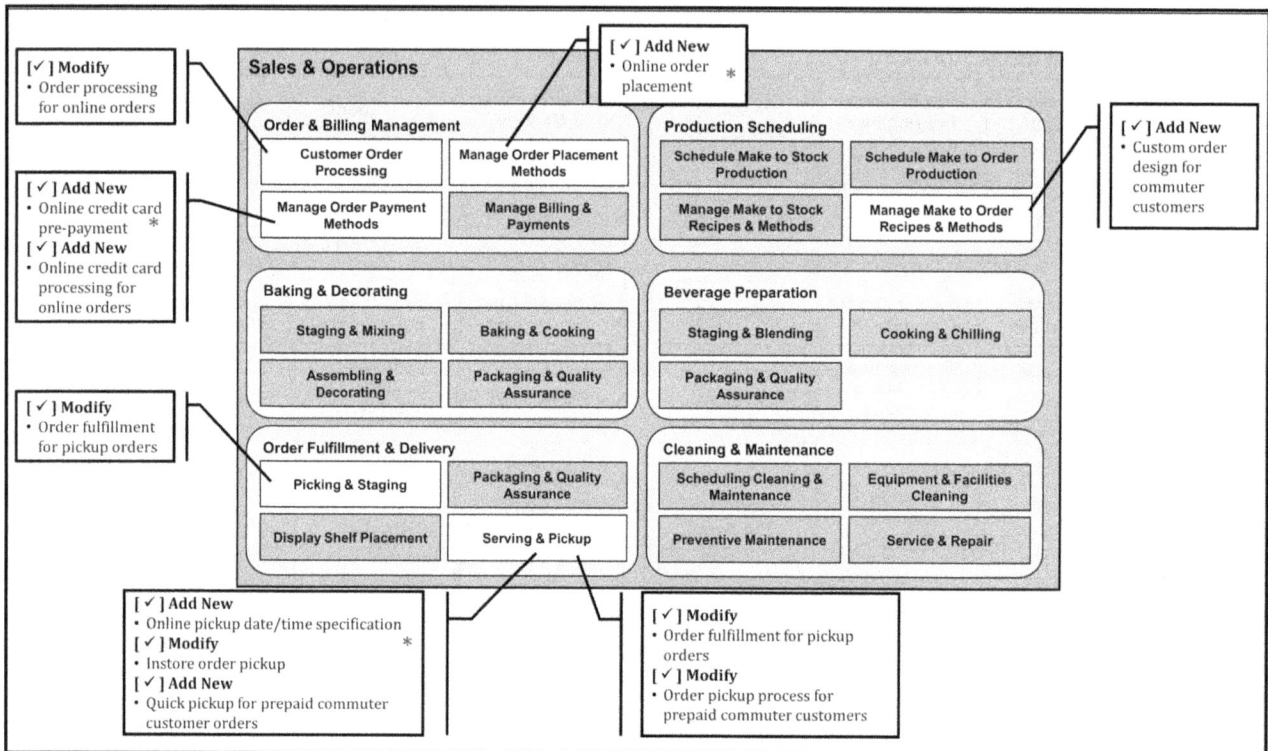

Figure 161: Let Us Eat Cakes Level 2 Sales and Operations Business Capabilities Model with Change Impacts

The capabilities to support online order placement, online credit card prepayment, and online pickup date/time specification for commuter customers can easily be extended to any customers who wish to order online for pickup at a date in the future. Let Us Eat Cakes was only considering the commuter customer segment problem, but their solution can easily be extended to address other customer segments. Focusing on specific solutions too early limits your ability to generalize to a broader purpose: the online/prepaid/pickup customer.

Leveraging the Business Capabilities Model

The business capabilities model can be further leveraged to identify new opportunities as well as address readiness issues.

Customer Loyalty Card

Let Us Eat Cakes used a customer loyalty card as part of their marketing promotions. Their customers were issued a small card that could be punched by the cashier whenever they made an in-store purchase. After ten card punches, the customer would receive a free cookie or doughnut and a new customer loyalty card. The customer loyalty card is part of the promotions capability under marketing management shown in figure 160.

By starting from the business capabilities model, Let Us Eat Cakes can consider whether/how each business capability needs to be adapted to serve the online/prepaid/pickup customer segment. For instance, the customer loyalty program can be extended virtually to record the number of times a customer has made a purchase using the new online ordering system. After ten online purchases, the customer would receive a complimentary item. This may have been missed altogether without a business capabilities model.

Drive-Through Order Pickup

One of the most significant readiness issues facing Let Us Eat Cakes is how customers who ordered and paid online would be able to quickly pick up their purchases. Today, all customers drive to the bakery, park, enter the store, and wait for a cashier to hand them their order. This is not a quick turnaround process and creates congestion in the bakery as well as the parking lot. Let Us Eat Cakes is attempting to address the new customer segment with the same order-fulfillment method used for their existing customer segments.

Let Us Eat Cakes can generalize the problem by starting from their business capabilities model. The "Packaging and Fulfillment Methods" capability under Product and Service Development (figure 160) is intended to address all packaging and fulfillment methods and not just in store pickup. Keeping that in mind, Let Us Eat Cakes can consider the best way to address packaging and fulfillment for the online/prepaid/pickup customer segment.

Given their limited store footprint and modest parking, Let Us Eat Cakes could consider the addition of a drive-through window for prepaid order pickup. This would eliminate both store and parking congestion and reduce the time it takes to fulfill a prepaid/pickup customer. There are of course other things to be considered such as traffic flow and building permits. However, the business capabilities model has freed them up to think beyond using existing fulfillment for the new customer segment. Furthermore, generalizing packaging and order-fulfillment capabilities might lead Let Us Eat Cakes to consider a delivery service at some point in the future.

Approaching Readiness in Your Company

Whether you're thinking about a transformation, actively leading transformational change, or evaluating the health of a transformation underway, you may be wondering how to approach the daunting task of readiness within your company or that of your client. This section closes the practitioner-level assessments and preparations by presenting strategies for approaching readiness in your own company.

Getting Started

If you are starting your readiness efforts at the beginning of a transformation, you are fortunate. The sooner you can begin, the better. However, the techniques presented in this book can benefit you wherever you are—even if you've completed your transformation and are hoping to realize the purpose and value. You begin by determining where you are in your transformation and then establishing a corresponding readiness plan.

Assessing Where You Are

All business transformations proceed through the three life cycle phases used to organize the readiness goals (see figure 40). Each of the phases was arranged into objectives, creating six distinct sequential groups of activities—repeated in figure 162 (below).

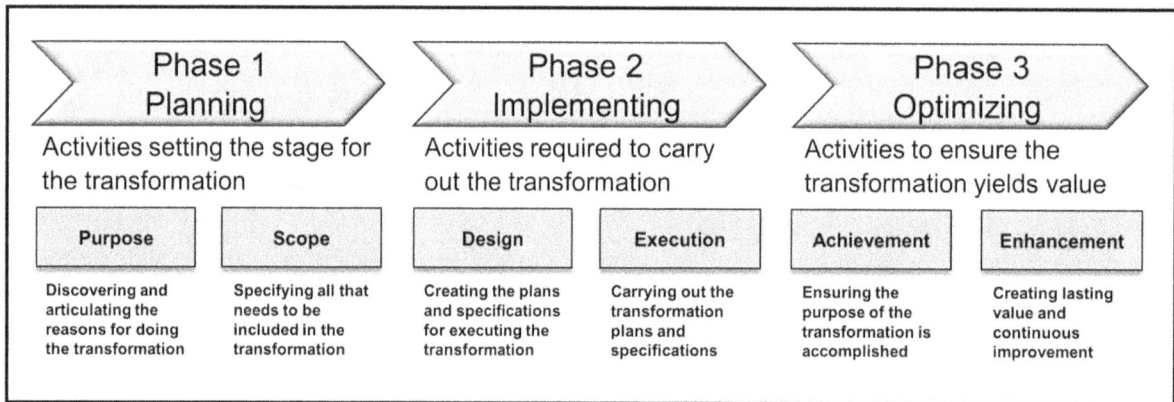

Figure 162: The Six Objectives of a Business Transformation

The flowchart in figure 163 (below) shows the high-level steps you can take to formulate your plan. Refer to this flowchart as you read through the descriptions of each step.

Step 1: Identify Phase and Objective

You first identify the current phase and objective for your transformation using figure 162 (above). This will be the starting point for your readiness plan. If it is not immediately obvious, you can review the description of the transformation phases and objectives in "The Three Phases of a Business Transformation."

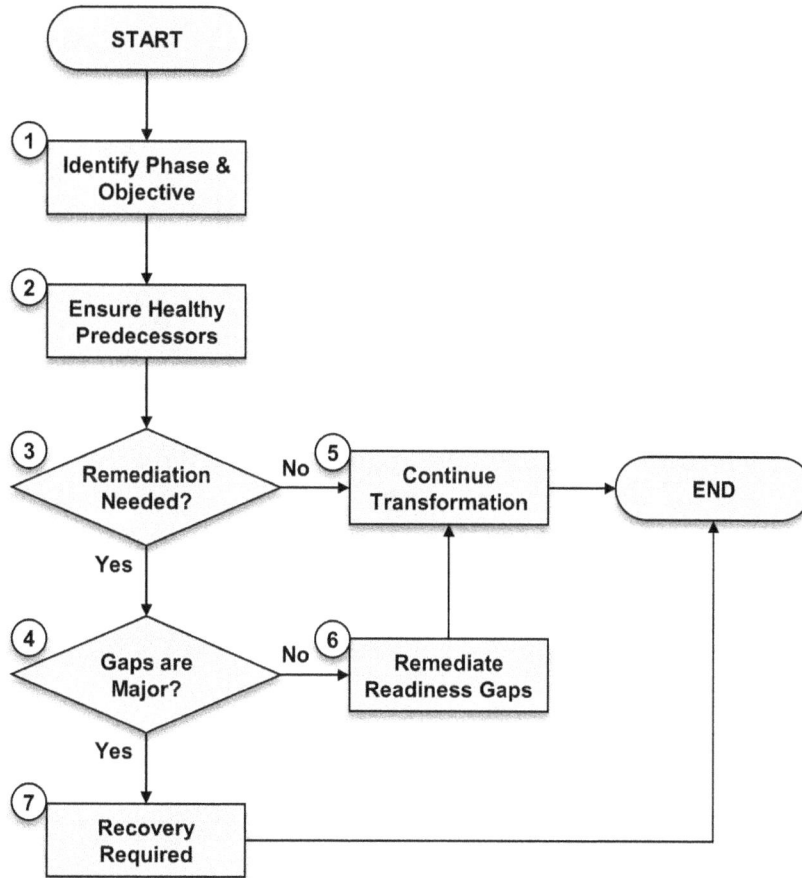

Figure 163: Getting Started with Transformation Readiness

Step 2: Ensure Healthy Predecessors

You must then determine if the readiness goals have been met for all phases/objectives prior to your starting point. Phase/objectives aligned readiness goals were given in figure 45. They are shown again in a slightly different arrangement in figure 164 (below). You can use the readiness assessments for each of the predecessor goals to determine whether your transformation is healthy up to your starting point.

Step 3: Remediation Needed?

After conducting the readiness assessments for the predecessor goals, either your transformation predecessors will be healthy—or you will need to remediate gaps in one or more readiness goals. If your predecessors are healthy, you can proceed to Step 5. If your predecessors are not healthy, you will need to proceed to Step 4 to understand the magnitude of your readiness gaps.

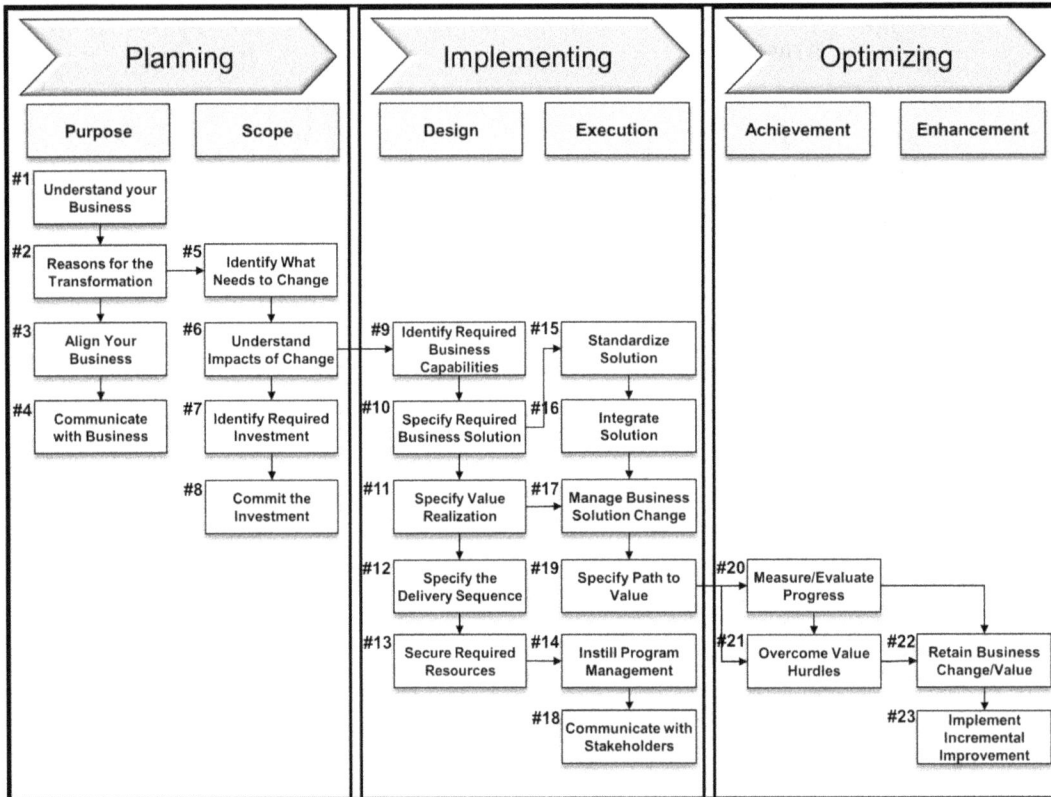

Figure 164: Transformation Life Cycle Readiness Sequence

Step 4: Gaps Are Major?

Your business transformation readiness gaps are major if the readiness standards for multiple assessments have not been considered at all. If the work behind the standards has been done, but the artifacts have not been fully documented, then the gaps are minor. You can proceed to Step 6 (below) if you have minor gaps. If you have major readiness gaps, it is likely you will need to consider some degree of recovery. This is addressed in Step 7 (below).

Where Do You Go?

Your transformation-readiness plan is a function of the state of readiness for your predecessor phases/ objectives.

Step 5: Continue Transformation

If in Step 3 you concluded that you had no readiness gaps, you can simply continue using the business transformation readiness techniques for all successor goals from your starting point.

Step 6: Remediate Readiness Goals

If in Step 3 you concluded that you had only minor gaps in some of your readiness goals, you can use the associated readiness preparations to close those gaps. After the gaps have been closed, you will have healthy predecessors and can move on to Step 5.

Step 7: Recovery Required

If in Step 3 you concluded that you had major gaps in some of your readiness goals, your transformation will require a recovery. The extent of the recovery will depend on which goals had major gaps and your starting point. This is taken as a separate topic in the next section.

Transformation Recovery

Recovering a transformation depends on where you are in the transformation (the starting point phase/objective) and the reason the transformation requires a recovery in the first place. Three reasons, called recovery types, will be considered here.

1. Major gaps. Your transformation has one or more readiness goals with major gaps.
2. Wrong track. Your transformation has evolved away from its original intent.
3. Stalled. Your transformation has ceased to move forward due to indecision or some other blockage.

When one of these recovery types occurs during a transformation, you will need to address it with one of four recovery responses.

1. Remediate in place. You can continue to work within the starting point phase/objective as you address the reason for the recovery. The recovery can be implemented in parallel with the progress on the transformation.
2. Pause, remediate, continue. You must pause the work within the starting point phase/objective as you address the reason for the recovery. The recovery must occur before you can resume transformation work.
3. Halt, redefine, restart. You must halt the work within starting point phase/objective and redefine the current course of action. Once this is complete, you can restart the transformation from the starting point phase/objective.
4. Halt, assess, redefine/restart, or discontinue. You must halt the work within starting point phase/objective and assess the current direction of the transformation. Once the assessment is completed, you will either redefine the current course of action and restart the transformation

from the starting point phase/objective or discontinue the transformation. The choice to redefine/restart or discontinue depends on what is discovered during the assessment.

Each of the recovery types can now be considered across all phases of the transformation life cycle to determine the most appropriate recovery response. You can refer to figure 165 as you read through the following sections.

Major Gaps

Planning Phase

Major gaps in the planning phase mean the purpose or scope objectives are at risk. If you have discovered gaps in one or more of these readiness goals, it is best to pause the transformation in its current state, complete the readiness preparation for the goals with the gaps, and then continue from the current state. The transformation is in its early stages so there will be little rework required, but it is vital to lock down the purpose and scope before going any further.

Implementing Phase

Major gaps in the implementing phase mean the design or execution objectives are at risk. If you have discovered gaps in one or more of these readiness goals, there are two possible recovery responses: remediate in place or pause, remediate, and continue. The best choice depends on which goal has the readiness gap.

- Goal #9: Identify Required Business Capabilities. Since business capabilities are primarily a form of documentation used in specifying the business solution, the most appropriate recovery response is to remediate in place.
- Goal #10: Specify Required Business Solution. Since the rest of the design phase depends on the business solution, the most appropriate recovery response is to pause, remediate, and continue.
- Goal #11: Specify Value Realization. Since value realization is essentially a form of documentation used in specifying the path to value, the most appropriate recovery response is to remediate in place.
- Goal #12: Specify the Delivery Sequence. Since the delivery sequence drives the implementation plan, the most appropriate recovery response is to pause, remediate, and continue.

- Goal #13: Secure Required Resources. The transformation cannot be effectively implemented without enough resources; therefore, the most appropriate recovery response is to pause, remediate, and continue.

- Goal #14: Instill Program Management. The entire implementing phase depends on formal program management. If this has not been completed, it is best to pause, remediate, and continue.

- Goal #15: Standardize Solution. The choice of solution elements will depend on the degree of standardization in place, but not every solution element requires standardization. The most appropriate recovery response is to remediate in place.

- Goal #16: Integrate Solution. Similarly, the solution will depend ultimately on the elements requiring integration, but not all solution elements require integration, so the most appropriate recovery response is to remediate in place.

- Goal #17: Manage Business-Solution Change. Since the success of your transformation is directly tied to effective management of the change related to your business solution, the most appropriate recovery response is to pause, remediate, and continue.

- Goal #18: Communicate with Stakeholders. It is preferable to have the communication plan formulated and executed as early as possible during the implementing phase, but it can be independent of any other readiness goals. Therefore, the more appropriate recovery response is to remediate in place.

- Goal #19: Specify Path to Value. Since the path to value must be completed prior to moving to the optimizing phase, the most appropriate recovery response is to pause, remediate, and continue.

Optimizing Phase

At this point your transformation has been implemented, but major gaps in the optimizing phase imply difficulty in demonstrating you've achieved your purpose and value objectives and can move beyond them. It is important to remediate these gaps, but they can be remediated without pause.

Wrong Track

When a transformation is on the wrong track, work continues to be performed, but the outcome is headed in a direction inconsistent with the purpose, scope, or value of the transformation. The ways in which a transformation can be on the wrong track are different in each phase—some of which were discussed in the sections on readiness preparation considerations.

Recovering a transformation that is on the wrong track requires more effort than recovering from a major gap. With a major gap, transformation readiness is actively assessed, and the gap is recognized by the assessors. This is followed by a readiness preparation to address the gap. However, when a transformation is on the wrong track, the issue is not readiness per se—but rather the quality of readiness. Poor quality readiness assessments or assessments that are ignored will result in future misalignment. Therefore, the transformation must be halted and some aspect redefined before it can be restarted.

Planning Phase

In the planning phase, there are several indications that your transformation is on the wrong track. Here are some for your consideration:

1. The purpose is inconsistent with the company's mission.
2. The transformation is based only on poorly defined motivators.
3. The transformation produces no discernable business value.
4. The key stakeholders are not aligned on the purpose or scope.
5. An existing capability, process, or other entity in the business conflicts with the new changes—and there are no plans to address it.
6. Your organization is not ready to tackle the changes initiated by your transformation.
7. The investment is not justified by the purpose and value.
8. Your willingness to make the investment in your transformation is eroded by an emerging or preexisting commitment.
9. Something has changed in the business environment during the planning phase and invalidates the purpose, value, or scope of the transformation.

There is certainly no point in continuing beyond the planning phase if you know your transformation is on the wrong track. The cost to redefine the transformation is much less than if it had reached the implementation phase. If the redefinition continues without end, your transformation may be stalled. This is considered a little later.

Implementing Phase

In the implementing phase, your transformation could either be on the wrong track due to activities in the implementing phase or due to activities in the planning phase. This section only addresses the activities in the implementing phase. It is assumed the transformation was set up correctly in the planning phase.

1. Your business solution is defined exclusively by the how dimension—technology, tools, applications, and methods—and excludes the other dimensions of change impact.

2. You cannot demonstrate how or why your business solution design achieves your value objectives.

3. The completion of a delivery in your delivery sequence depends on the completion of a future delivery in the sequence.

4. The executive leadership team is consistently missing leadership steering meetings; issues or decisions are not addressed in a timely manner or are not addressed at all; and program milestones are delivered consistently late or at a higher-than-expected cost.

5. Solution scope continues to expand during the implementation.

6. Off-the-shelf solutions were selected as part of the overall business solution, but customizations are frequently implemented without justification.

7. There is growing resistance toward adopting the business solution—and no mitigation in place to address it.

8. Something has changed in the business environment during the implementing phase that invalidates the purpose, value, or scope of the transformation.

The effort required to get a transformation back on track in the implementing phase depends on how far along you are and how far off track the transformation has drifted. The transformation must be halted and redefined. If the transformation's purpose/value are still justified with the added cost to course correct, then the transformation can be restarted. In cases where something has changed in the business environment, the transformation may need to be discontinued.

Optimizing Phase

In the optimizing phase, your transformation could be on the wrong track due to activities in all three phases. This section only addresses the activities in the optimizing phase. It is assumed the transformation was set up correctly in the planning phase and carried out correctly in the implementing phase.

1. There is no measurable progress, inconsistent progress, or frequent relapses in progress toward achieving the purpose and value of the transformation.

2. New business improvements are undoing the business solution implemented through the transformation.

While the transformational work has been completed by the time you are in the optimizing phase, the purpose and value will not be fully realized if the optimizing phase goes off track. Therefore, if either of the situations above should occur, the optimizing work should be halted, redefined, and then restarted.

Stalled

When a transformation is stalled, it means it is no longer achieving measurable progress. The transformation can be plagued with indecision, and/or progress on transformation work products has ceased. In some cases, a stall occurs because the transformation is on the wrong track, but this is not yet known. In other cases, the transformation is not right for the business. The stall is sensed differently in each phase, and the recovery is at least as extensive as in the case of a transformation on the wrong track.

Planning Phase

During the planning phase, transformation progress is owned by the CEO and the executive team. If the transformation is stalled, it means the executive team is not aligned on the purpose, scope, or value—or whether the business is willing/able to undertake the investment in the change. The stall may manifest as purposeful delay, indecision, or endless debate. If this is occurring, the executive team needs to halt work on the transformation and assess whether the cause of the stall can be overcome.

If the transformation is on the wrong track, and this is creating the stall, then the transformation can be redefined and restarted. However, if the stall is occurring because the business is unwilling or unable to proceed, it is best to discontinue the transformation until the cause of unwillingness or inability is removed.

Implementing Phase

During the implementing phase, transformation progress is owned by the implementation leadership team. If the transformation is stalled, it means the implementation team has reached an obstacle it cannot address. For instance, it may be insufficiently resourced—or it may have reached a critical decision requiring significant input from the executive leadership team. Whatever the case, the transformation should be halted until the obstacle is removed. This may require redefinition of some portion of the transformation as well. Once the obstacle has been cleared, the implementing phase can be restarted.

Optimizing Phase

During the optimizing phase, transformation progress is owned by the teams responsible for driving/ retaining/extending value. A stall during the optimizing phase means either insufficient resource has been applied to driving/retaining/extending value or there is an obstacle (intentional or unintentional) to overcoming the value hurdles. As in the case during the implementing phase, the transformation should be halted until resources are applied or the obstacle is removed. This may require redefinition of the optimizing phase objectives as well. Once the resources or obstacles have been addressed, the optimizing phase can be restarted.

The action plans for transformation recovery are summarized in figure 165 (below).

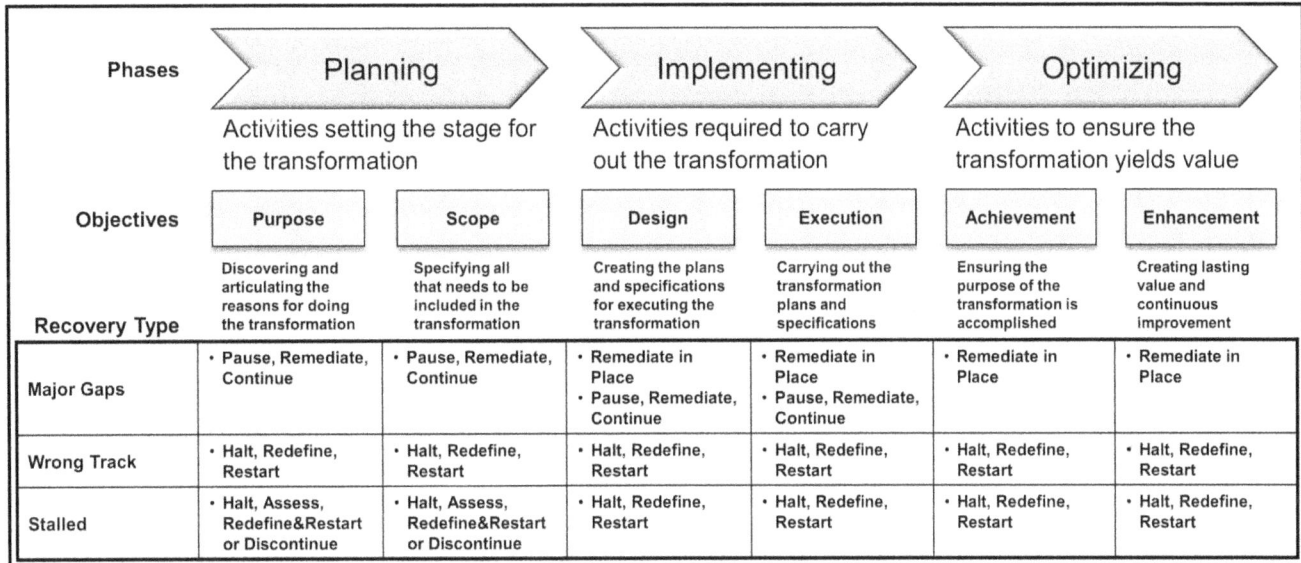

Phases	Planning		Implementing		Optimizing	
	Activities setting the stage for the transformation		Activities required to carry out the transformation		Activities to ensure the transformation yields value	
Objectives	Purpose	Scope	Design	Execution	Achievement	Enhancement
Recovery Type	Discovering and articulating the reasons for doing the transformation	Specifying all that needs to be included in the transformation	Creating the plans and specifications for executing the transformation	Carrying out the transformation plans and specifications	Ensuring the purpose of the transformation is accomplished	Creating lasting value and continuous improvement
Major Gaps	• Pause, Remediate, Continue	• Pause, Remediate, Continue	• Remediate in Place • Pause, Remediate, Continue	• Remediate in Place • Pause, Remediate, Continue	• Remediate in Place	• Remediate in Place
Wrong Track	• Halt, Redefine, Restart	• Halt, Redefine, Restart	• Halt, Redefine, Restart	• Halt, Redefine, Restart	• Halt, Redefine, Restart	• Halt, Redefine, Restart
Stalled	• Halt, Assess, Redefine&Restart or Discontinue	• Halt, Assess, Redefine&Restart or Discontinue	• Halt, Redefine, Restart	• Halt, Redefine, Restart	• Halt, Redefine, Restart	• Halt, Redefine, Restart

Figure 165: Transformation Recovery Action Planning

Chapter Takeaway Points

- We described how to use the planning phase readiness assessments and preparations (Goal #2, Goal #5, and Goal #6) to address the issues facing the Let Us Eat Cakes bakery.
- We described how to use the business capabilities model (readiness assessment and preparation for Goal #9) to identify new opportunities (customer loyalty card and drive-through order pickup) at Let Us Eat Cakes.
- We described practical methods for approaching readiness within your company—including how to get started with a transformation already in progress and how to handle transformations that require recovery—including major gaps in readiness—transformations that are on the wrong track, and transformations that have stalled.

Appendices

APPENDIX 1

SUMMARY OF BUSINESS TRANSFORMATION RESEARCH FINDINGS

The findings from the research studies compiled in chapter 3 are organized using the three-phase business transformation life cycle.

Reasons for Business Transformation Failure

Phase 1: Planning	Reasons for Failure
Purpose	1. Not establishing a great enough sense of urgency
	2. Lacking a vision
	3. Lack of focus
	4. Lack of CEO sponsorship
	5. Conflicting visions among executive leadership or decision-makers
	6. Lack of consensus on what digital transformation means
Scope	1. The future state is unknown when you begin
	2. Trouble in articulating the what and how of the transformation
	3. Too strong of focus on back-office and infrastructure issues
	4. Not creating a powerful enough guiding coalition
	5. Failure to understand the complexity of the operating model and the changes necessary to affect its transformations
	6. Undercommunicating the vision
	7. The future state is radically different than the current state—the people and culture must change to implement it successfully
	8. Lack of internal talent to spearhead or execute business change
	9. Change leaders need to first transform themselves

Phase 1: Planning	Reasons for Failure
	10. Missing the necessary skills and mind-sets to execute the transformation
	11. Talent deficit
	12. Inability to innovate or create the processes and budgets required for innovation
	13. Insufficient funding

Phase 2: Implementing	Reasons for Failure
Design	1. Failure to take a "business-value-first" approach to technology
	2. Not systematically planning for and creating short-term wins
	3. Resource/budget constraints
Execution	1. Isolating the digital transformation from the rest of the business
	2. Inflexibility—managing transformation with predetermined, time-bound, and linear project plans
	3. Inefficient execution or lack of formal process
	4. Lack of adequate technology
	5. Inability to execute the transformation and operationalize a new target operating model
	6. Integration challenges
	7. Not removing obstacles to the new vision
	8. Existing organizational culture was a barrier
	9. Resistance to change
	10. Lack of speed
	11. Lack of leadership continuity

Phase 3: Optimizing	Reasons for Failure
Achievement	1. Declaring victory before adoption has been completed
	2. Missing ongoing commitment to the transformation
Enhancement	1. Changes not institutionalized in company culture

Phase 1: Planning	Actions to Ensure Success
Purpose	1. Establish a sense of urgency—market and competitive realities, crises, or major opportunities
	2. Create a vision to direct change effort
	3. Focus on customer expectations
	4. Aspire: Where do we want to go?
	5. Communicate the vision
Scope	1. Stretch for company's full potential
	2. Form a powerful guiding coalition
	3. Assess: How ready are we to embark on the journey?
	4. Form the right executive-oversight team
	5. Bring on CTO to reinforce the executive team
	6. Active and involved leaders
	7. Appropriate, adequate resources from the start
	8. Change the cadence with a transformation office (TO) empowered to make decisions

Phase 2: Implementing	Actions to Ensure Success
Design	1. Plan for and create short-term wins
	2. Architect the steps that lead to the destination
	3. Assign the right employees to implement the project
Execution	1. Utilize strong program governance
	2. Manage the journey
	3. Simplify the solutions
	4. Adopt proven solutions
	5. Empower others to act on the vision—eliminating obstacles to change
	6. Learn to thrive on change—build agility into your organization
	7. Accurate timely feedback from employees executing the program
	8. Engage business to socialize transformation objectives, clarify scope and objectives, and manage expectations and acceptance
	9. Engage and empower employees
	10. Leaders communicate effectively, especially about transformation progress
	11. Remove barriers and create incentives to change
	12. Gather data for metrics during the process

Phase 3: Optimizing	Actions to Ensure Success
Achievement	1. Consolidate improvements and produce still more change
	2. Institutionalize new approaches
Enhancement	1. Create culture of continual innovation
	2. Embed new culture of execution to sustain the transformation
	3. Keep transformation moving after it is completed
	4. Implement continuous improvement after the transformation

APPENDIX 2

FIGURES USED IN THIS BOOK

References

Alie, S. S. (2015). Project governance: #1 critical success factor. PMI Global Congress 2015—North America. Orlando, FL: Newtown Square, PA: Project Management Institute.

Anderson, D., and Anderson, L. A. (2010). What is Transformation, and Why is it so Hard to Manage? Retrieved from Change Leaders Network: http://changeleaders network.com/free-resources/what-is-transformation-and-why-is-it-so-hard-to-manage

Basford, T., and Schaninger, B. (2016, April). The four building blocks of change. Retrieved from McKinsey Quarterly: https://www.mckinsey.com/business-functions/organization/our-insights/the-four-building-blocks--of-change?cid=podcast-eml-alt-mkq-mck-oth-1804&hlkid=cf5e96ee5b d94912aaa84d27d34f3349&hctky=10310971&hdpid=8769e49d-9697-4ff2-b51c-0c73ab1c7ea2

Basford, T., Schaninger, B., and Viruleg, E. (2015, September). Survey—The science of organizational transformations. Retrieved from McKinsey & Company—Organization: https://www.mckinsey.com/business-functions/organization/our-insights/the-science-of-organizational-transformations

Boulton, C. (2018, January 18). 12 reasons why digital transformations fail. Retrieved from CIO From IDG: https://www.cio.com/article/3248946/digital-transformation/12-reasons-why-digital-transformations-fail.html

Boulton, C. (2018, February 26). 16 real-world digital transformation success stories. Retrieved from CIO From IDG: http://cio.in/feature/16-real-world-digital-transformation-success-stories

Bucy, M., Fagan, T., Maraite, B., and Piaia, C. (2017, March). Keeping Transformations on Target. Retrieved from McKinsey & Company—RTS: https://www.mckinsey.com/business-functions/rts/our-insights/keeping-transformations-on-target

Bucy, M., Finlayson, A., Kelly, G., and Moye, C. (2016, May). The 'how' of transformation. Retrieved from McKinsey & Company—Retail: https://www.mckinsey.com/industries/retail/our-insights/the-how-of-transformation

Bucy, M., Hall, S., and Yakola, D. (2016, November). Transformation with a capital T. Retrieved from McKinsey & Company—RTS: https://www.mckinsey.com/business-functions/rts/our-insights/transformation-with-a-capital-t

Carucci, R. (2016, October 24). Organizations Can't Change If Leaders Can't Change with Them. Retrieved from Harvard Business Review—Change Management: https://hbr.org/2016/10/ organizations-cant-change-if-leaders -cant-change-with-them

CB Insights. (2017, April 13). When Corporate Innovation Goes Bad: The 110 Biggest Product Failures of All Time. Retrieved from CB Insights: https://www.cbinsights.com/research/ corporate-innovation-product-fails/

Chemko, H. (2018). Top 3 Reasons Why 84% of Digital Transformation Projects Fail. Retrieved from getelastic—The Future of Commerce—Enterprise Commerce Blog: https://www.getelastic. com/top-3-reasons-why-digital-transformation-projects-fail

Conner, D. R. (1992). Managing At the Speed of Change. New York: Random House.

Dewar, C., Blackburn, S., Nielson, A. B., Irons, E., Blackburn, M., Ulosevich, G., and Wood, C. (2011). How do I Transform My Organization's Performance? Retrieved from McKinsey— Insights into organization: https://www.mckinsey.com/~/media/mckinsey/dotcom/client_service/ public%20sector/pdfs/how_do_i_transform_my_organizations_performance.ashx

Difronzo, G. (2012). Transformation programmes: a PMO insight. Retrieved from PMI Website: https://www.pmi.org/learning/library/transformation-programmes-pmo-insight-6344

Drevets, T. (2014, January 23). 5 Companies That Have Stayed Relevant By Re-inventing Themselves. Retrieved from Valuewalk: https://www.valuewalk.com/2014/01/re-inventing-companies-wester n-union-ibm-n-geographic-lego-mcdonalds/

Drucker, P. F. (1994, September-October). The Theory of the Business. Harvard Business Review, pp. 95-107.

Erdman, D., Greenberg, E., and Harper, R. (2016, May). Geostrategic risks on the rise. Retrieved from McKinsey & Company—Strategy and Corporate Finance: https://www.mckinsey.com/ business-functions/strategy-and-corporate-finance/our-insights/geostrategic-risks-on-the-rise

Forbes Media. (2014). Transformational Change: What Works and What Can Doom the Initiative. Retrieved from Forbes Insights: https://images.forbes.com/forbesinsights/StudyPDFs/ Medidata_Transformational_Change_REPORT.pdf

Frankel, D., and Wagner, A. (2018, March). Resetting the cost base. Retrieved from McKinsey & Company—Digital McKinsey: https://www.mckinsey.com/business-functions/digital-mckinsey/ our-insights/resetting-the-cost-base?cid=other-eml-alt-mkq-mck-oth-1803&hlkid=6c78e2ef8b5 e4849bc14f547a19d5cc3&hctky=10310971&hdpid=9b81e422-d38e-4e99-8250-26e9e1e90d01

Isern, J., Meaney, M. C., and Wilson, S. (2009, April). Corporate transformation under pressure. Retrieved from McKinsey & Company—Organization: https://www.mckinsey.com/ business-functions/organization/our-insights/corporate-transformation-under-pressure

Jacquemont, D., Maor, D., and Reich, A. (2015, April). Survey: How to beat the transformation odds. Retrieved from McKinsey & Company—Organization: https://www.mckinsey.com/ business-functions/organization/our-insights/how-to-beat-the-transformation-odds

Jones, J., Aguirre, D., and Calderone, M. (2004, April 15). 10 Principles of Change Management. Retrieved from Strategy + Business: https://www.strategy-business.com/article/rr00006?gko=643d0

Kotter, J. P. (1995). Leading Change: Why Transformation Efforts Fail. Harvard Business Review.

Kotter, John. (n.d.). 8 Steps for Accelerating Change. Retrieved from John Kotter's Web Site: https://www.kotterinc.com/wp-content/uploads/background-photos/8-Steps-for-Accelerating-Change-eBook.pdf

KPMG. (2016). Three critical factors for business transformation success. Retrieved from Succeeding in Disruptive Times: https://home.kpmg.com/content/dam/kpmg/ph/pdf/ThoughtLeadershipPublications/SucceedingInDisruptiveTimes.pdf

Maven Training. (2011, October 11). Business transformation quick guide. Retrieved from Slideshare Website: https://www.slideshare.net/MavenTraining/business-transformation-quick-guide-10/10

McKinnon, T. (2017, January 12). 6 Companies That Give Real Meaning to "Digital Transformation". Retrieved from Inc.com Website: https://www.inc.com/todd-mckinnon/is-digital-transformation-the-real-deal-these-6-companies-think-so.html

Merriam-Webster. (2018, March 18). Dictionary. Retrieved from Innovation Definition: https://www.merriam-webster.com/dictionary/innovation

Morgan, R. (2008, December 22). HOW TO DO RACI CHARTING AND ANALYSIS: A PRACTICAL GUIDE. Retrieved from Project Smart: https://www.projectsmart.co.uk/how-to-do-raci-charting-and-analysis.php

Olavsrud, T. (2017, September 21). 10 tips for change management success. Retrieved from CIO From IDG: https://www.cio.com/article/3225505/digital-transformation/10-tips-for-change-management-success.html

Project Management Institute. (2018). PMBOK Guide and Standards. Retrieved from Project Management Institute Web Site: https://www.pmi.org/pmbok-guide-standards

Richter, M. (2016, July 17). The 3 most critical factors for successful business transformation. Retrieved from Expert Blog KPMG Switzerland: https://blog.kpmg.ch/critical-factors-for-successful-business-transformation/

Rogers, B. (2016, January 7). Why 84% Of Companies Fail At Digital Transformation. Retrieved from Forbes—Leaders hip: https://www.forbes.com/sites/brucerogers/2016/01/07/why-84-of-companies-fail-at-digital-transformation/#3cbf89be397b

Roos, D. (2014, January 10). 10 Companies That Completely Reinvented Themselves. Retrieved from How Stuff Works.

Siu, C. (2017, January 4). Key Success Factors for Business Transformation. Retrieved from CDC Synetics web site: https://cdcsynectics.com/2017/01/04/key-success-factors-for-business-transformation/

The Open Group. (2018, June). TOGAF Series Guide—Business Capabilities. Retrieved from The Open Group Publications: https://publications.opengroup.org/downloadable/download/link/id/MC44MDg0NjUwMCAxNTMyOTQ5Njk5MTg5Nzc4MTk4MzcyOTQz/

Vullings, R., and Heleven, M. (2015). Not Invented Here: Cross-industry Innovation. Amsterdam: BIS Publishers.

Westerman, G., Bonnet, D., and McAfee, A. (2014). Leading Digital. Boston: Harvard Business Review Press.

Wipro Digital. (2017, June 1). New Survey Highlights Leaders hip Crisis in Digital Transformation. Retrieved from Wirpo Digital Website: https://wiprodigital.com/news/new-survey-highlights-leadership-crisis-digital-transformation/

Young, L. (2007, June 19). Home Depot to Sell HD Supply for $10.3B (updated). Retrieved from MDM Competitive Intelligence for Wholesale Distribution: https://www.mdm.com/articles/4179-Home-Depot-to-Sell-HD-Supply-for-10-3B-updated-?page=2

Glossary

ability gap	A missing competency, license/permission or resource required to address a change impact.
business capabilities model	A representation of the skills, physical assets, relationships, or some combination that provide a commercial advantage to a business.
business change impact	Something that affects the key behavioral dimensions of a business (what, how, who, where, when, and why) resulting from a change that has been made.
business-solution element	A component of a business solution, including work products and services, processes/workflows, procedures, policies, knowledge, skills, tools, equipment, staff, and facilities.
business transformation	Complex, large-scale changes to a company's business capabilities and behaviors—to bring about significant improvement in performance.
Business-transformation change cycle	The four states of business change a company can experience: environment changes, business transformation, business changes, and change impacts.
change impact matrix	A table that expresses the change impacts that are induced during a business transformation—by either the business changes initiated or the transformation's business solution.
change impact profile	The potential change impacts that could be induced by the various types of changes initiated.
change impact profile metric	A quantified measure of the total potential change impact induced by the changes initiated in a business transformation.
change readiness assessment	A tool used to measure a company's level of preparedness to absorb the change impacts induced by a business transformation or the resulting solution.

change readiness gap closure	A method used to address or close a gap in a company's readiness to address a change impact.
common business changes	The set of business changes most frequently initiated during a business transformation.
competitive environment motivators	The reasons a company might undertake a business transformation originating with respect to its competitors and their objectives to win business within the segment.
custom business solution	A business solution that is tailored to a specific need.
delivery sequence	The ordered set of deliveries required to fulfill the business transformation scope, when it cannot be completed with a single delivery.
external environment motivators	The reasons a company might undertake a business transformation originating with respect to factors occurring outside of the company.
hurdle mitigation	An activity planned and executed to eliminate or reduce the impact of an implementation hurdle.
implementation hurdle	Impediments to achieving the implementation of your business transformation purpose, scope, or value.
implementing phase	The phase of the business transformation life cycle where the transformational change activities are carried out to achieve the purpose and scope defined in the planning phase.
implementing phase objectives	Design—creating the plans and specifications for executing the transformation. Execution—carrying out the transformation plans and specifications.
integrated business solution	An integrated solution is one where the workflows are both connected and coherent across solution elements.
internal environment motivators	The reasons a company might undertake a business transformation originating with respect to controllable conditions inside of the organization.
KPIs	Metrics that demonstrate progress in achieving your objectives.
measures	Unit-specific values quantifying the state of an observation.
metrics	Combinations of measures used to track and assess the status of a specific action or result.
optimizing phase	The phase of the business transformation life cycle where the value of the transformation is realized.

optimizing phase objectives	Achievement—ensuring the purpose of the transformation is accomplished. Enhancement—creating lasting value and continuous improvement.
path to value	The specification for how the value of a business transformation is achieved and validated.
phase-specific challenges	The reasons a business transformation can fail arranged by phase and objective. Phase-specific challenges are rephrased as readiness goals.
planning phase	The phase of the business transformation life cycle that establishes the foundation for the transformation, defining the purpose, what it entails, why it is needed, and the value it will bring.
planning phase objectives	Purpose—discovering and articulating the reasons for doing the transformation. Scope—specifying all that needs to be included in the transformation.
poorly defined motivators	A motivator that fails to articulate an objective business reason to undertake the business transformation.
readiness assessment	A method for evaluating achievement toward the preestablished standard of readiness associated with a readiness goal.
readiness assessment metric	Questions used to evaluate the attainment of the standard of readiness for a readiness goal.
readiness assessment standard	The minimum degree of readiness required to achieve a readiness goal.
readiness gap	A gap in a company's willingness or ability to address a change impact.
readiness goal	A state of readiness to be achieved during a business transformation and which addresses a phase-specific transformation challenge.
readiness preparation	A set of remedial actions a company can take to help it attain the standard of readiness associated with a readiness goal. A unique readiness preparation is defined for each readiness assessment.
readiness preparation action	The part of a readiness preparation that identifies what needs to be done to achieve the readiness standard for a given readiness goal.

readiness preparation step	Artifacts produced during a readiness preparation to carry out the preparation action and ultimately attain the standard of readiness for a readiness goal.
standard business solution	A business solution which contains a high percentage of predesigned/prebuilt content.
transformation life cycle	The natural states a business transformation moves through as it is carried out. The transformation life cycle is used to organize readiness goals, assessments, and preparations.
transformation motivators	The reasons a company undertakes a business transformation.
value realization	A mechanism for relating the value objectives of a business transformation to the required business capabilities—and their corresponding parts of the business solution.
willingness gap	Reluctance or uncertainty in addressing a change impact.